20/20
INSIGHT

20/20 INSIGHT

6 Keys to Seeing and Changing the Hidden Patterns That Control Our Lives and Limit Our Effectiveness

RANDY J. GIBBS

Daybreak® Books
An Imprint of Rodale Books
New York, New York

Jacket Designer: Andrew Newman
Jacket Photographer: Anthony Loew
Interior Designer: Faith Hague
Illustrator: Robert J. Frawley

Library of Congress Cataloging-in-Publication Data

Gibbs, Randy J.
    20/20 insight : 6 keys to seeing and changing the hidden patterns that control our lives and limit our effectiveness / Randy J. Gibbs.
      p.   cm.
    Includes index.
    ISBN 0–87596–519–9 hardcover
    1. Insight.   2. Gibbs, Randy J. I. Title. II. Title: Twenty/twenty insight.
    BF449.5.G53   1998
    158—dc21   97–43074

Distributed in the book trade by St. Martin's Press

2 4 6 8 10 9 7 5 3 1 hardcover

─── OUR PURPOSE ───

*"We publish books that empower
people's minds and spirits."*

Dedication

To my extraordinary wife, Cindy, truly a wife for all seasons and my best friend. Her deep love, support, and brimming optimism illuminates my life's journey. To our children, Karianne, Shawn, and Jamie, three of the most remarkable and good people I have ever known. I consider it a privilege to be their father and to learn from watching them live their lives.

To my precious parents, John and Joan Gibbs, whose lifelong faith and courage amidst difficult trials has always inspired me. And to my mother- and father-in-law, Ruth and Darwin Brough, whom I love as my own parents. Their amazing examples of enduring and unconditional love still moves me to this day. Had it not been for the combined love and encouragement of these wonderful souls, this book would never have been.

And finally, in memory of Dr. Gene W. Dalton, college professor, adviser, professional colleague, and most of all, dear friend. Gene's life is proof that intellectual giants can also have complete integrity and genuine caring and compassion for all. Many times I went to Gene discouraged and out of hope, I emerged uplifted and hopeful. You knew that Gene cared more about you and your challenges than anyone on Earth when you were with him. His humble manner made everyone who knew him immediately comfortable in his presence and uplifted by his genuine interest in everyone he met. This book and its message is dedicated to Gene and the lofty principles by which he so well lived his life. His legacy lives on even though Gene has moved along.

Contents

Acknowledgments

Writing a book like this one is a lot like a cross-country train ride that takes several years. Some people boarded the train when I did, making great contributions and then departing. Jeff Briggs, Lynn Whipple, and Preston Hunter provided such useful assistance early on. Without it, I would likely still be sitting at the station.

Others boarded halfway through the journey and stayed on until the end, making huge contributions. Dee Oviatt, a dear friend and brilliant colleague, was helpful so many times during the experience. His insights, feedback, and helpful suggestions added great depth to the book in ways that I cannot fully describe. He will undoubtedly be on other "journeys" with me in the future.

On a different level, Gene Eskelson was instrumental from an artistic standpoint. His creative mind and skillful hand developed the concepts for the graphics in this book, taking it to an entirely new level.

Finally, there were people who boarded even later, when we were near the end, but who also made important contributions. Kris Kristensen boarded, dove in quickly, and helped rewrite final drafts for the publisher. His friendship, skill, and genuine interest in this project helped bring it to a pleasant and satisfying close. I could not have finished without his able assistance.

I would also like to thank Karen Kelly and all the folks at Daybreak Books for believing in this project and its message and working patiently with me to pull it all together. Finally, thanks to my agent, Dave Robie, who really started it all. In so many ways all of these people, and others not mentioned, contributed to this project and made it an enjoyable and interesting experience that I will not soon forget. Thank you all for what you have done as you made the journey with me.

Preface

In 1963, my life took a distinctly unexpected turn. I was 10 years old and sat in the chair of a prominent eye surgeon, who could do little more than shake his head in disbelief. He had never seen such deterioration of the retina in a boy so young, and his prognosis was very gloomy.

Anxious questions raced through my head: "Will I go blind, or can this be corrected? Will my life change dramatically, or will all of this be over soon?" Amidst this uncertainty, one thing became crystal clear in the weeks and months that followed—my life was changing dramatically. In quiet retrospect, I now realize that I was embarking on a path that would make all the difference.

My concern about my physical sight was only the beginning of a lifetime of work and research in the area of mental vision, or how we see internally—in our mind's eye. My work led me to uncover natural laws of effective mental vision that have a profound impact on each one of us as we strive to improve personally and professionally. A journey that began with concern about my physical eyes has been transformed into the much broader view of vision that this book is about.

In many ways, this book is autobiographical. I share stories from across the range of my life, walking with you arm in arm through experiences that shook my soul and opened my eyes to things I could scarcely have imagined 30 years ago. But even though the book tells about me and my life, in many ways it is not about me at all. It is really about you, the reader.

In the introduction to his classic work *Leaves of Grass*, Walt Whitman wrote, "Most of the great poets are impersonal. I am personal. In my poems, all revolves round, concentrates in, radiates from, myself. But my book compels, absolutely necessitates every reader to transpose himself or herself into the central position and become the living fountain, actor, experience, of every page, every aspiration, every line."

So it is with this book. I have written much of myself into it, but I hope that as you stand in my shoes and see through my eyes, you will take the central position and experience the things I have experienced in your own way and thus see with new eyes. I promise that you will see things that you never before thought possible. In order for us to reach our highest potential and create a world filled with love, compassion, and meaningful achievement, we must begin by clearly seeing things as they really are and really can be. We must slough off the scales from our eyes and see in crystal-clear, undistorted ways who we are and who we have the potential to become. As this happens, we will change. We will begin to see a world that was always right in front of our eyes but that we could not see.

I am a firm and optimistic believer that words and ideas can and are changing the world. Thus, I plead with you to engage your God-given gifts of imagination and visualization to see yourself in the pages that follow. Use this book as an opportunity to rethink how you see the world and your place in it.

If I have a fear, it is that people will read this book and say, "Gee, this was a neat book. He sounds like a good guy with lots of interesting experiences." What I pray will happen instead is that you will say something like, "Gosh, this book moved me, touched me, and made me think. I saw myself in the stories Randy told, and they caused me to think differently about myself and my world and the way I live my life." This is my heartfelt desire for you as you read.

Part I
Principles of Inner Vision

Vision, Sight, and In-Sight

This is a book about attaining a life perspective that makes everything clear, which I call 20/20 Insight. Once developed, it enables us to see ourselves, others, and the world around us in new and profoundly different ways. Not only do we come to see differently, we come to be differently as well. All of this "seeing and being" causes us to experience life in ways that we never thought imaginable.

Two Kinds of Vision

Seeing with our physical eyes provides us with one type of vision. This book is about another kind of vision that has nothing to do with the clarity of our physical eyesight. This vision happens in the mind's eye and is reflected in how we perceive ourselves, others, and the world around us. Just as our physical eyesight can become blurred and affect the quality of our lives, our internal vision can also become distorted, affecting our lives in even more significant ways.

When our physical eyesight begins to falter, we quickly visit an eye doctor for help. The doctor, as part of the diagnostic procedure, determines which lens or combination of lenses allows us to see clearly. As he places various lenses in front of each eye, he asks, "Which is better, this one, or this one?" and at some point the right combination is found. The entire process is designed to accomplish one simple objective: to restore our distorted eyesight to complete clarity—to 20/20 vision.

The idea of lenses and how they influence what and how we see has fascinated me for years. Place a telescope in front of the human eye, and we are able to peer into distant galaxies that are invisible to the naked eye. Turn the telescope around, and objects near to us appear to be miles away. Powerful microscopes allow us to step inside a new world, one so small that we never notice it normally. We can examine tiny stems of bacteria that are all about us, moving, living, changing, and affecting us in ways we can scarcely imagine.

How we see with our physical eyes has a tremendous effect on the quality of our lives. Those who struggle with farsightedness have difficulty seeing things close up. They have to hold a newspaper at arm's length until it comes into focus. They find close detail work impossible unless they wear corrective glasses that bend the light so their eyes can see with focus and clarity. Those who struggle with nearsightedness have just the opposite challenge. When they look down a highway, distant road signs are fuzzy, and they have to wait until they are closer to the signs in order to read them.

Most of us will experience the frustration that comes with vision problems at some point in our lives. In most cases, distorted vision is correctable. Sometimes, however, deterioration steals vision, and it leaves some completely blind. For those among us who cannot see clearly and for whom corrective lenses are not helpful, how important is the ability to see? What would these people give or sacrifice if their vision could be restored to a perfectly clear state? If someone offered millions of dollars in exchange for our eyesight, would any of us make such a bizarre trade? Without question, the ability to see clearly is one of the most precious and important gifts we will ever receive, because it has such a profound impact on how we experience life and our ability to achieve the level of happiness and success we all desire.

As noted above, there is another kind of vision, one that I believe has even greater influence in our lives than our physical eyesight. Our internal vision, which is manifested in how we see ourselves, others, and the world around us, is the wellspring for the way we think, believe, interpret, and make sense of the world. This vision holds within it the ideas and interpretations we have of ourselves, the beliefs we hold about success and failure, and important assumptions about how to achieve the things we want most out of life.

We often refer to perfect visual acuity as 20/20. When you visit an optometrist, the measurement used to indicate perfectly clear, undistorted eyesight is 20/20. Whether with the naked eye or with the assistance of corrective lenses, we see perfectly and are free from any kind of distortion at this point. The world of physical sight provides a fascinating parallel with our internal vision, or what I call the mind's eye. Our hopes, dreams, assumptions, ideas, and methods for living flow out of this curious but real internal vision. Terms such as paradigm, perspective, frame of reference, point of view, viewpoint, and so on have all been used to describe this internal vision and the power it has to shape the quality of our lives and relationships. As important as it is to have clear physical vision, I believe that it is just as important and significant to learn how to see clearly with our mind's eye. Once our internal vision is clear, we come to see the world as it really is and really can become.

A person can have perfect physical vision but be stricken with distorted internal vision that makes him labor under a false view of the world. False views of the world, ourselves, and others prevent us from achieving what we most desire. Perplexity, frustration, failure, confusion, doubt, fear, and all sorts of unwanted emotions come upon us when our internal vision becomes unclear. We find ourselves struggling with important relationships. We are blind to what really is and what really can be, all the while being completely unaware of our blindness. Without realizing it, how we see becomes the root cause of what we create around us, and like the individual who needs new lenses to see clearly, we too need "lenses" to hold up in front of our mind's eye to enable us to see things as they really are and as they really can be.

The Power of the Mind's Eye

My own awareness of the power of the mind's eye has been growing for years. It came into focus some time ago with an experience that became the impetus to writing this book. It brought questions that had been in the back of my mind to a new level of awareness.

For nearly 20 years, I have been an avid and regular jogger. I started out running one mile, then two, and I finally worked up to five miles. That's how far I jogged: Rain or shine, in summer, winter, spring, or fall, I ran five miles, no more, and generally no less. I was clearly a five-mile man. Over the years, friends invited me to 10-K races, but I always declined because, well, it was too far.

Then a new jogging path opened near my home. Once it was ready for runners, I laced up my shoes and headed up the path. My wife, Cindy, was at home, and she said she'd see me when I got back.

As I ran, I found myself enraptured. The path led me beside a beautiful, rushing river that ran off the snow-capped peaks of the Wasatch Mountains. Birds sang in the trees overhead, and deer frolicked on the mountainsides on either side of the river. This was similar to one of those "out-of-body" experiences that you hear about. That day I experienced a true runner's high.

I reached the end of the path near a spectacular waterfall cascading off a rugged cliff to the river below. It was breathtaking. I made the turn and headed for home, still caught up in the beauty of Nature that enveloped me. I cruised home and into the house feeling better than I had felt in months after a run.

But my reverie was suddenly interrupted by my wife's serious question: "Where in heaven's name have you been? You've been gone over an hour."

I explained what had just happened to me and how terrific this new path was and how excited I was at the prospect of jogging it every morning.

"You have to be kidding," Cindy said. "You really went all the way up the path to the waterfall and back?"

This question only brought more gushing from me about the trail and the deer and the birds and the stream—and on and on. Then came more of her questions.

"Do you realize how far it is up there?" she asked.

For a split second, I was caught off-guard. Then the obvious answer came to me. "Well, I'm guessing it's about five miles because I did it, and I feel great."

She could only laugh at my answer. "Guess again, Buzz Walter." (This is a strange nickname that she calls me when she thinks I'm acting weird.)

"Well, think about it, Honey," I said, slowly formulating my argument. "It must be about five miles because that's how far I run. If it was much farther than that, don't you think I'd realize that or have noticed it while I was running?" I thought that would end the debate, until she threw in one last comment.

"I'll bet you it's 12 miles up to where you ran and back home. It's probably twice as far as you have ever jogged before," she asserted.

"No way," I replied incredulously. "If it were 12 miles, I would be dead right now, lying alongside the path somewhere." Back and forth we went, both guessing how far I had just jogged.

"Okay, Smarty Pants," Cindy smirked, "get in the car and we'll see how far it is." That was a challenge I was excited to accept. So we jumped in the car, set the odometer to zero, and drove parallel to the path all the way to the waterfall and back. As we pulled into our driveway, the odometer measured 11.8 miles.

I knew what she was going to say next—and she did. "I told you it was almost 12 miles up there and back." Then she asked me one last question that set me thinking: "When you took off this morning, didn't you realize it was that far?"

My answer and the world of reasoning that lay behind it opened the floodgates of questioning and introspection that have continued to this day. "Of course I didn't know how far it was. If I had, I would have never taken the path," I said.

My assumption that I could jog five miles and no farther had established limits on what I could and could not do. And I had accepted these limits for so long that I never questioned their accuracy. How is it then, that in spite of all of this, I was able to jog that 11.8-mile distance? The answer is clear: I did not know the true distance, but I acted as if I did, and by so doing, I broke my own self-imposed boundaries.

So many questions that I had been wrestling with in my professional life started coming into focus as I reflected on this experience over the following days. I realized that how far I jogged was completely governed by how far I *thought* I could jog. "What other beliefs do I hold that limit my ability to succeed?" I started to wonder. "In what other ways does the way I see myself and the world around me affect my ability to create successful experiences and achieve those things I want most in life?" The questions haunted me as I continued to reflect on many instances in my life in which I had seen people struggle with personal, professional, and social challenges. For years I had wondered why otherwise bright and capable people could find themselves so "stuck" when it came to resolving these challenges.

I have had the privilege of working with some of the best and brightest people in the world, yet these people are often completely stumped as to how to resolve some of the most important concerns in life. Here are some examples.

- The general manager of one of the largest divisions of a Fortune 100 company, who was responsible for thousands of people and millions of dollars, confessed that his success in the workplace did not carry over to his home and family. "My 16-year-old daughter ran away last month and is living on the streets," he said. "Our relationship has deteriorated to the point where we don't communicate anymore. I have no idea what I need to do to improve this relationship."

- A bright, promising law school graduate revealed that he had been plagued throughout his life by feelings of insecurity and uncertainty. He desperately wanted to succeed but acknowledged, "I doubt that anyone would really want to hire me." With everything to offer and boundless potential, he was stymied in his job search and was increasingly despondent and hopeless day by day.

• An extremely competent manager concluded, at the end of one of our workshops, "I've been able to deal with work-related challenges and manage these effectively. But all through the discussion, I couldn't help but think about my marriage. Frankly, it is falling apart, and everything I've tried only seems to make things worse. I don't want a divorce, but unless something changes, I know our relationship will never last. What do I do when nothing I try works?"

• Another successful salesman related, "I've always been successful in my work, but my biggest trial is working with difficult people. You always run into a few, but lately it seems like I'm surrounded by difficult people, and I'm tempted to just blow them all off. But as I've listened today, I'm beginning to wonder if in many cases I've actually created some of the difficulty in others by my approach to them. Can I really be contributing to my own problem?"

These individuals all have one thing in common. They are bright, competent, and talented but are unable to effectively resolve the most important problems they face. In every case, they are unable to see things clearly, thus limiting their ability to improve the situation. Their inability has little to do with IQ, education, or financial standing. It has everything to do with the clarity of their internal vision. Because this is so, they become blind to the possibilities before them and are trapped in patterns they cannot understand and have no idea how to change. Their internal vision is cloudy and filled with distortion and blind spots, preventing them from seeing things as they really are and really can be.

One central and compelling truth has shone through my own experiences and my observations of others striving to achieve success in life and relationships: *How we see creates the world we experience.* The beliefs and ideas that we hold in our mind's eye translate into the way we interpret the events around us and drive our actions. The pictures that we hold in our mind's eye and all the complexity of our thoughts, ideas, interpretations, and beliefs in large measure determine who we are and dictate our ability to get what we want out of life. I proved that jogging 11.8 miles was something I could do. It had nothing to do with my physical ability to perform; it had everything to do with how I saw myself and the beliefs I held in my mind about what I could and could not do. I came to understand that if we could find ways to change how we see, we could create a different world and experience ourselves, the world, and others in new and transformational ways.

This single experience set into motion years of unanswered questions about the keys to creating peace and happiness in life and building effective relationships with others. In the days that followed, the central and powerful role that the mind's eye plays in our lives came into focus for me. It was as if someone had lifted a veil and I was able to see things in an entirely new way. When my vision changed, I changed as well.

What Is 20/20 Insight?

The focus of 20/20 Insight is to attain a crystal-clear perspective of ourselves, others, and the world around us. My experience over the years is telling. Bright, intelligent, and competent people continue to wrestle with sticky problems that seem to have no effective solution. Personal effectiveness is undermined, interpersonal relationships grow worse, and critical business goes unresolved, not because people don't have the skills but because they cannot clearly see the pathway ahead. We need an organizing principle or framework that helps us understand and resolve the most important dilemmas in life—at home and at work. We need an approach to help gain a solid handle on things, to unravel and reduce confusion, to open up new possibilities and produce significant results.

Such an organizing principle needs to be simple but not overly simplistic. At bottom, this principle, or lens, should allow people to make quantum leaps forward in their personal and professional lives. Such a view should provide us with crystal-clear views of things as they really are and produce significant insights about the things that matter most. It is 20/20 Insight.

Although *20/20 Insight* is a new term, the ideas that comprise it are timeless. Insight takes place in the mind and heart, reflecting how we see ourselves, others, and the world in general. It is a form of discovery, a new and sometimes sudden realization that patterns exist about which we were unaware. Insight is not just knowledge about the way things are, it is also increased wisdom about the way things can become. When we acquire greater insight, we are able to see possibilities that we could not see before and understand that which was unclear or confusing. Deep, rich insight is essential to increase human effectiveness and create harmony and success with others.

Developing perfectly clear insight, or 20/20 Insight, is a promising new breakthrough in addressing life's greatest challenges. We need to be able to see clearly to identify foundational causes of problems, to determine why painful problems persist, to recognize real possibilities for dealing with problems in new and effective ways, and to break through the barriers to success with others. This kind of insight bursts upon us in powerful ways, opening up new vistas and illuminating the confusing landscape in ways scarcely imagined. When we attain 20/20 Insight, we see, experience, and live at an entirely new level of understanding. It may be the single most important achievement we ever make.

An Overview

As we build on the parallel between physical eyesight and internal vision, the analogy of lenses continues to be a useful one. *20/20 Insight* is presented in three parts, including six highly integrated chapters or "lenses" that come together to produce greater understanding. While each lens is presented individually as a single point of greater clarity, the interplay between the lenses is supremely important; for it is the cumulative effect of all six that enables our vision to grow in breadth and piercing clarity.

First, in this chapter, my goal is to provide a necessary backdrop upon which the individual lenses of 20/20 Insight are viewed. The next chapter titled "Your Head Creates Your World" outlines perhaps the single most important principle in this book. Once we understand that, in large measure, we create the world we experience and therefore can create a different world by seeing it differently, we immediately are imbued with power and understanding unlike anything we have ever experienced. This is the basic principle upon which *20/20 Insight* is firmly built, and it lays the foundation for the rest of the book.

In part two, "Personal Vision," the first three lenses of 20/20 Insight are discussed.

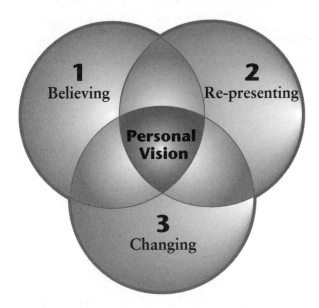

Lens one, "Beliefs Create the View," describes the critical role that beliefs play in shaping how we see and experience the world around us. Understanding how beliefs are formed and how they affect what and how we see helps create greater insight into human behavior and the processes of transformational change.

Lens two, "Re-presenting the World," discusses the ways in which we process life's experiences, interpret events as positive or negative, and shape the world around us by our responses.

Lens three, "Focusing on Change," explains the power that we all have to change the world by changing how we see it. These three lenses are highly interdependent and come together to produce clear personal vision.

Part three, "Interpersonal Vision," builds on part two and shifts the focus to relationships with others. Like lenses one through three, lenses four through six are highly interdependent. It is the combination of these three lenses that increases the clarity of our interpersonal vision and allows us to see ourselves and others in more productive ways.

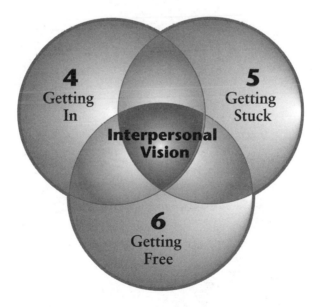

Lens four, "The Dance of Doom—Getting In," describes the dynamics that are produced when relationships go bad. I call this interplay the dance of doom. Negative, frustrating relationships and difficult people become part of an interpersonal drama that is very much like a dance.

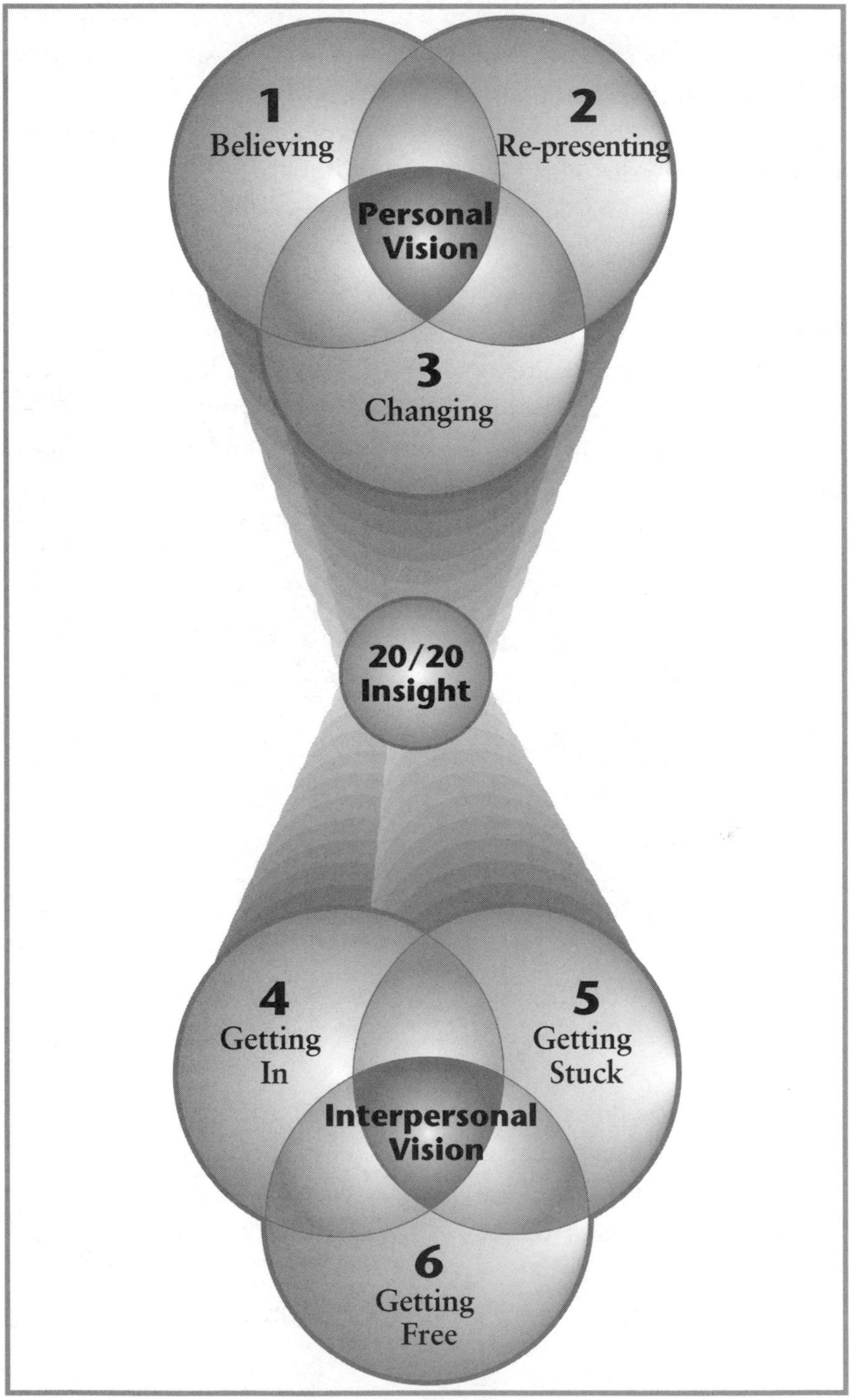
1
Believing
2
Re-presenting
Personal
Vision
3
Changing
20/20
Insight
4
Getting
In
5
Getting
Stuck
Interpersonal
Vision
6
Getting
Free

Lens five, "Dancing the Dance—Getting Stuck," answers the question: Once we are in a difficult and painful relationship, why is it that we can't seem to turn it around? Often people feel trapped, with no real answers about what to do next. In effect, they are stuck in a pattern that they can't seem to surrender, so they continue to fight a battle that they can never really win. Knowing why we get into these problems (lens four) and understanding how we get stuck (lens five) help us develop greater insight into all interpersonal relationships.

Lens six, "Dancing a New Dance—Getting Free," answers the most important question of all: Once we are in a difficult relationship, how do we dance a new dance with others, a dance of harmony and caring in which both parties are happy and the relationship is productive? Knowing how we get into the dance and get stuck helps us know how to get free from the entanglements of the dance of doom.

The three lenses of personal vision and the three that comprise interpersonal vision combine to produce 20/20 Insight. It is the cumulative effect of all these insights that broadens and deepens the clarity of our vision and allows us to see possibilities never before imagined.

Although each lens represents a specific point of clarity, when taken together, their combined effect allows us to see ourselves, others, and the world in amazing ways. Each lens builds on the previous one, and their coming together makes up 20/20 Insight and brings it together into one whole view.

Finally, the epilogue, "Rediscovering Who We Are," discusses who we are and how we can rediscover our greatest possibilities. How we journey through life is largely dependent on the clarity of our vision. We will discuss change in a way not typically considered and recognize how we are designed for peace, happiness, and success, all of which lie before us if we can only come to see things as they really are and really can become.

Developing a Sense of Wonder

Not long ago, I was teaching a workshop in a large organization on the West Coast. Over the course of this four-day program, we touched on various aspects of leadership and management and the keys to creating significant change. We discussed our vision and how it becomes filled with distortions that limit our effectiveness so that we fail to recognize the real causes of our problems. During one of the breaks, I noticed a man standing alone by the window and looking out at the nearby ocean. He was deep in thought when I walked up to see how he was enjoying the workshop.

"How is this all working for you?" I asked. He continued to stare out the window, thinking about my question. Finally he spoke, and I will never forget his words.

"I wonder if what you are telling us is true, because if it is, we are talking about some of the most central ideas in life," he remarked. "We're not just talking about making small changes in our behavior but remaining the same inside—we're talking about making fundamental shifts in how we see ourselves and the world around us. That is powerful."

I fully agreed with him, reaffirming my belief that these are the kinds of ideas that change us, and everything around us, if we so desire. Then he added one more brilliant insight.

"It's not that we've talked about anything totally new that I've never heard before. It's like hearing things that I've always known were true but had somehow forgotten or overlooked. This experience is allowing me to focus on them again, and it feels like I'm rediscovering something I always knew, kind of like coming home again to a very comfortable familiar place that feels right."

I couldn't have said it better myself. I do believe that when we come to see ourselves and others clearly, it is like coming home. It is as if scales fall from our eyes and we are able to see and understand things that confused us before. Thus it is that 20/20 Insight comes as we approach life with a deep sense of wonder about how things might be and could be if we could learn to see things in new and clearer ways. Those who experience significant breakthroughs are deeply immersed in awe and wonder, and it is this sense of wonder that invites deeper, more tangible insight and clarity of thought.

Polish-american rabbi and philosopher Abraham Joshua Heschel once wrote, "There is only one way to wisdom—awe! Forfeit your sense of awe, let your conceit diminish your ability to revere, and the universe becomes [nothing more than] a marketplace for you. The loss of awe is the great block to insight."

Sir Isaac Newton had a true and honest sense of wonder that led him to some of the greatest discoveries in history.

"I don't know what I may appear to the world," he wrote, "but to myself, I seem to have been only as if a boy playing on the seashore, and diverting myself now and then, finding a smoother pebble or a prettier shell than ordinary, whilst the great ocean of truth lay undiscovered before me." The world that Newton saw was a world that others simply could not see, not because they were less intelligent or less educated but because they would not question the world and experience its wonder. Newton's brilliance came not solely from his intellect but also from an enduring sense of wonder, which led him to seek new insights about everything, opening the eyes of his understanding to see what few others were able to perceive. By having a sense of awe, like Newton's, we can begin to see things as they really are and really can be.

Insight is not something we can buy or order from the Internet like parts for our computers. We can't have it installed into our subconscious minds in a way that makes us see and experience life in different ways. Deep, honest insight, as we will discuss, comes upon us as we are open to it and are willing to accept, just for a moment perhaps, that there is much we can learn if we remain honest and willing to consider things in new ways. It is awe and wonder that help create the kinds of insight woven into each of the chapters that follow. The poet Robert Frost once wrote:

> *For, dear me, why abandon a belief*
> *Merely because it ceases to be true.*
> *Cling to it long enough, and not a doubt*
> *It will turn true again, for so it goes.*
> *Most of the change we think we see in life*

Is due to truths being in and out of favor.
As I sit here, and oftentimes, I wish
I could be monarch of a desert land
I could devote and dedicate forever
To the truths we keep coming back and back to.

My hope is that this book will represent for you, the reader, truths that you can continue to come back to, like pure water that quenches your thirst for the solid insights that so many search for these days. It has been for me.

How Your Head Creates Your World

Every spirit builds itself a house and beyond its house a world and beyond its world a heaven. Know then that the world exists for you. For you it is the phenomenon perfect, what we are, that only we can see. All that Adam had, all that Caesar could, you have and can do. Build therefore your own world.

—Ralph Waldo Emerson, American essayist and poet

It was a beautiful summer afternoon, with a soft, warm breeze blowing through the towering trees around the baseball stadium. I loved this game and had played it from as early as I can remember. Over in the dugout sat all my best buddies from school, kids with whom I had grown up and played baseball nearly every day. Baseball was our one true love.

On this day, our team was to play its first game as a C-League team. We had all played Little League, but now the entire game was about to change. The players ranged in age from 12 to 14. The bases were farther apart, and it was farther from the pitcher's mound to home plate. The pitchers were older and taller, and they could throw faster than any of us had previously experienced. This was no longer Little League; we were now playing in the "big show."

As I stood anxiously in the on-deck circle watching a lanky 14-year-old take his final warm-up pitches, I said to myself, "You can hit off this kid, Randy, you know you can; now get up there and rip the ball." Two years before, I was diagnosed with a rare retina disease that was robbing me of my central vision. The progression of the disease was very slow, and so far I had been able to continue a normal life, including playing the game I loved. But I knew that there would come a day when I would no longer be able to play. Little did I realize that this was to be that day.

Talking about my eyesight problems was not something any of us kids did in those days. All my friends knew that I had trouble reading books and seeing the baseball, but it didn't seem like something we needed to discuss. They knew, and I knew that they knew, and that was good enough. After all, we were 12-year-old boys, all heading for the big leagues someday. For me, however, that lifelong dream was slipping away.

As I stepped into the batter's box, my heart pounded. "Will I be able to see the ball?" I wondered to myself as I waited for the first pitch. Would I be able to play baseball for another year? Time stood still for those few seconds as I waited. I prayed that I would just be able to see the ball well enough to get some kind of hit.

A wave of anxiety swept over me as I stared toward the pitcher's mound. It seemed a hundred miles away, and the pitcher looked 20 feet tall. My coach's final words to me before I stepped to the plate still ring in my ears: "Come on, Randy, you can do it. You've always been a great ballplayer, now get up there and knock the socks off that ball. I know you can do it." As I stood waiting for that first pitch, I hoped and prayed that he was right.

I had scarcely stepped up to the plate when it was all over. Three blazing fastballs came so hard and fast that I hardly knew what happened. I saw nothing. I stood there motionless for those few seconds, trying to see the ball coming toward me, but I couldn't. The only way I knew that the ball had even been pitched was by the eerie thud as it popped into the catcher's mitt. I'll never forget that day or the prophetic words of the umpire as he cried, "Strike three—you're out of there!" He was right. I was "out of there" in many more ways than anyone really appreciated.

I also recall that long walk from home plate back to the dugout, where all my friends sat. I could feel the sobering reality of what had just happened welling up inside me. I wanted to cry but didn't. I just took my seat at the end of the bench, barely hearing the supportive words of my buddies. In spite of their kind words, we all knew that everything was not all right. Something was very, very wrong.

I sat on that bench and stared at the ground, trying to make sense of what was happening to me and what this all might mean. That strikeout was not just an ordinary strikeout; it was symbolic of something that I had hoped I would never face. As I sat there embarrassed, alone, and afraid, I realized that all the encouragement in the world could not bring back my failing eyesight. It was out of my hands.

Two Kinds of Vision

As you were reading that story, you were exercising one of the most amazing powers in the world—the power of visualization. In your mind's eye, you were able to picture the events of my last day of baseball and even sense how it might have felt to be in that situation. In a very real sense, you were there, able to "see" the entire experience on the stage of your mind just as if you had actually been there. This ability to see in the mind is one of the most profound of human endowments.

On the stage of our mind's eye, we see ourselves and the world around us. It is there that our dreams begin, our desires originate, and our emotions and attitudes—fears, discouragement, doubt, anger, happiness, love, hope, and wonder—are formed.

Most of us rarely comprehend that vision takes place in the mind, let alone understand how it does. Regardless of what we know, it remains that the images that form in our mind's eye have tremendous power over our attitudes and actions. In order to be effective in any endeavor, we do not need to develop habits or skills; these are merely reflections, or natural outgrowths, of our internal vision. What we need is to better understand the power that our internal vision has to create success and failure. We need to more clearly understand the role that our internal vision plays in our everyday lives, how it can lead us to greater effectiveness or continual discouragement and disappointment. It all begins here, on the stage of our minds, where we see ourselves and the world around us.

My last day of baseball was eventful on many levels. First, I realized that my ability to play the game had slipped away and that the passion I felt for the sport could no longer be expressed on the field. My deteriorating physical eyesight prevented me from accomplishing the things that at that time were supremely important to me.

Something else happened that day that proved to be even more serious and significant in my life. In my mind's eye, I began to form a picture of the world that was based on this and other experiences in my young life, a picture that was heavily influenced by these experiences and the emotions they created. My way of seeing my experiences began to form a lens that uniquely distorted my view of the world and everyone in it, based on my pain and disappointment. On that day, I not only suffered the loss of a sport I had grown to love, I also lost my ability to see myself and others in clear and productive ways.

Somehow in the confusion and disappointment of those early years, I began to see a world that was cold, heartless, and jarring. It became very clear to me that other people prevented me from doing what I wanted to do. Kids at school who teased me or had probing questions about why I couldn't read the blackboard or play sports became a source of resentment. I turned inward, fearing what others might think if they found out about me—the real me, the blind Randy. Classmates and acquaintances became a source of anxiety as I spent every day wondering if people could tell that I had poor eyesight. I developed the ability to lie my way out of tight spots in which people were determined to know why I looked at them the way I did.

When my friends and I turned 16, the questions started about why I didn't drive and when I was going to get my driver's license. "I just don't want to get it right now," I said, trying to appear disinterested in driving, or "I got it, but I lost it, and I have to take the test again."

Every day in every class at school I felt the pressure that came with having to put on an act—an act that I now call blind-man's bluff. I wanted more than anything not to have this problem, and the only way I knew how to deal with it was to pretend that it wasn't real, that it didn't exist.

I didn't realize that I was creating a world of anxiety, dishonesty, defensiveness, and resentment by my response to what was happening around me. Those who asked questions and who "exposed" me became my enemies. I vividly remembered the names and faces of those kids who were determined to tell everyone that "Randy is blind. He can't see. That's why he doesn't drive. He's blind." I felt as if I were waging a secret war against the world, trying with all my heart to present a fully sighted image and hoping that I could pull it off. The world I experienced was one I helped create, and in a very real sense, the world I saw was my own creation.

Lenses of the Mind

It has been said that the world we see is the one we are conditioned to see, based on our experiences. That means that there is no "real" or "objective" world that we must learn to see clearly. The world is what we create, and how we create it is based on what we have learned to see and how we have been taught to make sense of life events. How we choose to see the world also has much to do with our ability to be effective personally and in relationships with others. The diagram on page 24 shows how all of this operates.

We know that various factors come together to create the lens or lenses through which we view reality. Our backgrounds, where we grew up, who raised us and our relationships with them, our race and ethnic origins, and our language all create these invisible lenses through which we view the world. My experiences as a young boy going blind created a lens that caused me to see nearly everyone as a threat and some people as real enemies. Innocent questions from innocent people were translated as attempts to embarrass and expose me. I saw well-intentioned teachers as my greatest source of danger be-

HOW WE SEE

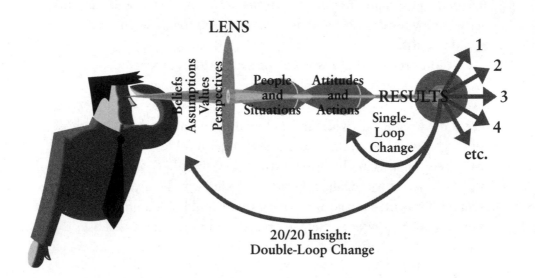

LENS

Beliefs
Assumptions
Values
Perspectives

People
and
Situations

Attitudes
and
Actions

RESULTS

Single-
Loop
Change

1
2
3
4
etc.

20/20 Insight:
Double-Loop Change

cause they seemed completely insensitive to how embarrassing it was for me to be found out in public. The lens of my creation forced me to live under a shroud of secrecy, to sneak around like a thief evading the police.

How we see is the root of how we behave. Our behavior and decisions are based on what we see. When I was a teenager struggling with deteriorating vision, my lens prevented me from seeing even honest acts of kindness for what they were. I interpreted every act as a clandestine attempt to expose me, which would cause me embarrassment and great anxiety. Not only was I quickly becoming physically blind, I was also becoming blind to honest acts of care and concern. I created a world in which I was under constant pressure to perform flawlessly lest someone find out about the "real me."

We see examples of this every day. A woman marries a man who is cruel and violent. The marriage ends in a bitter divorce. The pain and frustration the woman feels build a lens through which she now views all men. She rejects even honest attempts to help her by concerned neighbors, thinking, "You don't think I can do this on my own, do you?" She is bitter at what has happened to her and devastated by the emotional scars left behind.

The world she now sees and experiences each day is far different from that of the woman across the street who is happily married and has a healthy and productive life. Even though they live only 100 feet apart, these two women are actually living in two very different worlds based on how they see and what they experience. Actually, the first woman is blind to the fact that life could be fulfilling and rewarding. To her, life is a sorrowful place, and others are not to be trusted.

We see it in the workplace as we observe how corporate managers choose to respond to the challenges they face. A manager of 30 people, for instance, views his employees as lazy and manipulative, the kind of people who need to be motivated to do anything. He hovers, checks up, tracks their work meticulously, and does everything he can to make sure that they toe the line. He's sure it's just a matter of time before they screw up. He believes that if he stays close by, maybe he can catch the mistakes before they cause too many problems. When people perform well, he translates it as an exception, something unexpected. He even sees good behavior as a possible ploy by the employees to win his favor rather than as honest efforts to do well.

This manager now lives in a world that creates the very behavior he fears. He doesn't hear the comments his employees make about how frustrated they are to be working under such a micro-manager: "If he's going to stand over us like a hawk and watch every move we make, we might as well lay back and let him do our jobs, too."

As the diagram illustrates, our lenses cause us to interpret events around us in specific ways, and these interpretations lead to our actions or responses to what we think and see. Thus, the results of our view tend to reinforce behavior and expectations. Our lenses create our world. That's why it is so hard to stand back and look at how we are seeing. Our lenses are so much a part of how we think and so deeply embedded in our mind's eye that we don't even recognize that we have them. But changing our vision will bring greater effectiveness and peace.

The connection between our internal vision and the results we ultimately produce is constant and direct. In a sense, the quality of the results we produce in life is merely a manifestation of the clarity of our internal vision. If we continually find ourselves frustrated, angry, disappointed, confused, depressed, or any of a host of other negative emotions, it is only because we see ourselves and others in a particular way. Our mind's eye is where our ability to produce effective results is first born, for if we start out viewing the world in distorted, ineffective, and counterproductive ways, we will automatically produce results inconsistent with what we really desire. The boon for change takes place at the level of inner vision because from there, everything else flows like a river from its source. If the headwaters are tainted, the river that runs out of them will be equally toxic. What we see is always what we get.

Single- and Double-Loop Insight

The diagram on page 24 also shows two different learning loops, which I call single and double. When we learn at the single-loop level, we observe the results we are getting and we consider our actions and try to change them to get different results. This is simple, straightforward learning that never causes us to question the clarity of our internal vision—our beliefs, assumptions, or values. How we see the world remains unexamined. The only thing that changes is our method or strategy for trying to get what we want.

For example, the manager I mentioned earlier believes that the best way to motivate people is to create tight structure and keep the reins short so that people will not fail. He believes in establishing control and keeping it. Once you lose control, you've lost everything, he believes. This reflects his worldview, or at least a piece of it. As he interacts with his people, his attitudes about them and their performance flow from this belief system. What happens then when things do not go as desired and he feels that results are slipping? At the level of single-loop learning, he simply changes his behavior to create a different method of ensuring tight control. He never examines his fundamental belief.

Examination is what double-loop learning, or 20/20 Insight, involves. It leads us to ask questions behind the question, to step back from what we are doing and ask what it is that drives us to do what we are doing. In the above example, the manager may reflect on what is happening with his people and begin to recognize that everything he does, all his communication and approaches, is designed to maintain control. "Why do I do this?" is a legitimate question that he could ask himself. "What am I afraid will happen if I don't personally stay on top of these people?" As he begins to ask deeper, more basic questions about the beliefs and assumptions he holds, he will begin to understand his behavior. This kind of learning is rich and filled with high-leverage possibilities because the manager is finally doing something that will immediately influence how he feels and what he does.

Hence, behavior is really a fingerprint or a clue to the more basic internal vision that we hold. When we begin to ask these deeper questions, we discover important insights that illuminate our understanding about ourselves and those with whom we interact.

The single most important insight that I know of for creating happy, productive lives and for building powerful and effective organizations and families is to fully and deeply understand the idea that our heads create our world. The world is not already created for us to figure out or manipulate in our favor. Learning to see in new ways, at higher levels, with greater clarity and truth than ever before, is essential, since so many other things flow from it. The great secret of 20/20 Insight is so easily lost in vigorous efforts to change others and to create strategies to get what we want. In so doing, we forget to step back far enough to include ourselves in the pictures we see. As we learn to stand back and gain a wider view of the world, we begin to see important connections between our own thinking and actions and the world that we are creating for ourselves day by day.

Making Sense of the World

Several years ago, I met a man who taught me about how our experiences shape and filter what we see and how we make sense of these experiences. I met him when he picked me up from an airport in New Jersey.

Vladimir Krucocov was born to poor Russian farmers in the Soviet heartland. Life was hard, and he dreamed of something better. In those days, the Cold War between the United States and the former Soviet Union was as frigid as ever, but in his heart, Vladimir yearned for the day he could travel to America.

His dream came true in 1975 when he set foot on American soil at New York Harbor. Thirty years old, he arrived with no money, no job, no friends, and absolutely no English. Still, as he looked around him, all he saw was opportunity. "There is plenty here," he said to himself, "and I will prosper."

Prosper he did, and in 10 years he had not only mastered English but had graduated from a university with an engineering degree. He was eventually hired by a large aerospace company in New Jersey. Because he wanted to earn extra money to bring his aging parents to America, he also drove a limousine at night, and that's how I met him.

Vladimir wrote to his aging parents back in Russia about his new home and job and freedom in America, but they never answered. When he finally talked with them, they told him that they could not believe what his letters had said. After being exposed to decades and generations of anti-American propaganda, Vladimir's parents found it impossible to believe that their son could go to America and find happiness. They had been told time and time again that America was filled with terror and disorder, that if you went to America, you would starve and be ruined. Now their son was writing about great success and personal happiness a world away from the poverty and strain of Soviet life on the government farms.

Finally, after months of planning and persuasion, Vladimir flew his parents to the United States for a visit. He was eager to show them his home and neighborhood and tell them all about life in America. They were cautious and suspicious, still believing that it just couldn't be true.

On the way home from the airport, they stopped at a local supermarket to pick up some things for dinner. Vladimir took his aging father's arm as they walked around the store. His father looked with amazement at the stacks of food of every kind, shape, and size. As they strolled through the fresh fruit and vegetable section, he stopped and stared. In most Russian stores near his home they usually had potatoes and sometimes carrots, but often there was nothing. Now he looked up and down rows of fresh food the likes of which he had never before seen. He simply couldn't believe his eyes.

As they drove home, Vladimir's father leaned up and patted his son on the shoulder. "Son, thank you for taking me to the food museum. It was beautiful!"

"What do you mean, Father? Food museum?"

His father then explained that this store must be a museum for food, brought in from all over America for people to see.

Vladimir laughed. "No, Father," he said with a smile. "We have stores like that all over America. That's what our grocery stores are like here." Vladimir pointed out several other large supermarkets on the way to his house, and his father sat in silence, staring in wonder out the car window.

Then they stopped at a shopping mall to pick up some new trousers for Vladimir. After 15 minutes in J. C. Penney, Vladimir told his wife that they didn't have what he wanted.

His father was incredulous. "Son, they have pants of all kinds, rows and rows. What do you mean they don't have what you want?" Vladimir explained, and his father listened in disbelief. In all his long, hard life he had never seen such plentifulness, such prosperity.

Truly our minds create our world; Vladimir's father's world looked nothing like this one. Where there was a grocery store, he saw a food museum. His previous experiences, his environment, and his surroundings created a world out of the facts that he knew. Vladimir's father literally could not see his son's world. Only after Vladimir's attempts to explain what these things meant to him could his father begin to see it.

Two individuals can see and experience the same world in radically different ways. In this case, two men went to a food store in New Jersey. They both saw the store's design and lighting and what was sold there, but their ways of making sense of those facts caused them to come to two very different understandings. Vladimir's father's initial interpretation led him to believe that it was simply a place for viewing various kinds of food products, not a place to purchase food.

Developing 20/20 Insight increases our field of internal vision, thus expanding our options, helping us to see possibilities that we could otherwise not see, and allowing us to see where we were previously blind. This expanded viewpoint enables us to be more effective as we learn to respond in new and more productive ways.

Many of the examples thus far have pointed out the downside of distorted, blurred vision, in which people are blind to what could be. I recently heard the life story of the wonderful Russian comedian Yakov Smirnoff, which points out how positive, meaningful experiences can shape in wonderfully productive ways how we see the world.

When Yakov and his parents landed at New York Harbor, they had nothing to their name and only $50 in their pockets. To make matters worse, no one in the family spoke any English. Their first challenge was to find a place to live, and so they searched and searched for an apartment until they finally found an old run-down apartment building with a small room for rent. There was, however, one major problem: They had $50 and the rent was $250. The kind, elderly landlady, Mrs. Landow, saw the plight they were in and offered to pay the difference out of her own pocket until they got settled. Yakov and his parents were deeply moved that this woman, who had very little herself, would reach out to them in such a kind way.

But that was not the end of Mrs. Landow's kindness. She quickly went around to the rest of the apartments in the building, telling people about the new Russian family that had moved in. A few days later, the Smirnoffs heard a soft knock at their door. What they saw when they opened it brought them to tears. There stood Mrs. Landow and a group of neighbors. Each one bore some gift of food, an article of clothing, a kitchen item that they needed, blankets, bedding, pillows, or whatever else they could pull together for this new family.

"We did not know these people and they did not know us," Yakov said, "but they did it anyway because they cared. We stood there in disbelief at what these people had done for us, and we could do little more than weep for joy."

This single experience at such a desperate time for the Smirnoff family formed a lens of kindness and decency that has remained with Yakov to this day. "I learned that day that this is what America was all about—helping one another and reaching out to those in need." Yakov is still reaching out whenever he can around the world to bless the lives of millions. It all began with a small, selfless act of kindness by Mrs. Landow, who set in motion a lifetime of service for Yakov and his family. Over 25 years later, he still speaks of her with great affection and emotion. What that woman did was far more than bringing food and blankets. She helped create in Yakov and his family a vision of what it means to be an American and, perhaps more important, what it means to be a human being.

She brought 20/20 Insight to the Smirnoff family in places where they were previously blind. Yakov is still seeing the world through those special lenses and making a difference wherever he goes.

The Mountain Man and *Field of Dreams*

Several years ago, I was on an airplane, in a seat near the door, half asleep and waiting for takeoff. A hulking, beefy man appeared in the doorway, attracting my attention. He stood about six feet six inches tall and probably weighed 300 pounds. But that wasn't what caught my eye. He had an Abe Lincoln beard that hit him about midchest and covered his upper body like a woolly rug. He wore a red hunting cap with fuzzy earflaps and a red-and-black-checked hunting jacket. He was a huge mountain of a man, and he sat right next to me. He looked as if he'd fallen off the cover of *Field and Stream* into this first-class compartment full of men in business attire. I was intrigued.

"Who are you and where are you headed?" I asked as casually as I could. He told me that he was a hunter from Appalachia. "No kidding," I thought. (I knew he wasn't a dentist!) He had been on the hunting expedition of a lifetime in the Rockies. As a boy, he had grown up hunting squirrels and raccoons and other small animals, and he had saved for years to go to Colorado to hunt big game. Then his eyes widened and his voice grew louder as he described in gory detail all the animals he had shot in the mountains of Colorado. "I got me a bear and a deer and a moose," along with several other creatures, he boasted.

But his hunt hadn't been a complete success. To his great disappointment, he had failed to bag an elk. "I'll be back as soon as I can make it to get me an elk," he said confidently.

After we had dinner and I had listened to a few more hunting stories, the flight attendant came down the aisle with headphones for a movie. *Field of Dreams* was one of the selections, and the mountain man asked me if it was a good movie and if he should watch it.

"You might not like it," I thought. "It's all about baseball, and I don't think it has any killing in it at all." What I actually told him, though, was that I had seen it and enjoyed it very much.

He moved to a vacant seat on the aisle across from me where he had his own TV screen, and the movie began. As it progressed, I could hear the mountain man chuckling, and I figured he had probably grown bored with the dumb baseball movie and changed channels to a comedy that was also being offered.

Near the end of the movie there is a particularly poignant scene that always reaches out and grabs my heart. Ray Kinsella, played by Kevin Costner, has been led by a voice to Minneapolis to locate Moonlight Graham, played by Burt Lancaster. When Ray arrives, he finds that Moonlight has died, as has his wife. But Ray talks with locals who knew him, and they all describe him as a good, decent man who was the best doctor the town ever had. When children needed eyeglasses, he would fit them for free. He did everything he could to serve people in the community. He had made a difference in this town.

Ray is confused. Why was he sent to find a dead man? Back home, he's losing his farm because he has plowed under a large amount of land to build a baseball field. Everything is unraveling. Bewildered, he goes out for a walk. As he walks, he is transported to an earlier time.

He looks up at a movie marquee and sees that *The Godfather* is the feature film. He bends down to inspect the sticker on a car license plate, which reads "1972."

He sees a man with a hat and an umbrella walking down the street in the pale moonlight. He suddenly realizes that it is Doc Graham, formerly known as Moonlight Graham, the baseball player. Ray jogs across the street, introduces himself, and is invited into Doc's nearby office to talk.

"Why did you quit baseball?" Ray asks.

"I had one chance in the major leagues and struck out," Doc tells him. "I was so afraid that they would send me to the minor leagues that I decided to quit." He talks of his deeply satisfying life in Minnesota and how much he has loved being a doctor.

Ray can't believe it. "You came this close to your dream and let it pass you by?" Ray says with amazement, wondering how any man could do it. Doc explains what a tragedy it would have been if he had been a doctor for only five minutes instead of playing baseball in the major leagues for five minutes.

Ray won't leave it alone. "But isn't there something you've always wanted to do, some dream you've always had that is still unfulfilled?"

"Yes," Doc answers. "I'd love to play baseball again and stare down a big-league pitcher and knock the ball out of the park, turn a single into a triple, and slide headfirst into third base. Yes, that is what I would like to do. That would be my dream. And now, my friend, is there enough magic in the moonlight for you to make that dream come true?"

"Yes," Ray answers. "Just come to Iowa."

I had seen this movie three times before and cried through most of it. This time I was hit with a wave of nostalgia like never before. Listening to Doc Graham talk about his dream of playing baseball again, I started recalling my days in Little League. As I sat on this plane 35,000 feet above the ground, the past became the present in my mind's eye. I could smell my old Brooks Robinson baseball glove. I recalled my baseball uniform and how I loved to wear it long after a game was over. I felt like a real big-leaguer in my uniform. "Syracuse Colts," it proudly declared. That was my team, the only team I ever played on.

I remembered how I loved to play baseball and how excited I was the day of a game. I could see myself running the bases and fielding grounders. I re-experienced the thrill of playing well and winning. It all came back, clear and sweet and real as I was transported back to earlier days when I played the game I loved more than anything. In my mind's eye I was there. Tears rolled down my face as I relived those tender memories.

Meanwhile, the mountain man was having the time of his life, clapping as if he were at a rodeo or a boxing match. I was absolutely certain now that he wasn't watching this movie. He couldn't be; it was impossible!

Finally the movie ended. As I was wiping my eyes and blowing my nose, the mountain man leaned across the aisle, tapped me on the shoulder, and said, "I appreciate you telling me to watch this movie. It was one of the funniest shows I've ever seen."

I couldn't believe my ears. "What did he say?" I thought in amazement. "The funniest show he has ever seen!" While I sat there in a pool of tears and a pile of handkerchiefs, he was watching a comedy! Unbelievable! He had told me he was from the mountains of West Virginia and lived in a rural community, but surely he had seen movies before, hadn't he? If this were his first and only cinema experience, then *Field of Dreams* could possibly be the funniest movie he had ever seen. But I was in shock.

I was still stunned as I walked off the plane. As I sat in the airport waiting for my ride, I pulled out a notebook containing points that I wanted to cover in my presentation the next morning. Then I read these words: "We do not see the world the way it is, but instead we see it as we are conditioned to see it based on our experiences and how we made sense of those experiences when we had them."

I had repeated this statement to people hundreds of times. This time, however, it struck me more forcefully than it ever had before. I had always understood the idea, but suddenly it came alive because I had just experienced it. My mountain man friend and I sat next to one another on an airplane and viewed the same movie. We heard the same dialogue and observed the actors playing their parts, and yet in the end, we each had a very different experience. Our physical eyes and ears may have witnessed the same material, but we experienced it much differently.

The Rest of My Story

I began this chapter with part of my story, perhaps the part that has had the most significant impact on me over the years. Now I'd like to complete it. I hope that once you hear it, your own personal history will come more clearly into focus and you will understand how profoundly powerful our inner vision or worldview is and how it affects us in fundamental ways every day of our lives. As I have shared my story around the world, others have shared their own experiences with adversity and achievement. I have been stirred by their courage and insights. I believe that, in essence, we all have the same story; only the characters are different.

I was born in 1953, a healthy, normal baby. As I grew, I developed a love for sports, particularly baseball. I was the little kid at family reunions with a Little League baseball cap on and a miniature bat that I would pound on everything. As a three-year-old, I would give demonstrations of my amazing baseball ability by letting people watch me hit. I was good, and I loved the game.

As I grew older, my love for baseball intensified. Every summer I played daily with my neighborhood buddies. I was the pitcher. Blair Davis down the street was my catcher, and his little brother Garth shagged the balls that we missed. I don't think Garth ever liked the position we gave him, but somebody had to chase the ball when it got by us, and he was the littlest.

Baseball was my passion, and regardless of the weather, rain or shine, we found a way to play. In the winter we played catch in our basement, and in the process drove my mom crazy. "But Mom," I said more than once, "we're not going to break anything!" I'm sure we demolished our share of pottery and other delicate things in our house, but they should have never been there anyway—right in the middle of our playing field.

Back in those days collecting baseball cards was a hobby, not a way to build a financial empire, and I had them all—Maris, Mantle, Koufax, and the rest.

Life rolled along beautifully until age 10, when my parents and I noticed that I was having trouble with my vision. I was holding books closer to my face and couldn't read the blackboard from the back of the classroom. We both thought that I just needed glasses. No big deal, right? Wrong. What we learned in the days and weeks that followed would change all of our lives.

The first optometrist we went to was baffled by what he saw. "I've seen this condition in older people whose vision deteriorates with age," he said, "but never in a boy this young." He didn't even know what to call my problem and recommended a specialist in Salt Lake City. My parents were stunned by the news, and I'm sure they lay awake many nights wondering where all this was heading.

The specialist had a name for my condition. It was retinitis pigmentosa, a fairly rare retina disorder. It was a degenerative disease; he could not predict how much deterioration would occur, and worst of all, it was untreatable. He said that we should go home and hope for the best.

Before we left, the doctor told me, "Randy, you need to know that there are several things you will never be able to do. You will never be able to drive a car."

"Who cares?" I thought. "I'm only 10 anyway and can't even reach the steering wheel." Little did I know that six years later, being able to drive would become the most important thing in my life.

"You also won't be able to read without significant help and some powerful magnification," he said.

This didn't bother me, either, because I really didn't like school much anyway except for recess and lunch. At recess I played baseball with all my buddies, so if I simply had trouble reading, that wasn't so bad. It took me a few years to understand just how much this would challenge me and the problems it would present as I grew older.

Then came the big blow. "Is there anything else you really like to do?" he asked.

"Sure," I said. "I love to play sports, mostly baseball."

He leaned back in his chair and thought for a moment before he said carefully, "I'm not suggesting that you quit playing baseball, but you may find that, in the years ahead, it will become impossible for you to continue."

That day as we drove home, I was angry and scared. "I don't care who this guy is," I said furiously. "There's no way I'm quitting baseball. I don't care what he thinks." My parents were wonderful and assured me that there was no reason to curtail any of my activities as long as I felt I could do them. So I continued to play baseball.

I played Little League for the next two years while my vision slowly grew worse. I lost all my central vision and had to use peripheral vision to play. When I pitched, I could no longer look directly at the catcher but had to look off to the side. I remember being tested by more than one kid who wondered why I looked at third base rather than at the catcher. But I learned that there was a significant competitive advantage to this style of play. The batter would come to the plate and see me looking at third base. While he waited for me to get ready, not knowing that I already was, he would stand there ill-prepared for the fastball that I blew past him. Batters soon learned that when they got to the plate, they'd better get ready fast because I was ready then! I think I struck out more batters that year with the peripheral approach to pitching than I did in my earlier years using conventional methods. I also took a lot of flak for it.

At about age 12, when I was finished with Little League, it was time to move on to C-League, or Pony League. I was now the youngest kid on my team. The coach, an old family friend who knew of my problem, put his arm around me at the first game and asked me if I could play. I assured him that I could, and he decided to put me in right field. "If you play right field, you won't have to worry about catching the ball much because no one hits it out there," he explained. I knew this, but I also knew that right field was where you always put your worst players. I had gone from being a star pitcher on my Little League team to playing right field. Despite what I'd told the coach, I didn't know for sure what I could still see. But the coach was willing to let me play, so I grabbed my glove and ran to right field.

The test came in about the third inning when the batter took a late swing at a fastball, slicing it high and long to right field. I never saw a thing. I actually heard it hit the ground and knew it was very close, but I still couldn't see it. I froze, not knowing whether to run forward, backward, or sideways. The other team screamed with excitement as I panicked. The runners raced around the bases while my team screamed at me to pick up the ball. Finally, my friend in center field ran over, picked up the ball, and threw it in. By then the other team had scored three runs.

I recall standing way out in right field feeling like everyone was staring at me and asking, "What's wrong with Randy? Why does he act like he doesn't know what's going on? Isn't there someone else you can get to play out there?" All this was going on even as I was wondering what I was doing on the field. I realized in those moments that I could not play outfield because I simply could not see the ball. But I wanted to play more than anything in the world.

When the inning finally ended, I walked slowly into the dugout and sat on the bench with my buddies. I had played with these guys for years, and they all knew what was happening with me. Some came over, patted me on the shoulder and said, "It's all right, Randy. You'll catch the next one." Others didn't know what to say, but they somehow knew that inside I was dying. I played the rest of that game, and luckily, no more balls came to right field.

I did no better at the plate. No matter who was on the mound or what he threw, I couldn't see the ball. In my heart I realized that this would be my last baseball game. Just thinking about it nearly broke my heart. Even now as I think back on that day and the disappointment I felt, the memory stirs sad, haunting thoughts of how it felt to stop playing the game I loved so much.

The events of that day have played themselves out in my mind's eye a thousand times over the years. The embarrassment was real enough, and so was the fact that we ended up losing that game partly because I couldn't see well enough to hit or field. But worse than all of that was what that experience and the days that followed did to me and how I was affected by those painful events.

The world that I was to live in over the next 20 years began to take shape that afternoon. Often, negative, traumatic experiences have deep and lasting effects on how we see the world and the conclusions we draw about reality. Before we realize it, a filter colored by our experiences has formed, causing how we see the world to be distorted and blurred in some way. That day my world began slipping into a colder, less tolerant place. I grew more anxious about what other people would think of me if they learned about my eyesight. I became almost paranoid about the things that people might do should they find out. Suddenly others began to appear nosy and overly curious about me and why I did what I did—why I couldn't read in class, why I never drove a car, why I always double-dated with friends, and endless other questions.

Filtered through the pain of my teenage experiences, innocent questions took on a new light, and I grew more and more nervous about what others might want to know about me. All of this caused me to turn inward and become more shy and less confident. I was more fearful of others and how they might hurt me or, even worse, expose me. In the years that followed my retirement from baseball, I became a polished liar. It was the only way I could protect myself from all the questions that people persisted in asking about my eyesight.

What kind of world did I create for myself? How did my assumptions, beliefs, and experiences shape the world I saw? Predictably, the more I saw others as something that could possibly be harmful to me, the more my world became a place I needed to defend. If we see other people as a possible threat to our safety or happiness, we will treat them with suspicion and caution. What do we create in the process? Generally, people who respond to us just about as we pictured them to be. In all of this, we unwittingly create the world we see and begin a self-fulfilling cycle in which our worldview is reinforced by the way we interface with it. If I send out love, generally I receive love back. If I send out fear and anger and resentment, in many cases this is what comes back to me.

The Path to 20/20 Insight

My story and the others illustrate the focal point of this chapter—that our heads create the world we experience. To really buy into the fact that we create much of what we experience in life is more than a casual nod, as if to say, "Yeah, I see what you mean." If understood deeply and clearly, it is an insight like few others, one that will open the door to making significant breakthroughs in life. I suggest that when we come to see things as they really are and really can be, the results of such clear insights are astounding.

But there's more. When we understand that we create much of what we experience, we also come to realize that we have incredible power to change how we experience the world and ourselves. If you struggle with self-doubt and hold a distorted self-image in your mind's eye, you can create a different view of yourself—a view that truly reflects who you are, want to be, and can become. You will unleash your capacity to change and will make significant leaps in your personal and professional effectiveness. You'll no longer want to live the false pretenses that informed your life up to this point. By abandoning false and self-limiting beliefs, you can rescript self-limiting ideas with effective, purposeful, and powerful thoughts and beliefs. The power was there all along. Hence, truly understanding that your head creates your world is one of the most significant insights there is, for it leads to so many other important insights.

I have met many people over the years who wonder if they can ever really change. They have tried nearly every formula and technique imaginable to move forward in their lives and improve their relationships with others. Often they experience a short-term surge in their optimism and feelings of hope, but they generally slide back into the same old rut. These are smart, talented, educated people who honestly desire to become more effective in all areas of their lives, but something stands in their way, and in most cases, they don't know what it is. They yearn for a place of peace, a feeling of well-being that cannot come from working harder or from watching TV. They are engaged in an honest search for substance, real nuggets that they can hold in their hands and that can illuminate the landscape of life. These people want to see their way to better problem-solving with others. Building harmony within and between others is high on the list of things that they care deeply about. Their searching questions usually reflect a gnawing sense of frustration: "What am I missing? What am I failing to see?"

After reading my story of blindness, you might wonder what happened to me and how I learned to see myself and the world differently, to see with 20/20 Insight. The answer is much more simple than you might expect. Over time, I came to see that the results I was producing—personally, professionally, interpersonally, and the like—were far short of what I desired. I kept running into myself, discovering that my methods for success were actually leading me to disappointment and pain. The love and support of a wonderful wife and good friends also helped me to look at myself differently and question the conclusions I had drawn about my limitations and the ideas I had about how others saw me.

Questioning how I saw life was not something I had ever honestly done. Like most people, I truly thought that I was seeing things as they really were, not as I had been conditioned to see them based on my many experiences. The dawning slowly came about as I started to experiment with new ideas and different beliefs; in time I created a different lens through which I saw the world. As I did, I instantly began to experience a different world. People responded to me in ways that I never imagined they would. I found that instead of rejecting me, nearly everyone I met showed great interest and compassion, with a great desire to help me succeed in any way they could.

All of this was a huge surprise to me and was inconsistent with everything I had ever believed. This disparity between how I saw and what I was now experiencing shifted many of my dearly held views of myself and those around me. As my internal vision cleared and the blind spots were lifted, I literally saw a different world than I had ever seen before, but this change did not happen overnight nor as a result of any single experience.

When physical eyesight slowly begins to worsen, it is natural to become accustomed to it after a while. We know we don't see as well as we used to, but it isn't that bad, and we soon adapt. We make the best of the situation. We simply go and have our vision corrected with glasses. Even so, we learn to accept and adapt to situations in life that are less than perfect, all the time wishing they would get better.

When our internal vision is blurred with distortions that obscure how we see ourselves and the world, we rarely notice because it is so subtle and transparent. We simply learn to adapt to worsening insight and to live life as best we can. We need some kind of signal or indicator that tells us that how we see a situation is the problem and that changing how we see is the critical and necessary solution.

What are the signals that may indicate that our world is being distorted by how we see? Here are a few questions to get you started.

• Is the way I view myself healthy and productive, or do I see myself in ways that limit my potential?

• In my work and family life, am I getting the quality of results that I really desire?

• Are my relationships harmonious and satisfying and free from blame, resentment, or conflict?

• When I do have a problem, am I able to stand back and see clearly how I might have contributed to it?

• How am I seeing the situations of my life? Are my points of view, beliefs, and assumptions leading me forward in more effective ways or not?

These questions focus our attention on outcomes that we are experiencing on many levels. It is a helpful place to begin to assess to what extent your internal vision is in need of corrective lenses.

Part II
Personal Vision

Lens One
Beliefs Create the View

People act on ideas they accept as true, whether or not this is so. Hypnosis demonstrates this phenomenon. There is no difference between being hypnotized to accept a false idea as true and acting on mistaken notions we accept as true in our lives. The ideas are still false.

—Maxwell Maltz, author of *Psychocybernetics*

The anxious audience hushes as the hypnotist appears on the stage. They've heard about the mystical powers of this hypnotist and what people do under his spell. Now they are about to experience it firsthand.

He first moves to a table where two husky college men are seated. After placing them under hypnosis, he calls out, "There are two pencils before you. Try as you may, you will not be able to pick the pencils up. They are much too heavy. Now, if you can, remove them from the table!" The two men reach out and grasp the pencils but are unable to lift them. Their faces redden and their muscles bulge as they tug and struggle to move the pencils around, but it is impossible. The hypnotist snaps his fingers and brings them out of hypnosis; they easily lift the pencils. They have no recollection of what just happened.

Next he calls a woman out of the audience and asks her how she likes performing. "I hate to be in front of audiences. It scares me to death," she says nervously. He places her under hypnosis and tells her that she is an opera star and has performed all over the world. She starts to belt out a tune with great emotion in front of what she believes are thousands of her hysterical fans, as if she had done it many times before. Once out of hypnosis, she quickly returns to her seat, embarrassed to be in front of the audience.

The hypnotist calls two more young men from the audience and asks them to sit at the table. Once they are hypnotized, he tells them that their hands are glued to the table in front of them. No matter what they do, they will be unable to remove them. The audience howls as they watch the two men tug and stretch and pull. No matter what they do, they are unable to free their hands. It all seems too unbelievable.

Another audience member is told that she is a chicken. She clucks and struts all over the stage as if she really were a chicken. The hypnotist then tells the woman's husband that he is a dog, whereupon he falls to all fours and barks. The audience laughs uncontrollably.

Documented studies on hypnotized subjects are just as remarkable. When people under hypnosis are told that they are at the North Pole, their actual, measurable body temperatures drop in reaction to the cold that they think surrounds them. In another case, a hypnotist tells someone that his finger is a hot poker. As he touches the subject's skin, a small blister appears as if the subject were really burned. Obviously, the hypnotist's finger is not a hot poker, but the subject believes that it is, and his body responds accordingly.

How do we explain such seemingly bizarre and amazing things? How is a hypnotist able to get otherwise normal people to do such strange things? Hypnotists know one amazing truth: Whatever the human mind believes to be true is accepted as true, even if it is completely false. The people who believe that they are at the North Pole act as if they were actually in frigid conditions. This is not role-playing or something that they are pretending to believe.

By believing certain things to be true, these people create a different world for themselves, although the real world around them undergoes virtually no change. This is their personal vision. The fact that the hypnotist's finger was not a hot poker is irrelevant, since research has shown that the brain does not know the difference between a real hot poker and a finger that someone believes can burn them. Such is the power of belief to create the world around us in very real and significant ways.

In 1963, Maxwell Maltz wrote a fascinating book about this power of the mind. Maltz was a plastic surgeon who saw people come into his office day after day, wanting him to change their appearances in the hope that the results would change their lives. Most were experiencing some kind of insecurity, low self-esteem, sinking confidence in themselves, or similar personal struggle. They felt that their appearance was the cause of their lowered self-esteem and lack of success, so almost all of them felt that they would be happier and more successful if only they looked different.

This opinion made sense to Maltz, yet early in his practice he noticed a pattern that initially confused him and eventually caused him to shift his professional emphasis from the body to the mind. Much to his surprise, not everyone experienced increased self-esteem and more confidence as a result of surgery. Some did, and their lives were helped immeasurably by having plastic surgery. But others who had the same surgery still felt insecure and unattractive.

Maltz was perplexed by this inconsistency and began to study it. His findings and his exploration of many other fascinating questions are recorded in his landmark book *Psychocybernetics*.

"How is it," Maltz queried, "that two people can undergo plastic surgery hoping it will improve their lives, and one person undergoes a miraculous change while the other experiences no change at all in his confidence and self-esteem? Both receive the same treatment, but one is affected in astounding ways and the other remains unaffected, as if there had been no surgery performed at all."

The illustration on page 48 shows this fascinating phenomenon. Maltz discovered that the surgery was not the controlling variable. The only way he could explain why some people changed so dramatically and others did not was that those in the first group experienced a change in their self-image and those in the second group didn't. In the first group, the participants' mental pictures of who they were changed as a result of surgery.

The difference between the two kinds of people was minimal yet

Person A comes for surgery: "I need a face-lift."	Person B comes for surgery: "I need a face-lift."

Surgery is performed successfully. Patient looks great!	Surgery is performed successfully. Patient looks great!

CONCLUSION

Experiences a mighty change. Is more confident, friendly, and outgoing. Sees herself as a new person.	Sees no real difference. Still feels insecure, inferior, and ashamed.

OUTCOME

Person A moves ahead with renewed confidence. Finds great success.	Person B is not affected by surgery. Still feels stuck where she was. No improvement occurs— "Surgery didn't help!"

very profound. With surgery as the impetus, those who were able to change their mental pictures of themselves and what they could accomplish underwent dramatic changes in their lives. For others, even when a look in the mirror confirmed that they appeared different, their mind's eye continued to show them the same person, full of inferiority and insecurity and lacking confidence in their ability to succeed.

Maltz describes patients with facial disfigurements that created great challenges throughout their lives. They felt inferior to others and lacked confidence in interpersonal situations. Many were inhibited socially and lacked the confidence to work effectively at their professions. The disfigurements were far more than skin deep. They seeped deeply into people's mental pictures of who they were, how they saw themselves at their innermost core. When Maltz performed plastic surgery on their faces, he was also performing surgery on their souls, significantly affecting how they saw themselves. After surgery, Maltz's patients' former symptoms vanished, and they came out of the surgery not only with new faces but also with new images of themselves and new outlooks on life.

In the cases of those people who emerged from surgery unable to create a new mental picture, it was because the surgery had changed nothing psychologically, although everyone could see a wonderful transformation in their physical features. Some patients would even look in the mirror and say, "I can see that I look different, but I don't feel any different at all. I'm not sure if this helped in any way." And even when family members and friends commented on the great improvement, the patients could not see it. They were unwilling or unable to accept the fact that this change of physical features could really change them inside. They still thought, "I'm unattractive, always have been and always will be, no matter what kind of surgery I undergo."

There is very little difference between people who are actually hypnotized and individuals who have accepted false ideas about themselves and the world. Since they are unaware that their personal vision is false, they act on their ideas as if they were true, and they fail to see the impact of their beliefs.

Are You Hypnotized?

Consider the following real-life examples of people who believe false ideas and accept them as true. Perhaps you can relate to some of the situations.

• A young man graduates from law school with honors and begins looking for work. His search, however, produces few results, and in most cases he doesn't even go to interviews because he thinks "they won't hire me anyway." When he talks about his employment challenges, he uses words like "can't, won't, wish I could, wish I were more like so and so." He sees himself as inept and incompetent, someone whom real employers would not want to hire. With all of his ability and knowledge, his own beliefs about himself and the world prevent him from getting what matters most at this time in his life.

• A vice-president of a small electronics company publicly announces his belief that people only work for a paycheck. All of his decisions—how he sees morale and motivation problems and his interpretation of lags in new product design—flow from this fundamental belief about people and what turns them on to work. He is confused when he reviews the generous bonuses paid out the previous year and compares them with the turnover rate: He pays his people well, yet they don't stay very long with the company. He cannot see how his beliefs about people at work color everything he does.

• A salesman spends two days each January setting goals for the coming year, but no matter what happens, he never seems to achieve what he sets out to do. In spite of his best efforts, he cannot break through a financial ceiling, and his efforts to improve customer relations end up in a pile of good intentions. When asked, he has no idea what it is that stands in his way. Could it be that his subconscious beliefs are self-limiting and sabotage his ability to get what he really desires?

All of these people have at least one thing in common: They have adopted a belief system that prevents them from achieving at their highest potential. Like the hypnotized patients, they all behave in ways consistent with their beliefs. Their personal visions are false, but they accept them as if they were true. Consequently, they produce the very behavior that reinforces their beliefs. Moreover, unless or until they recognize the erroneous assumptions that they labor under, they will continue to struggle with the very problems that their beliefs help create. Their deeply held beliefs set the limits for their achievement, happiness, and success. However skilled or well-educated they may be, it is their basic beliefs about themselves, others, and the world that have more impact on their success than any other single factor. Identifying and changing false beliefs therefore becomes one of the most important activities they will ever undertake.

Beliefs Defined

The first step in understanding how our minds create our world is recognizing that the beliefs we hold have real-life consequences. This is the point of the hypnosis examples. Beliefs are those ideas, principles, concepts, and information that we hold in our unconscious minds and that predispose us to think, feel, and respond in certain ways. In this way, our beliefs are the basic operating system for our lives. The illustration below shows this concept.

INSIDE/OUT

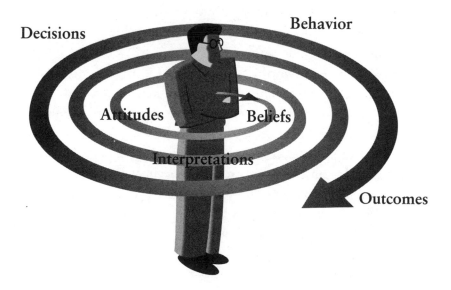

A simple, everyday example illustrates just how this works. Suppose you were at home alone and heard an unusual noise in the next room. If you believed that someone had broken into the house, how would you feel? Most likely, you would be fearful and anxious. These emotions would lead naturally to several possible behaviors, including calling the police, leaving the house, getting a gun, and so on. However, suppose you believed that the noise was caused by a gust of wind through an open window. The emotions stemming from this belief would obviously be different. You would not feel the same sense of anxiety and fear; consequently, you would not call the police or go running from the house. Instead, you would simply go into the room and shut the window.

As you can see, it is an individual's beliefs that give rise to attitudes, emotions, and behavior. Thus, since so much springs from what we believe to be true, any effort to make significant and honest improvement in life must begin at the level of beliefs.

Our basic beliefs also create a backdrop against which everyday experience plays out. What is relevant, important, and significant to us flows from our basic belief system. Ineffective or unproductive beliefs differ from effective beliefs in that they are rigid, inappropriate, and excessive. Although transparent to most other people, beliefs also act as premises that lead to thought processes.

Basic premise: "If I don't have love, I am worthless."
Specific case: "Jon doesn't love me."
Conclusion: "I am worthless."

To the individual who holds such a deep belief, none of this is very apparent. Such beliefs have been woven so deeply into the person's self-image that they are now reflected in the way she automatically thinks. And this is the core of the problem. Because our beliefs, thoughts, conclusions, and interpretations occur with virtually no conscious thought, we become completely unaware that they are operating in our lives at all. The most basic beliefs we hold, which give so much meaning to everything else in life, are in most cases invisible to us. That is why it is so important that we discover ways to uncover and change beliefs that may serve as barriers to our success and effectiveness.

In the above example, the person is certainly aware of how she feels (the conclusion) and often aware of the specific case ("Jon doesn't love me"); she may be thinking about possible ways to change his mind. But she is completely unaware of the basic premise that gives meaning to the specific case and causes her to think, feel, and behave the way she does. Even so, it is at the level of beliefs that the rich deposits of insight are buried; once uncovered and understood, they hold tremendous promise for making significant improvements in all areas of our lives.

Beliefs Run Deep

The key role that beliefs play in life is difficult to accurately describe and fully comprehend, in large measure because the beliefs lie at the subconscious level. They seem to operate independently of choice or conscious thought. They become the wellspring from which so many other things flow, yet we remain largely unaware of this powerful connection. Because we are so unaware, we are unconsciously controlled by something that we can't identify.

I have a friend whose life provides a vivid example of how our deeply held unconscious beliefs prevent us from achieving the success and happiness we desire. Doug grew up in the streets of Detroit. His father left when the family was young, and he was raised by his mother. During those formative years, experiences were being stored in his memory bank that caused him to see the world and his place in it in a particular way. These beliefs played out every day in his adult life, coloring his self-image and his view of the world around him.

He became a real estate broker. One year he set a conscious goal to make $100,000, and he made $85,000. The next year he set the same goal. By August he had made $91,000, with five potentially productive months left to reach or exceed his goal. He ended the year with $93,000.

Year after year Doug would fall just below where he wanted to be, and he was frustrated at being unable to break the $100,000 barrier. A friend, seeing his concerns, recommended a hypnotist who could help.

Doug's experiences with the hypnotist were much different from the strange behavior on stage mentioned at the start of this chapter. He was placed under hypnosis, and the conversations he had with his therapist were recorded so that he could listen to them after the sessions.

After several visits, some themes began to emerge, the most central of which was Doug's basic unconscious belief that he did not deserve to make $100,000—his personal vision was that as a street kid from Detroit, he didn't deserve that kind of money. Also, when he was a child, his mother had told him many times to make enough money to get by and not be greedy. He could recall none of these parental injunctions consciously, but they were still lodged deep in his subconscious mind, where they constantly affected how he felt about himself personally and professionally.

The next year, unencumbered by self-limiting beliefs, he made $360,000. This experience launched him into tremendous professional success, and more important, a better understanding of the role that beliefs play in our lives minute by minute, hour by hour, day by day.

Deeply held beliefs formed early in life grow more elusive over time, until we have no idea that they are operating. What's more, because we cannot with integrity act incongruently with our beliefs, we do the very thing now that reinforces those beliefs, causing them to become even more deeply rooted in our subconscious mind.

Once rooted, beliefs fulfill two very basic and far-reaching functions. First, they form the frame through which we view ourselves, others, and the world around us. They serve as a filter that causes us to "see" and perceive events in a particular manner. How we think, feel, behave, make decisions, and handle various daily events in life are, in every case, consistent with our deeply held beliefs, even though these beliefs remain at the unconscious level.

Second, our beliefs are a "deflector shield," deflecting any input that runs counter to what we believe. This deflection process takes place all the time as we interact with life.

Most people do not experience beliefs as separate from who they are and what they think. Because the beliefs operate at the subconscious level, it's difficult to access them, as illustrated above. Trapped by our own ignorance, we experience our beliefs as "the way things are" and think that we are seeing ourselves and others clearly. Most of us fail to consider that negative emotions such as fear, frustration, anger, resentment, and blame are usually signals that a basic belief is operating in us, giving rise to such negative emotions. Attitudes, emotions, reactions, and interpretations are little more than manifestations of our beliefs, and when we come to understand that, we move to a higher level of insight and understanding—20/20 Insight.

Unfortunately, we tend to hold on to false and distorted beliefs even in the face of mounting evidence that they are incorrect. A manager, for example, holds a basic belief about people at work that goes something like this: "People are basically lazy, they're out to get you and take advantage of the company, and they cannot be trusted to do good work."

His belief was formed during his 30-year military career, and he took it with him into corporate life. He firmly believes that he is innocent of any distorted thinking because he systematically filters out any evidence that contradicts this belief. If an employee performs at an exceptional level, the manager writes it off as a rare exception to the "rule" that he had formed years before. What's more, his lack of awareness causes him to create the very circumstances that reinforce the belief.

Finally, another characteristic of deeply held beliefs is the twisted logic that surrounds them. Part of the "program" is to disconfirm anything that challenges the present belief system. This is what makes beliefs self-sealing and self-reinforcing. Hence, we "behave ourselves" into the very problems that we most complain about and so become the prophets of our own destiny. We predict what will happen and then create the evidence to validate the prediction. This is what is known as self-fulfilling prophecy.

Beliefs as Self-Fulfilling Prophecy

Self-fulfilling prophecies occur when we believe that something will take place based on our past experience and then behave our way into that very outcome. We do the very thing that produces the evidence we need to say, "I knew it would happen." In so doing, we fail to comprehend that we have put ourselves into the very pickle that we now complain about. Hence, we fulfill our own prophecy, and at the same time, we reinforce the accuracy (as we suppose) of our belief.

Most flawed and distorted beliefs lead to self-fulfilling results. If, for example, someone in the workplace genuinely believes that she will not be happy unless she is given special attention, then she will not be happy if recognition is denied her. The very act of predicting the consequences serves to bring this about. There is great irony in all of this, for our beliefs trap us into the very behavior we are trying to avoid. We may want to be happy and successful, but because we believe that this will not happen and we predict that outcome, we never will be. This takes place when we are unaware of the part we play in the sad drama, and it is our unwitting participation in such situations that defeats us. Consequently, we continue to create ineffectiveness in other situations—and then complain about it.

Years ago, I worked for a large food distributor that had hundreds of sales representatives all over the world. These reps called on individual grocery stores to sell their line of dessert treats. In one district there were 21 salespeople. One day I asked the sales manager of this team, "Who are your best people, Tim?" Without hesitation he listed the three or four people who he thought were outstanding. Then we started talking about what made these people so much more effective than the others. We talked about education level, work experience, the number of training programs each had attended, where they grew up, and various other possible explanations for their success. Then he got to the heart of the matter.

"You know," he said, "I think none of those things matters as much as the individual's own self-image. I can put these four people anywhere in my district and they'll find a way to succeed. I have others that I can put anywhere and they'll find a way to stay average, and I have still others that no matter where they are, they stay right near the bottom." Then he told me about Frank.

Frank had been with the company for nearly 22 years, all in one major city in the Midwest. Frank was "a good soldier"; he didn't really blow the doors off anything, but he plugged along month after month, putting in his time. "I noticed after I was Frank's boss for two years," said Tim, "that he made just about as much money as he wanted to."

"What do you mean?" I asked.

He showed me Frank's sales figures for the past three years. Frank had been in four different areas in those three years, but his commission amounts had changed very little. Tim noted that for eight months, Frank had been put in one of the hottest areas in the city, where he could really shine, but he stalled out. Then he was moved to one of the slowest areas in the city; there he picked up the pace. He surged or stalled depending on where he was, but in the end, he made almost the same amount of money every single year.

It was as if Frank was bound and determined to be average, and there was nothing Tim could do about it. Put him in an area of high growth with opportunity dripping from the stores, and Frank slowed down, coasted, and ended up just where he had been in his last area. Give him an area with little growth, and he would push harder and increase his sales to bring him up to where he had been previously. In four different areas with dramatically different kinds of potential, Frank stayed right in the middle of the pack, no matter what.

Frank's story proves once again that what you see is what you get and that everything happens first in the mind's eye. Frank's personal vision led him to believe that he was an average salesman, and he produced the evidence to support this belief. Average was acceptable to Frank.

Now imagine that Tim sits down with Frank and says, "Frank, you know, you have so much potential. You need to get out there and make things happen. You could do so much more than you now do if you would just apply yourself. Work on the things you can control, and don't worry about all the other distractions. Be proactive, Frank!"

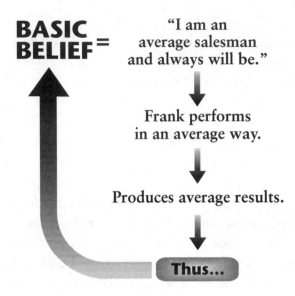

You can almost see the confused look on Frank's face as he listens to Tim's spirited pep talk. To Frank's mind, he is doing all that he can to succeed. He looks at the sales reports for the three previous years and sees without question that he is an average salesman. Even if he wanted it to be otherwise, that is where he is: The figures can't lie. After all these years and his consistent performance record, it must be plain that he performs as well as he can. When Tim tells Frank that he can do so much better if he'll just try harder, it sounds ridiculous to Frank. After all, he's doing everything he can to improve. What else is there?

Frank obviously does not consciously say to himself, "I'm average, always have been, and always will be. I want to improve, but I can't." His beliefs about himself are not consciously available to him. He is unaware, blind, as it were, to seeing that his own mental picture is the only thing separating him from greater success. More training, encouragement from Tim, longer hours, all may help, but until he can see himself differently, he will never change the quality of the results he produces. When Frank's view of himself changes, he will see that he has all the ability in the world to achieve at significantly higher levels.

It all depends on and is governed by his beliefs, which set the limits for his performance in very real and predictable ways.

Four Types of Beliefs

Our understanding about beliefs and how they operate deepens as we begin to look at them more closely. There are four basic types of beliefs.

Type 1: Beliefs about Cause

What causes us to feel the way we do about something? What causes so and so to be successful? Why do some people succeed and others don't? What causes those around us to behave the way they do? By asking ourselves these questions, the basic beliefs that we hold about cause become evident. Obviously, if we believe that people who are successful achieved that success through sheer luck, with luck being the root cause, we think and behave much differently than if we feel that they earned it fairly. Beliefs about what causes other things to take place drive so many of our emotions and actions. Why would a person who believes that successful people lucked into their success put forth any effort to succeed? Why would a person who believes that he will be rejected if he interviews for a job even dress up for the interview?

Beliefs about cause reveal our mini-theory about how the world "works" from our perspective, and this moves us to act in predictable ways. Furthermore, beliefs about cause are usually based on previous experience, which in turn makes us repeat it again and again. Tiger Woods, the great young American golfer, believes red is his lucky color. After he won the 1997 Master's Tournament in Augusta, what color was he wearing as he accepted the hefty winner's check? You guessed it—bright red. So the cycle begins and is reinforced, and you can bet your four-iron that he'll wear red whenever he feels that victory is on the line. Ridiculous as it may sound, the beliefs held in our conscious or subconscious minds lead us to think and behave in very predictable ways and so reveal our deeper beliefs.

Type 2: Beliefs about Meaning

Beliefs about meaning operate in the interpretations—positive or negative—that we place on events. A college student receives a "C" in a course and is devastated. Why? Because to her, it means that she will not be able to get into graduate school, a goal toward which she has been working for four years. It is not the grade itself that has any real meaning but what that grade represents.

What does it mean if you create your own business and then fail? What does it mean if you set a goal to lose weight but gain weight instead? Our beliefs lead us to "see" events in certain ways, and how we interpret those events has a great deal to do with our ability to achieve those things that are most important.

Type 3: Beliefs about Identity

Beliefs about identity are those that we hold about who we are—what kind of people we are, what potential we possess, and so on. It's easy to predict what people will do once they reveal their belief about their own future potential. Some believe that they are gifted in a certain field of endeavor and pursue it with vigor, believing that it will bring them joy and allow them to do what they really want to do. Others believe deep in their hearts that they are worthless rejects. This consuming image of self and identity colors everything they see and creates a world of frustration and pain. All of it is driven by their beliefs about identity.

Type 4: Beliefs about Truth

What do you believe to be true about yourself, others, and the world around you? What do you believe is false or incorrect in some way? Beliefs about truth direct us to pursue some paths while avoiding others. They are manifest in what we value and care about and how we spend our time and money. They serve as criteria when difficult decisions are made. Like the other types, beliefs about truth cause us to act in ways that are consistent with what we believe to be true. Hence, they become an indicator of deeper beliefs about what is true.

There were some ancient cultures that believed that there were many gods who had power over all things, including the weather. Farmers believed that unless they pleased the gods—through offering sacrifices, paying tribute, praying, and worshiping—they would be punished with unfavorable weather. This caused them to engage in numerous religious practices that they believed would please the gods. And what happened when the weather turned ugly or a mighty windstorm destroyed half of their wheat? Consistent with their beliefs, they would predictably redouble their efforts by offering more sacrifices, tithing more of their income, and praying more often than they did before. This was all based on the related belief that they must have done something wrong or the gods would have blessed them with good weather.

Negative Thoughts and Beliefs

Certainly not all beliefs are counterproductive and lead to negative outcomes. When we hold productive beliefs, they enable us to move forward, create successes in our lives, and form productive relationships with others. It is the negative and distorted beliefs we hold that stand in our way and cause us to live under the burden of false ideas that we accept as true.

Negative thoughts and beliefs have some very specific attributes.

• They are automatic and occur as if without any prior reasoning. We don't experience our beliefs as something that "happens" that we are aware of. They seem automatic and involuntary.

• They are unreasonable and ineffective, often leading to poor outcomes. One of the best ways to "see" beliefs is by the outcomes they produce. A negative outcome in most cases has its roots in negative beliefs and thoughts that led us to think, feel, and act in negative, counterproductive ways.

• They are accepted as completely plausible and valid, even though they lead to negative outcomes.

• Because they seem involuntary, many people have difficulty turning them off. A person who believes he is worthless feels his worthlessness throughout his entire being. Often he doesn't like it and doesn't like the way it makes him feel, but he experiences it as something outside of his direct influence or control. That is why negative thoughts and beliefs usually lead to discouragement and depression. They often lead to a cycle in which we unconsciously do those things that make us continue to see ourselves in false and distorted ways. This is shown in the illustration below. We do become our own worst enemies.

At first glance, beliefs appear to be so automatic, unconscious, and untouchable that we are locked into whatever beliefs we currently hold. How can we examine a thing we never knew? But just because we are not now consciously aware of our beliefs does not mean that we cannot bring them to the surface and examine them in systematic and powerful ways.

Over time, our beliefs fall into the background of life, rarely thought about or considered until that moment when someone says,

DISTORTED VIEW OF SELF

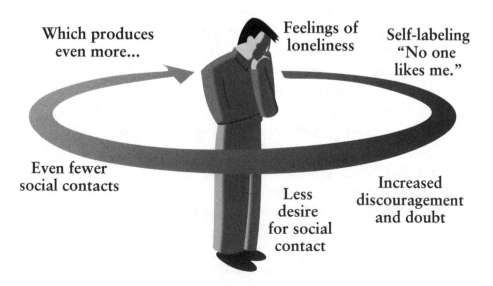

Which produces even more...

Feelings of loneliness

Self-labeling "No one likes me."

Even fewer social contacts

Less desire for social contact

Increased discouragement and doubt

"What do you think of this?" or "Why do you believe that way?" Many people have no idea why they think the way they do and what experiences have led them to draw the kinds of distorted conclusions they draw. In most cases, beliefs and thoughts are so automatic that we are unaware that we are even drawing any conclusions driven by any particular belief. We must undergo a process of dehypnotizing ourselves from false and self-limiting beliefs. This means that we must set our current beliefs up for scrutiny and change. This kind of work is high adventure, because in my experience, we begin, often for the first time, to work at a level where unbelievable power can be discovered and utilized. By seeing our false and distorted beliefs and replacing them with productive and transforming beliefs and thoughts, we tap into a power that can change us in profound ways.

Examining Our Beliefs

Our objective in this chapter has been primarily "to part the curtains and look in" at how our beliefs help to shape the world we create. It is difficult, if not impossible, to articulate just how much our lives are influenced by deeply held beliefs about ourselves and others. They give rise to emotions, attitudes, and automatic thoughts that cause us to behave in ways that are consistent and congruent with those beliefs.

Examining beliefs and understanding more fully the role they play in our search for personal excellence is vital work, for we cannot think, feel, or behave in ways that are inconsistent with those beliefs, however unconscious or unknown. They operate in the background of our lives, filtering out certain things and causing us to see other things in certain ways—some productive and others counterproductive. Beliefs can either elevate us to the highest level of human achievement or limit us to lives of quiet desperation, held back somehow by a power we do not understand. The most liberating idea we can hold on to as we close this chapter is the realization that beliefs can be identified, carefully examined, and changed—with productive, empowering results.

Lens Two
Re-presenting the World

> *If circumstances had the power to bless or harm, they would bless and harm all men alike, but the fact that the same circumstances will be alike good and bad to different souls proves that the good and bad is not in the circumstance, but only in the mind of him that encounters it.*
>
> —James Allen, author of *Aftermath*

Several years ago I had an experience that altered the direction of my life. I was conducting a workshop with a large telecommunications company on the East Coast. I had presented the material many times and felt comfortable with my knowledge and command of it. I had received high marks for presentations and had developed a healthy sense of confidence in my ability to deliver the material in an effective and compelling way—until that day.

When I arrived at the training room, I saw that it was being used for another workshop; I soon learned that we had been moved to a large conference room down the hall. As soon as I walked in, I knew I was in trouble. The room was poorly lit, the tables were spread all around the huge room, and the high ceilings made it feel as if we were in an aircraft hangar.

As I stood there watching the participants file in, I grew more nervous. I had always presented in small workshop rooms with good lighting that allowed me to see people well. For years I had stood in front of people and had never told them the truth about my eyesight. I had figured out ways around that uncomfortable conversation and had maneuvered pretty well. As I stood thinking about this situation, however, I found that I was fresh out of good ideas.

"I just want you all to know," I said a few minutes later, "that a few weeks ago I had eye surgery and I'm still recovering. If I don't happen to see your hands, just call out my name." And then for further clarification, I added, "But it's not a big deal, and I should be fully recovered in a month or so."

"That ought to do it," I thought as I turned to begin the presentation. "Now they know, and I don't have to tell them anything further." Unfortunately, it was all a lie, a fabrication for the purpose of letting people know about my poor vision without telling them about my real eye problem.

I knew that I was being dishonest, but I had always gotten away with it before. In this case, however, I didn't know that my eye-surgery story would not have the desired effect of making people aware that I might not see them well enough to acknowledge their questions. It was only later, after I found out the price of my dishonesty, that I realized what I should have done. I should have honestly admitted my limitations and contacted someone in charge so that I could explain the problems I anticipated in the large, poorly lighted space and ask to have the seminar moved to a smaller room. Of course, I didn't do that because I was so reluctant to let anyone know how severe my eye problems were.

The seminar went along with few unusual occurrences, and then I flew home. A week later I received a phone call from the director of training for the company. "We received your course evaluations, and they aren't good," he told me. "You've always done well in the past, but I'm afraid something happened here that we cannot allow to happen again."

He was confused and concerned, and I was shocked. As he read some of the comments from people about how insensitive I was to their efforts to get involved and how they raised their hands but were not called upon, my face reddened with the realization of what had happened. I could barely speak as I thought back over the experience.

I left work early that day and walked all the way home to give myself time to make sense of what had happened. When I arrived home, my wife was waiting for me and was ready to listen.

"I can't believe this," I said, feeling genuinely confused by the feedback. "I don't know what happened."

"Well, what did you tell those people back there about your eyesight?" Cindy asked.

"What do you mean?" I said, although I knew what she meant, and I knew the answer to the question. I was just afraid to talk about it truthfully. After hemming and hawing about what I had really said, I finally got it out.

"I told people that I had just had eye surgery and was recovering, but everything was going pretty well and I expected a full recovery," I explained.

My wife sat speechless for a moment and then asked, "Why did you tell them that? You never had eye surgery. What made you tell them about your eyesight that way?"

The next few minutes seemed to move in slow motion as I sat thinking. I was confused, distraught, emotionally sapped, and afraid of what was happening. Her question lingered in the air, awaiting an honest answer, but I found it hard to find one. Finally it started to slowly roll out in the form of a story.

"When I found out as a young boy that I could no longer play baseball, I decided to focus on basketball. I tried out and made the first cut for the ninth-grade basketball team, but one final player needed to be cut so the coach would have the required number of players. It came down to me and a friend, Lynn Shimada, both guards and both good players. To settle the issue, the coach held a one-on-one scrimmage between us. By the end of the scrimmage it was clear that I had won. I knew that I had proven to the coach and myself that I was good enough to play on the team and that my failing eyesight no longer stood in my way.

"Two days later, when the list of players was posted on the coach's door, I saw that I had been cut. I couldn't believe it. I had been certain that I had made the team and had been looking forward to playing in front of the entire school. But the coach had chosen Lynn over me. Late that afternoon I learned what had happened from a good friend who had made the team.

" 'Do you know why Coach cut you from the team?' he asked me in the hallway.

" 'No, I don't,' I told him. 'I really thought I was a better player than Lynn.'

" 'I know,' he said. 'Coach told me that he had heard about your eyesight problem. He was afraid that you might have trouble seeing the ball in games and decided that it would just be better to cut you from the team.'

"The news struck me like a fist to the stomach. Those words rang in my ears for the rest of the day as I thought about why I had been cut. The answer to me was simple: The coach had found out about my eyesight. If he had not known about it, I would have made the team. That was how I made sense of that experience and how I explained it to myself in the months and years that followed. I decided that what I needed to do was make absolutely certain in the future that people didn't find out the truth about my eyesight, because if they did, bad things would happen."

My wife sat patiently and listened to this story of discouragement and disappointment that had taken place more than 20 years earlier. Then she said, "I'm just trying to understand all of this, Honey, but let me ask you a question. Are you telling me that because of how you were cut from the team in ninth grade, you told these people in your workshop a lie about your eyesight?"

Cindy has a way of getting right to the heart of the matter. Even so, I found it difficult to answer her question. On the one hand, at a rational level, it all sounded dumb and illogical that something that happened so long ago could still be affecting my thinking. But deep in my heart there still lived the pain and disappointment associated with losing my eyesight as a young boy and all that it meant I could not do.

Simple logic was running smack-dab into deep emotion, and the result was some kind of mental and emotional "brain cloud."

As I sat there staring out the window and wondering what all of this really meant, she posed another question: "Are you really afraid that if you tell people the truth about your eyes, they will reject you like your basketball coach did?"

This time the answer came much more quickly. "Yes, I guess that's it. I'm afraid that if I tell people the truth, they will think less of me or reject me in some way. I know it may not make sense, but that's what terrifies me to this day, and that's why I told them the story about the eye operation."

As we pressed forward, we talked about why I felt the way I did, and I shared several other experiences that had reinforced that belief. I had never told my best friends for the same reason—fear of rejection or of being treated differently somehow. I had never told a girl I had dated before meeting my wife out of fear that she would reject me or not want to date a "blind man." Fear of rejection became the dominant theme in all my stories, along with the belief that I had developed about the need to protect myself from others by doing whatever was necessary to prevent them from knowing the truth about my eyesight.

Although I shared many different stories with Cindy that afternoon, everything seemed to go back to that significant emotional experience in ninth grade. That event, along with the experiences that forced me to stop playing baseball, set me on a path of deception and dishonesty that lasted more than 20 years. Clearly it wasn't the event itself that was significant to me as a handicapped boy of 14. Rather, *it was what that event meant to me*—how I had interpreted it and experienced it.

Several other players had also been cut from the team. Most of them were disappointed, but they moved on with few repercussions. For me, however, it meant far more than simply not making the team. It was all wrapped up with my fear of what being blind would mean, the fear that it would prevent me from being a normal boy and doing the things that other boys did. It was deeply rooted in the belief I held that perhaps I was a reject, that I was somehow defective because of my vision.

That basic belief and the fears associated with it led me to interpret this experience in a way specific to that belief. The way I made sense of the experiences I was having as a boy would prove to influence the way I interpreted events years later. What started out as a seemingly disappointing but harmless event became the launching point for so many other decisions to follow, including the experience of telling people I had just had eye surgery when in fact I had not. I still felt such a strong need to protect myself from possible rejection that I was willing to misrepresent myself and lie to anyone who I perceived could reject me in any way.

As Cindy and I concluded our discussion, much of this began to fall into place for me. I had been protecting myself for so long that I had lost sight of how it all began and what it was turning me into. Not only had I become dishonest about myself but I was also creating a world of secrecy, fear, and great anxiety out of fear that in spite of my deception people would still somehow discover the truth and, as I supposed, reject me.

"Do you really think that if you just told people the truth, they would reject you or stand up and walk out, as if to say, 'Unless this guy has perfect eyesight, we're not going to sit here for another moment and put up with him?' Do you really think that would happen?" Cindy asked.

I knew what she was getting at. I had spent so many years being fearful of what the truth might bring that I had stopped telling the truth. Lying had become much easier than telling the real story. Somehow I knew that this experience was about to change me in significant ways, many of which I could not fully imagine at the time.

My boyhood experiences shaped and colored my life and my mental pictures for years because of the process I employed to respond to them. I proved what social scientists have been saying for years: It is not what happens to us that matters but rather how we interpret those experiences. Events occurred, I formed an opinion of them, and I consequently created for myself a cycle that looked a lot like the following illustration.

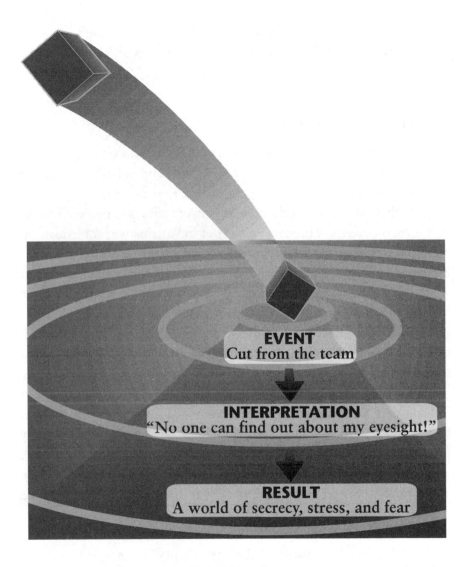

Some experiences are like pebbles thrown into a pond in that they have ever-expanding ripples or consequences. My story illustrates just how far-reaching our response to certain situations in life can be. The original event is the stone hitting the water, but the impact creates ripples that grow continually, covering a larger and larger area until finally the whole surface of the pond is disturbed. One event in junior high school, processed as it was, had far-reaching implications for me at various ages and stages of my life thereafter.

How we choose to respond to any given situation is the difference between happy, productive results and negative, destructive outcomes. The decision is ours. The choice rests ultimately with each one of us and no one else.

Re-presenting Events

The interpretations that we make of people and events flow automatically, effortlessly, and predictably from our beliefs. Hence, we don't see the world the way it is; instead we *re-present* it.

Another intriguing cycle is created every time we place an interpretation on events. This cycle plays out in various ways. First, intrapersonal outcomes change as we perceive and interpret events that influence how effective we are and affect our ability to achieve what we desire. How we interpret events and people today shapes how we will see things in the future.

A lonely teenager, for example, fears that she is not popular or attractive. She believes she is unwanted socially. When she is not asked to the Junior Prom, what does it mean? To her, it means that truly she is not liked or popular and that boys don't want to take her out. She feels deeper insecurities and retreats further into her shell. She goes to fewer dances, remains uninvolved in school activities, and shies away from any experience that might cause her to feel rejected. This choice, although understandable, makes it even less likely that she will be asked out. Others see her less often or withdraw from her because she is quiet and unapproachable. This in turn reinforces her basic belief that she is unlovable.

The teenager is unaware of the part she plays in helping to create and perpetuate the world she experiences. From her myopic point of view, this is just "the way things are," and she feels precious little power to change them. Because she cannot see the pattern that she is part of, she continues unwittingly to do the very thing that continues the pattern. It is not the event itself that affects her but the way she *processes* the event that causes everything to happen.

Seeing the patterns that we are part of lies at the very heart of 20/20 Insight, for it enables us to see things in new and more expansive ways. Standing back from everyday experiences provides us with useful perspective and helps us to separate ourselves from events that we are part of. When people are unable to separate themselves from events, they become entangled in a way that prevents them from seeing things as they really are.

A frustrated math student fails a test and draws the conclusion that he is stupid and can't do math. He stops doing his homework (after all, why should he persist at something that he can't succeed at?) and begins to fall farther and farther behind. When test time comes, he's not ready and fails again. All of this provides rock-solid evidence that he can't do math, that he is stupid. In desperation, he and his parents decide that he should drop math, reinforcing his initial belief about the subject.

Such ironic patterns are not limited to confused teenagers. I am often called in to visit with disgruntled employees who have received poor evaluations from their bosses. The employees thought that they were performing very well, but the bosses saw it differently and rated them lower than the employees anticipated.

With these two sets of differing expectations, the cycle begins. An engineer I know received a far worse rating than he thought he deserved. What did that rating mean to him? He decided that his boss was stupid and unfair and that he, the engineer, would never succeed in that organization. How did this interpretation cause him to feel? Discouraged and angry, he was resigned to spending his days in frustration unless he did something quickly. These emotions, fueled by his interpretation of the initial event, led the engineer to conclude that the only smart thing to do was to look for another job, which he did. Six weeks later he was gone.

The illustration above depicts the only possible way that this experience could have played itself out. It is based on a single interpretation, which produced the rest of the pattern. What if the engineer had made a different interpretation of the events? I have asked people in similar situations, "Do you have any idea why your boss sees your performance so differently than you do?" People never have an answer to that question. They have concluded that the boss is simply out of

EVENT
Engineer receives poor evaluation

INTERPRETATION
"The boss is unfair.
Now I'll never succeed!"

ATTITUDES
Anger, fear, frustration
and resignation

REINFORCEMENT
Beliefs are reinforced.

DECISION
"I should start looking for a new job."

touch with what they really do, and if he realized all the good work that they do, he would never have given such a poor evaluation. I also pose other questions, such as, "Have you ever talked with your boss about your performance, making sure he knows what you are doing and the contribution you are making?" Rarely have people had such conversations. Of the many different ways in which they could interpret this event, they often choose the interpretation illustrated above, which more often than not leads to the kind of outcome shown.

False Self-Esteem

Most of us have met people whom we describe as having low or poor self-esteem. Usually they are people who have little self-confidence and little regard for their own opinions or ideas. They have a tendency to stand back and wait for others to take the lead because they don't value themselves highly enough to step forward. They often compare themselves to others and find themselves coming up short.

Your self-image was formed effortlessly by the experiences you had in the past and how you interpreted those experiences. Some were positive and caused your self-confidence and self-regard to soar. With this came greater confidence in your ability to succeed personally and with other people. Positive experiences in childhood and adolescence helped each of us create a true picture of our potential and possibilities.

Most of us have also had disappointing or even traumatic experiences in childhood that shaped our self-images in blurred and distorted ways. A child who suffers under the wicked hand of abuse by an adult is often weighed down by various forms of self-deprecation and criticism. Many of us have had experiences that led us to see ourselves in a particular way and to form opinions of ourselves that are completely inaccurate. I call this false self-esteem or a false self-image. It is the personal vision that we create from experiences that cause us to distort our own worth and potential. Such experiences lead us to hold certain beliefs about our strengths and weaknesses and serve as a lens through which we interpret the world around us.

False self-esteem happens effortlessly and unconsciously as experience after experience creates within us an image of who we think we are and what we think we can achieve. Like a crazy mirror in a carnival, it doesn't change how we really appear or who we are, but it distorts the image that we see.

I will always remember Nancy, a financial analyst in one of America's leading food product companies. When I met her, she was a participant in a seminar I was conducting on personal effectiveness. From early in the seminar, it was clear that she was suffering. She sat near the front of the room and said very little; when she did make comments, they were filled with negative, cynical, and depressive overtones. After the first day of the workshop, I was clearing up my things when she came up to me and asked if I could meet her in the hotel lobby after dinner so we could talk. I had no idea what it was about, but I knew somehow that she needed the chance to share her story.

Two hours later I found myself sitting near the huge hotel fireplace listening to a woman who was miserable. Nancy told me her story of coming to this company with expectations of making a real difference. However, she felt that she was being beaten down by her boss, a man I knew quite well. They had reached an impasse several months earlier and now she was playing the waiting game—waiting to see what would happen. As we talked about her feelings and her options, she spent most of the time convincing me that there was nothing she could do that had not been done. The more I listened, the more it became crystal clear that she had done very little except stew and worry and keep everything inside. She felt that she could not talk with her boss for fear of what he would do—discipline her in some way or fire her. I had found him to be pleasant enough in my work with him, but she was terrified of what he would do if he knew how she felt.

As we discussed her background, I learned more about how numerous difficult life experiences had created a dark and obscured lens through which she saw herself. Beneath her rough, cynical exterior was a woman who had no self-regard. Nancy saw herself as a loser, incompetent, and unworthy of success, and her recent experiences served as a grim reminder of what she had felt all along—"I'm no damn good." She could see very little of the cycle she was part of, beginning with false and blurred images of herself that were mirrored in self-defeating beliefs that caused her to see everything and everyone as "out to get her." Her fears became more manifest as we talked about what she could do to fix the situation. "I can't fix it. It's too far gone now. I've decided to move on." In her voice was dismal resignation, acknowledgment that this was yet another rotten experience that she could chalk up along with so many others in the past. To her, it all spoke volumes about herself, her potential to succeed, and her negative perspective of other people.

She had developed a false self-image, filled with self-defeat.

Around every turn and with every failure, another stone was added to the already-heavy burden that she carried around. Worst of all, she felt that there was nothing that she could do to change it.

I met with her several times over the next few months and watched her slow but steady progress. We talked about self-image and how she saw herself in relation to work and personal success. She shared her beliefs with me, things that she had not articulated to anyone in years and concepts that she herself had never fully considered. In order for her to "get behind" depression and the beliefs that spawned it, we explored some other significant emotional experiences that had helped shape her lens of life, distorted and dark as it was.

It was extremely hard for her to accept the fact that she was in large measure creating her world by the way in which she was seeing it and that people actually do see themselves falsely. As this light began to dawn, it brought renewed hope that maybe things could be different. She had lived so long under the black cloud of doubt and self-deprecation that she had lost all hope that she could feel any differently. In fact, it had become such a deep-seated pattern of thought that she felt that it was locked in, that it was "just the way things are."

I assured her that her self-image had been formed from negative experiences and that it was possible to redefine herself in positive, productive ways. Hope began to glow from her eyes as she started to see herself in new ways. This hope led to greater confidence in her ability to change, and over the weeks that followed, she talked with her boss, negotiated a new position, and turned both her work life and her personal life around.

Nancy's story clearly illustrates a powerful and sobering principle of perception and self-image that undergirds any attempt to explain individual behavior. In her mind's eye, she was incompetent and unworthy of success, someone whom others would not want to know. She thought that she was seeing herself clearly; instead she had a distorted, blurred image of her real self. This belief and the negative self-image it created controlled her life. Her self-image literally set the boundaries for her entire life. Like a lens through which she looked at every situation, her mental picture distorted everything she saw. More-over, her behavior and the results she produced in life flowed directly from this picture of who she felt she truly was.

It is important to understand that this same process goes on inside each of us, not just people like Nancy who have obvious emotional challenges. We are all affected on a daily basis by how we see our-selves, what we think our talents are, and who we think would like a person like us. One common example is the feeling of self-doubt many of us experience during public speaking. Our fears that we are not good public speakers may cause us to become so nervous that we have difficulty during the speech. As a result, our original belief seems to be confirmed (see illustration).

I once read about a severely handicapped boy who had every reason in the world to be down on himself and retreat into a lonely, introverted life. He chose not to. He saw himself as important and spe-cial; he saw himself as someone whom others would like if they could only get to know him. While so many others like him gave up early and failed to try, he saw himself as a winner. He had girlfriends, dated, and lived a normal life.

SEE "I am not a good public speaker. I can't express myself well, and it scares me to death."

DO "I overprepare or procrastinate. I worry and fret about the upcoming speech. I'm so nervous. I'll look like a fool!"

"I work myself into a lather. My knees knock and my voice shakes."

GET "I lose my place. I feel like an idiot. I'll never do this again!"

EVIDENCE

Proof That I'm No Good!

What is the difference between him and a thousand others like him who become entrenched in negative, self-defeating thinking and behavior? The only significant difference is in the way he looked at himself. How he saw himself made all the difference in the quality of his life and the kinds of relationships he had with others.

Amazingly, we behave ourselves into producing a result that is matched perfectly with how we see. The sobering reality now jumps out. Until we can modify our self-images and learn to see differently, we are permanently locked into producing results that are anchored to our present images. Is there any way to break such a self-defeating cycle and produce more effective results, consistent with our deepest values? The illustration on the opposite page answers that question in part. *Until our internal image of self changes, we will never be able to significantly change the results we produce, since what we get is nothing more than a reflection of how we see.*

The Interplay of Past and Present Interpretations

Although rarely recognized or fully appreciated, our interpretations of past events and present experiences are tightly woven together. Interpretations that we have made previously create a filter through which we see present challenges, and before long we have created a predictable and consistent way of seeing the world. This is a cycle that feeds on itself, constantly providing reinforcing evidence to us that we are seeing things "as they really are." Without countering evidence, we become unconsciously trapped by the fuzziness of our thinking, creating a world much different from that which we want.

This sad cycle is similar to the others we have examined in that it is self-sealing. We think it's real and that we're seeing clearly, but our self-image inaccurately reflects our true potential and nature.

What makes the cycle so pesky is how difficult it is to "see" what is happening when we are standing in the midst of it all. How do we correct a pattern such as this when we finally come to see it for what it truly is? It begins with a recognition that moment by moment, we are making interpretations regarding personal worth and competence,

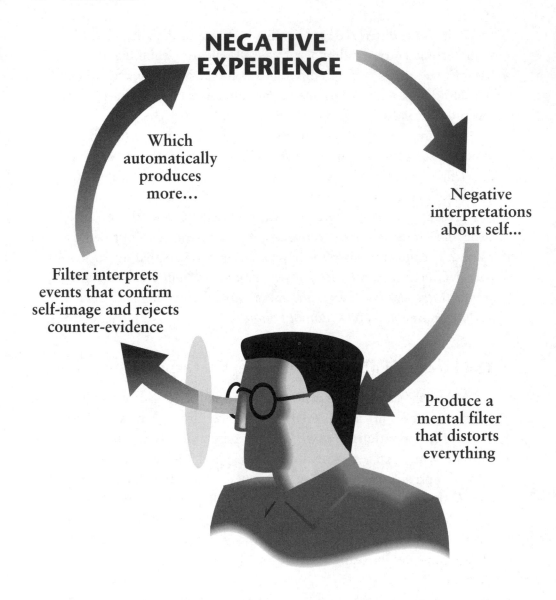

NEGATIVE EXPERIENCE

Which automatically produces more...

Negative interpretations about self...

Filter interprets events that confirm self-image and rejects counter-evidence

Produce a mental filter that distorts everything

about others' behavior and their motives, and about the world around us that we interact with. From there, we are free to make alternative interpretations of events and produce different outcomes. What we need is countering evidence that disconfirms our current self-image and causes us to question the clarity of our thinking and the accuracy of the interpretations we are making.

I recall a conversation I once had with a frustrated college student who struggled with a clouded image of herself. She had come to see herself as incompetent, inept, and somehow missing something that others had. This distorted and obscured self-image caused her to interpret events around her in predictably negative ways.

As we talked, she told me that one of the most popular and powerful professors in her college program thought that she was a reject. As proof, she produced an essay she had written for which she had received a "C," along with "critical" comments that the professor had written about the essay and its "weaknesses." She was devastated by the grade and the teacher's comments. What's more, she labored under a nagging belief that she could not succeed at college. This belief and the fear it produced predisposed her to interpret events in predictably negative ways, and this grade was ample proof that, just as she feared, she could not succeed. At the time we talked, she was getting ready to drop out.

"Do you think this grade reflects your true ability?" I asked. She thought for a moment and then told me that she had written the paper at a time of great anxiety when other papers were due and her life was very hectic. She had not taken the time she felt she should have taken. After a few minutes she recognized and admitted that it did not reflect her best effort and that before she drew too many hard conclusions or made a rash decision, she needed to place the grade in context with what was going on when it was written.

I was also concerned about the frequent reference to herself as a "reject." "Other than the interpretation you have made about the grade, what are some alternative explanations you could give?" I asked her. Although it was difficult at first, she finally listed several other ways in which she could interpret her grade. We listed them on a white board and then I asked her to rate each alternative explanation for believability. Here is her list and her rating for each on a 1 to 100 percent believability scale.

1. "I am incompetent when it comes to English, and a reject."— 90 percent
2. "The professor dislikes female students and has demonstrated discrimination against me."—10 percent

3. "This wasn't a bad grade for this kind of difficult assignment."—3 percent
4. "I did my best considering that the professor is a very tough grader."—2 percent
5. "The professor doesn't think I'm a reject, and his comments were an honest attempt to help me learn how to be a better writer."—10 percent

We discussed each one of these at length, and she decided that before dropping out of school, she needed further information from her professor. By talking with him, she learned some very interesting things. First, he did not think she was a reject, and it turned out that most of the class had received a "C" on the assignment. He also told her that he felt she had more promise as a writer than many of the other students and offered to tutor her after hours for a few weeks. She was shocked by all of this "new input," and when we talked again, she had decided to stay in school and was feeling better about her future in English than ever before.

This simple story is everyone's story in some ways. Because of past experiences and their impact on how we see ourselves and events around us, we develop a negative bias toward events, causing us to interpret them in counterproductive ways. Rarely if ever are we aware of what we are doing or of the consequences that accompany our erroneous conclusions. As I talked with this struggling student, I wanted her to consider other possible ways of interpreting her grade and to assess how realistic these explanations seemed to her. To me and perhaps any outside observer, her interpretation was simplistic and rash. But to her, after years of seeing herself as a reject, negative interpretations and the accompanying discouragement came automatically and effortlessly.

I have known people who have had a single memorable negative experience that spreads into so many other corners of their life. They are failing a class, for example, so they simply drop out rather than try to improve. Discouragement builds, and within several months they drop out of college altogether. Dragged down by disappointment and embarrassment, they lose confidence in their abilities in general, and it starts to show up in the kind of people they associate with and how they spend their time. A single, significant emotional event, accompanied by a certain kind of interpretation, serves as the beginning of many other unwanted experiences. As we strive for excellence in life and wrestle with honest desires to improve and achieve at higher levels, we need to clearly see how our beliefs cause us to translate events around us in all manner of negative and unproductive ways. Those who seek 20/20 Insight are continually aware that they are making interpretations daily and that they have the power to see things differently, to interpret life in more positive and productive ways, and to create a different outcome by interpreting events from fresh points of view.

Limitless Possibilities

Let's pause and look back over the territory we have just traveled. There have been several critical road signs that we have driven by that must never be forgotten.

Our heads really do create our world. Whatever it is that we experience, we can rest assured that in most cases, we have had a hand in creating it, sustaining it, and causing it to roll on as it does.

A basic building block of the notion that we create our world is the role that our basic beliefs play in our lives. They form the frame through which we see the world and predispose us to "see" things as we do. Beliefs therefore become the wellspring of attitudes, opinions, thoughts, decisions, and behavior, all of which work together to produce the outcomes we experience. It is a symphony played out daily in our mind's eye, reaching a crescendo in the life decisions we make.

It is impossible to think about our beliefs without also thinking about what those beliefs lead us to do. How we *process* life, the ways in which we make sense of things around us, reflects our basic beliefs, however subconscious they may be. As the basic engine that drives so many other phenomena, beliefs are most readily manifest in how we see things—the way we interpret life as filtered through the lens of belief.

With this in mind, we finally come to see with greater clarity and truth our own role in the events and relationships around us. Our sharpened 20/20 Insight enables us to "see" the connections between how we think and believe and how we create the outcomes we do. We also recognize our central role in the dramas unfolding about us and for the first time grasp the power of pure and honest understanding.

As we come to see and accept the power that we have always had to create a different world, we are able to take hold and exercise our divine gift to act. For some, this means a chance to act differently and by so doing to produce different, more positive outcomes. Without this kind of understanding, we are blind to what is really taking place around us. With added 20/20 Insight, we can see unlimited possibilities, thereby achieving at entirely new levels. We literally can change our world by changing ourselves.

In all of the stories in this chapter, including my own, so many other options were available that were never even considered. In my story, for example, there were clearly a dozen different ways that I could have chosen to interpret my not making the basketball team, but I didn't. I could have blown it off and never thought about it again. I could have gone to the coach and asked for more input as to why he thought I shouldn't be on the team. That conversation might have led to all kinds of other opportunities. But I never went to the coach, so I'll never know.

Another possibility is that someone, perhaps a friend or family member, could have sat me down and said something like, "Randy, I understand how this might feel and appear to you. I know you are afraid and disappointed. But keep in mind that this is not how everyone sees you. Many others will not reject you because of your eyesight. Many will respect you, and their courage will increase because of yours." Such a conversation might have changed the course of my life in untold ways. But it never happened.

One person could have made a difference as I stood confused at that crossroads, as many have done at other crossroads of life. The years of pain and frustration could have been avoided if I had elected a different interpretation of that one seemingly innocent event. As explained earlier, it was not the event itself that had meaning but how I *experienced* it that made all the difference. How I made sense of it and translated it through the filter of my own belief system set me on a path of deception for years. I created it all—the lies, the defensiveness, the rejection from others, the pain of trying to pretend that I was something I was not, and the pressure to keep up the front in the face of mounting evidence. I carried around a heavy burden of self-imposed baggage that could have been largely avoided had I chosen a different response and elected to translate that experience in a more productive manner.

Lens Three
Focusing on Change

The greatest discovery in our generation is that human beings, by changing the inner attitudes of their minds, can change the outer aspects of their lives.

—William James, American philosopher and psychologist

Years ago I was asked to speak at a large Las Vegas convention. Hundreds of people from dozens of different companies representing many different industries were invited to a conference about change. They all shared one experience: Rapid and relentless change was upon them, demanding some kind of response.

As I walked up on the stage to take my seat, the atmosphere in the room was electric. Hundreds of people from various smaller sessions were now filing in for the keynote presentation on "Creating Transformational Change." That's where I came in.

From my early days in college, I had always been interested in the dynamics of change. Personal change, interpersonal improvement, and finally, broad, large-scale organizational change had always fascinated me. It became the underlying theme of all my work through several different college and work experiences. Now I was ready to stand in front of nearly 3,000 people and tell them what I had learned about this most compelling and timeless topic.

In spite of my experience and interest, the task before me was a bit daunting. These people had come looking for real answers to their most plaguing questions about how to produce personal and organizational change. Simplistic, snake-oil platitudes would not work with them. They were in the throes of significant international pressures that required them to rethink how they did business. I knew I had to talk about "weightier matters" with regard to change if I was to make a difference.

I certainly don't recall everything I said on this occasion, but I did share with them something about the following key points.

- The business world in which you now operate is in part your own creation. As our heads in general create our world, so the ways in which we lead and manage organizations create the kind of competitive climate you live in and how you respond to it. Your destiny therefore lies largely in your own hands.

- Change has much to do with the basic beliefs we hold about what brings about significant change. False and distorted beliefs about change can prevent it from ever taking place, even though we claim that it's something we must do. Deeply held beliefs about what makes business work and what doesn't may in fact be at odds with the kinds of things needed for positive change.

- How we see events currently sets the stage for our business experiences in the future. Today's decisions pave the way for to-morrow's results. Thus, if we want to produce certain kinds of re-sults, we must learn *now* to see in new ways. We can't do the same old things and just hope that things will work out.

- Unless we can learn to see things more honestly, all our ef-forts will result in unintended consequences. We can't start down the wrong road and end up at the right place, any more than we can plant oats in the spring and harvest tomatoes in the fall.

I shared a few stories, made a few more supporting points, and ended with a powerful quote about change and the power we all have to bring it about. Then I sat down. The crowd seemed to like my mes-sage and applauded generously. I felt as if I had opened their eyes to new possibilities that maybe they had not considered before. Later, the letters began to arrive.

Amidst the letters telling me that I had presented a very compelling message were several from people who simply could not accept what I had said. The notion that we create the world around us and that by learning to see things differently we could create a different reality was too much for some. The essence of their input can be summarized by the following letter that I received from a senior manager of a midsize manufacturing company.

> *You made some very interesting points, and I must admit it got me thinking. In all honesty, however, I must say that I cannot accept your premise that our heads create our world and that change is in large measure something that begins in our mind's eye as we see things in new ways. As I sit with my management team day after day, working over thorny operational problems, thinking at a new level and seeing things in new and more productive ways is the last thing on our minds. We are up to our eyeballs in a swamp filled with alligators, and you come along and tell us to see things in a different way. If we had the time to do that, it might be an interesting exercise, but the daily pressures of keeping the business going prevent us from making the kinds of changes we might otherwise make. Your message makes great sense and is intriguing, but impractical.*

I had heard this before. For many years I had worked with people who felt trapped by their present circumstances and were unable to make the changes they longed for. As a counselor, I had seen married couples and individuals who felt hopelessly trapped in situations that they honestly felt they had nothing to do with bringing about. They wanted things to be different but felt that making things different was beyond their control or influence. Lectures on taking personal responsibility seemed to fall on deaf ears as people pointed to various reasons why they had no power to change because of some person or situation "out there."

In my organizational consulting work I had spent years with clients who were determined to turn their organizations around, only to discover a year or two later that they had largely made no movement at all. After dozens of meetings and hundreds of man-hours working on change teams and committees, the fundamental ways in which their organizations functioned had not changed, in spite of agreement up and down the hierarchy that change was critical. The letters from my Las Vegas friends only reinforced a sentiment I had heard many times. In essence, people everywhere want to make needed changes personally or inside their businesses, but they are perplexed as to how to bring them about.

After receiving these letters, I did some serious reflection. I had spent my entire professional career thinking, studying, designing, and attempting to orchestrate changes at various levels and still, after all of this, bright, capable people responded with skepticism and serious reservations about whether change can actually take place.

I understood part of what they were saying. Organizations are complex and represent various divergent points of view. Bringing everyone to a common viewpoint to create the necessary energy for change is not easy, but I have seen it happen many times. The letters suggested that many of these people had not seen this kind of change. Furthermore, I had witnessed miraculous changes in individuals as they came to see themselves truthfully and free from distortion, guilt, defensiveness, or deception. What was the difference between my understanding and that of people who did not see the changes? Why was it that so many people still felt powerless to produce change?

One theme thundered through all of the letters I received and through my various experiences with cynics over the years. In every case, these people held several beliefs.

   • They believed that they couldn't affect people and circumstances around them and didn't have the power to do anything about things needing change.

   • They believed that when circumstances were not what they would have liked them to be, they had little or nothing to do with helping to produce them. They placed blame on others. Their focus was almost always outside of themselves, causing predictable feelings of helplessness and angst.

   • They believed that even if they did know how to change something, they wouldn't be able to bring it about. Even when motivated, they had little confidence that they could actually affect change. They felt that it wasn't about personal motivation but about ability.

A related theme has to do with how we view our place in the situations we are currently in. Do we see ourselves as individuals who can act or simply as objects that are acted upon by external situations and pressures? Put another way, do we believe that we can choose differently or not? If we believe that the power to choose is not something we can exercise, then we are trapped by our own thinking.

The power to change and create a different world is not something we either have or don't have as much as it is a power that we either access or turn away from. Why do we turn away? Because in our heart of hearts, we do not *believe* that we have such power at our disposal. If I believe, for example, that I can't stop smoking, why would I begin a smoking cessation workshop? If I believe that I can't change the nature of my interaction with my boss at work, why would I try to do so? And furthermore, if I believe that I have little to do with the current situations I am faced with, why would I engage in any effort to change? After all, the situations have little to do with me and my choices.

Whether people believe they can change and whether they can affect the situations around them has everything to do with whether they initiate any effort to do so. Hence, the power to choose to change is before our eyes at all times, but it might as well be a thousand miles away if we do not see things as they really are and really can be. When internal vision clears, as it must at some point, we will see that when we were born, we were endowed with precious gifts of choice that no one and nothing can take away. This is the truth we must ultimately embrace, for anything less is living dishonestly with ourselves and results in inevitable feelings of hopelessness. This kind of debilitating emotion serves to reinforce our flawed belief that we are not responsible and are incapable of making the changes we desire.

As our internal vision clears and over time is sharpened to 20/20 Insight, we are able, often for the first time, to see ourselves clearly and honestly and to see others in similar ways. When we do, possibilities are seen that were hidden from our view. It is not as if they were not there all along, for they were. It is simply that our blind spots or distorted vision did not allow us to distinguish them, so they went unnoticed.

This is never more true than in the way it applies to our power to implement all of the ideas presented in this book. Often we are held down by false and distorted ideas about our individual power to make things different, to create the world we honestly desire for ourselves and those we work with. Our own experiences have dulled our ability to see clearly the phenomenal options that are available to us as human beings imbued with truly amazing powers for good.

It is my deep conviction that we come "hardwired" to progress and make things better, and when we become convinced that we cannot do this for whatever reason, we experience the natural emotions that accompany false ideas—confusion, dismay, and frustration. Over time, these emotions may be the most important indication we have that we have tried to give away our God-given power to choose and change. Conversely, the same emotions vanish when we embrace truthfully the power we always had but failed to embrace. 20/20 Insight includes the ability to see this important truth clearly and keenly and then embrace it with enthusiasm and conviction.

Breaking Free from Insanity

Years ago I heard an insightful little phrase that has stuck with me. It says much about what this chapter is about and the power that we all have to produce different outcomes in all areas of life. It's about insanity: *Insanity is continuing to do the same old thing day after day and hoping for different results.*

It is absolutely insane for anyone to believe that if they continue to do things as they have always done them, they will produce different results. Can it get any more straightforward than that? Results are always the product of action, of choices and decisions we make. Thus, if I do not change my methods and I believe that things will get better, I am completely insane. Even so, as I have worked with people over the years, it has been obvious to me that many of us secretly hope that without any changes on our part, things around us will change dramatically in our favor. We hope that the previous maxim is false, that people and circumstances will change and we will have to do nothing. What a country! There are more crazy people than I thought.

Some specific stories come to mind that vividly illustrate just how insane we sometimes are and how blind we become to real solutions to real problems.

Years ago when I was doing marriage counseling, an interesting couple came to my office. They were in their fifties and had just celebrated their 30th wedding anniversary, but all was not well in Mayberry. When they came into my office I invited them to sit down, but the husband came closer to me and whispered, "I'll just leave Marge here and be back in an hour."

I was almost too shocked to comment, but then words came. "What do you mean?" I asked. "I thought this was *marriage* counseling."

"I know what you mean, but you don't understand," he said. "Marge has numerous personal problems and has had them for years, and even though I'm married to her, I think she needs personal help."

I grabbed his arm firmly and said, "Frank, I don't fix wives. I do marriage counseling, and that means you stay." I led him to a chair and plopped him down. He thought that this was a fix-it shop for people who were sick, but that he had no personal responsibility for the problems in his marriage.

The next couple of hours were interesting. I learned that he had been a Marine Corps colonel, and a tough one at that. In fact, he had been active in the Marines for over 25 years, and as I watched him interact with his wife, it was clear that to him she was his dutiful private. He told his side and she cried as she told hers, a story of years of verbal abuse from him that had left her beaten down and defeated.

He scoffed at her apparent weakness as if to say, "No Marine of mine cries like a baby." My heart ached for her because of what she had suffered but also for him for the deep degree of his internal blindness. He was unaware that he had any part in helping to produce this quivering woman who sat before him. He saw her as weak and brainless. What he did not see was what was killing their marriage.

"How long has the relationship been this way?" I asked them. They both agreed that it had been nearly intolerable for more than 20 years. Twenty years—day after day, doing the same old things and yet hoping that things would somehow, someday get better. In their own way, each was sowing the seeds of discontent and yet secretly praying that the relationship would magically improve. When it did not after all those years, they began talking about divorce, and that's about the time they came to my office.

"What would you like to see happen?" I asked them after hearing their sad story of insanity. With little hesitation, they each answered similarly: "We want to be happy again, to feel love, to like one another, to find a way to stay together, and to have some sense of harmony again. That's what we want and have wanted for years." I wrote their answers on a flip chart (see illustration).

Then I asked a follow-up question: "Would you say that either of you has been doing anything that would logically produce these kinds of results?" We reviewed again that they had been engaging in blame, resentment, fighting, anger, avoidance, and other ineffective strategies, none of which would naturally produce any love, respect, or harmony. In fact, they agreed, they had been doing the very things that would almost guarantee that the marriage would get worse. This was an important insight, for it helped nail down the importance of the insanity principle.

"Well, if you, or anyone else for that matter, wanted to create these kinds of outcomes, what would you need to be and do in order to produce them?" They knew the answers and we listed them on the flip chart alongside the outcomes they had discussed a bit earlier (see illustration on page 96).

After discussing what they currently were doing to one another and the results or outcomes they each desired, I said, "I hope you can see one obvious truth: You simply cannot get there from here! You cannot be angry, vindictive, impatient, critical, and the like and then hope for some inane reason to create love, respect, and harmony. You cannot plant one crop in the spring and then harvest a totally different one in the fall. On the farm and in life, the law of the harvest is always

DESIRED OUTCOMES

Happiness,
companionship,
friendship, love

Able to
communicate better

No fights or arguments;
mutual respect

Feelings of peace
in marriage

operating, even when our own insanity would have it disappear. You always reap exactly what you sow—no matter what."

Did this couple have the power to change the nature of their interaction and create a different kind of relationship? Certainly, but in the midst of the heat of a withering relationship, such choices rarely rise above the mess that is being produced. It is in these moments that we must always remember the insanity principle, for it never fully goes away.

As we discussed the nature of their current interaction, this couple began to see things differently. They could each describe various reasons that they were not happy, and coincidentally, each reason placed blame on the other party.

"Each morning when you wake up," I said, "you make choices about how you will respond to one another. You have talked about what you want to create, what you wish you had in this relationship. My guess is that early in your marriage, you possessed such harmony and spontaneity. Now the question is, are you interested in re-creating that?"

This is not a simple question for people in trouble to answer. After years of pain and frustration, they are often worn out by the weight of a difficult relationship. Some are not willing to try anymore. In this case, however, both partners were still interested in doing what they

LAW OF THE HARVEST

BE		HAVE
Loving	→	Harmony and Love
Caring	→	Happiness
Forgiving	→	Openness
Kind	→	Kindness
Selfless	→	Compassion

could to create the happiness they had missed for so long. I asked them to go home and write down the kinds of things they could each do to help create the kind of relationship they wanted. "Decide what each of you must be and do in order to have what you want," I said. "This is the way we will rebuild your marriage."

Luckily, there was enough love left, and they followed through. In several weeks, progress was evident. Even though they still had areas where they differed widely, they had learned some new ways of seeing their relationship and were growing more aware that whatever they were experiencing, they had been the ones to create it. Choices produce results, and their marriage was the proof of that.

This couple learned what one author, J. Allen Peterson, teaches: "Most people get married believing a myth—that marriage is a beautiful box full of all the things they long for: companionship, sexual fulfillment, intimacy, friendship. The truth is that marriage at the start is an empty box. You must put something in before you can take anything out. There is no love in marriage, love is in people, and people put it into marriage. There is no romance in marriage. People have to infuse it into their marriages. A couple must learn the art and form the habit of giving, loving, serving, praising, keeping the box full. If you take out more than you put in, the box will be empty."

Keeping the box full is not just a principle for marriage relationships. It is true for all social interactions. If what you have created is not what you want, then you must either want what you have or do something different. You cannot neglect any relationship and then expect it to flourish. This single principle eludes many as they hope for love, respect, acceptance, and esteem yet fail to plant the seeds that produce it.

Knowing that we can choose something other than what we are now choosing is an integral part of this process. If any relationship is not what we would like it to be, we have a great deal to do with where it is headed and what it will become. Doing nothing other than what we have always done has a predictable result: Everything stays the same or erodes even further. In many ways, relationships are like flowers. If we fail to care for them, they don't just remain beautiful; they wither and die. Choosing to respond to others in ways that nourish them and fill them up causes withering relationships to re-blossom and grow. You get just what you give in the end.

When we decide that change at any level is needed, choice becomes a critical element in the process. We do have the power to change the endings and produce different outcomes. Such power lies within us to choose differently and in so doing, stop the insanity trap that we sometimes fall into. We often hope that things will improve and even talk about it to others, but at the end of the day we really act very much as we always have. So we continue to do the same old things and hope for different results. Changing the ending requires changing ourselves—how we see and believe, how we make sense of events around us, and how we behave based on these interpretations.

If we ultimately refuse to embrace this central truth, we give ourselves up to the forces and situations around us, inviting the dulling affects of hopelessness and helplessness to take over. Beliefs can be carefully examined. Interpretations of events and people around us can also be scrutinized in ways that enable us to determine if we are interpreting the world in ways that help us produce the outcome we care most about. We can reflect on our thinking and re-script it with fresh and productive ways of seeing and experiencing the world for significantly greater effectiveness. When we come to see with such crystal clarity our own ability to share the world around us in ways that lead us to our goals, our internal vision has sharpened to the level of 20/20 Insight. We see things regarding change as they really are and as they really can be, and the results are stunning. This process of dehypnotizing ourselves from false beliefs is what we will focus on for the remainder of this chapter.

A Father and a Son

My good friend George and I were talking about his struggling teenage son, Tyler. Tyler was, in his father's mind, making all the wrong choices. He was not going to school regularly, not doing his homework, and basically failing all his classes. His test scores proved that he was very bright and had ability. He just didn't want to do the work.

As George visited with Tyler's teachers, he formed an image of Tyler that was something like this: Tyler is lazy, unreliable, dishonest, and chronically disorganized, and he has poor study habits. For further evidence that he had captured Tyler accurately, he talked with teachers who all agreed that Tyler was bright enough but simply too lazy and apathetic to do the work. Some saw him as resisting any adult authority, and the quasi-clinical theories spread from there. It was clear to my friend and everyone who knew Tyler that this was "the way he was."

Like most responsible fathers, George went to work to create a system to make sure that Tyler did his work and got better organized at home. At school, a checks-and-balance system was established that almost ensured that Tyler would "have to" do his work and hand it in or be called on the carpet.

Clinically speaking, Tyler's father was accurately describing Tyler's behavior. In so many months Tyler had proved many times over that he was in fact "lazy, unmotivated, lackadaisical, and unreliable." Evidence abounded of these "facts," and George felt confident in his description of his son. But the problem was not getting better. In fact, after several months of hard work on George's part, his son had changed little, which only served to reinforce his belief that his son was even lazier and resistant than first believed.

After all of his thinking and planning and working, George had caused virtually no change in the outcomes he desired from Tyler. Ironically, what was driving him crazy was the fact that things were actually worse than ever; it sent him into a fit of frustration and confusion. This was when the following insight came to him and ultimately changed the true heart of his and Tyler's relationship forever. I'll share this in his own words.

> *After several weeks of watching Tyler, the accuracy of my perception deepened, at least in my mind, and the strength of my certainty that I was seeing him accurately strengthened. I knew he was lazy because I had so much evidence to convince me of it. I didn't just think he might be lazy and unreliable and resistant—I knew he was that way, and it was on that belief that I acted. It all fell apart when I started to see that nothing I was doing was helping and that the nature of the outcomes I wanted so badly was not coming to pass. Early on I believed that if I worked hard enough at it, made him more responsible, and got his teachers more involved, it would all turn around. When this did not get better but in fact got steadily worse, I began to question the accuracy of my viewpoint. That's when things began slowly to turn back the other way.*

Naturally, this experience was deeply frustrating. This good and decent father was spending so much time working with Tyler that when he began to see that things were sliding backward, he questioned what he was doing. And this is a question that all of us should consider: "Is what I am doing working? Am I producing the kind and quality of results I desire?" If we are working hard but seeing no progress, it is often evident that the way we are seeing the situation and our beliefs about the people involved are twisted and inaccurate. This is exactly what George came to realize.

One night, he heard a speaker talk about how we see our children: "Often we come to view our children as problems that must be fixed, and we go about trying to fix them." This was something that my friend could easily relate to. "But what happens when we do that?" asked the presenter. The entire audience muttered to itself, "It never works." This is a hard lesson to learn, but a valuable one. "See your children as real people who are trying to do good and be successful," the speaker advised. "Your role is to let them know that you are there to help them. If they need your help, they will ask for it, if your relationship is open."

These realizations led George to sit down and talk to his son, openly and honestly, for the first time in months. He stopped trying to change Tyler and started to love and accept him as he was. His focus shifted from changing Tyler to helping him.

"Son, I know school has not been going well for you lately, and I've been trying to help but have not. Is there anything I can do that you would like me to do, that would be helpful?" George asked. This was a much different question from "Did you do your homework like I told you to?" The emphasis shifted and Tyler began to turn around, stop resisting his father's assistance, and take responsibility for improving his work at school. Much to George's delight and surprise, things began to improve as soon as he backed off. All of his assumptions and beliefs about raising kids were tossed up and shot at in this difficult relationship with Tyler, but in the end, he was able to see both of them in a new light, and it changed them.

It is absolutely true that difficulties with ourselves and others result from a distorted view of reality. One key to greater success is a clearer view of things as they really are. In this example, George came to see that his viewpoint of Tyler was in large measure leading him to do things that were actually making things worse for Tyler, not better. Often we feel that we possess a correct view of reality because so many times in the past we have "nailed" it by indicating that another person was a jerk and they turned out just as we said. This builds our confidence in our ability to read people, and after a while, we stop questioning the accuracy of our beliefs. Truth is revealed when the outcomes roll in and we come to see that in spite of how accurate we thought our view of another person was, we are unable to produce the results we desire.

Here's the 20/20 Insight discovered by Tyler's father: Even when we believe that our perceptions of another are "dead on," we need to temper our beliefs in two ways. First we must accept the ever-present possibility that we could actually be wrong. For a long time this possibility never presented itself to my friend. He was too certain that he was right to entertain the thought that he could be mistaken about Tyler. Often the strength of our feelings can be misinterpreted as meaning that our conclusions are accurate. The stronger our emotions about the other person, the more accurate we believe our viewpoints to be, particularly when we infer the intent of another person by predicting their reaction (what he will say, why he feels the way he does, what he will do next, what he is thinking, and so on). There is a likelihood that we are only partially accurate.

Second and most important, we must see that the outcome of the interaction is far more important than the accuracy of our beliefs about the other person. If we are technically "right" in our assessments but the relationship remains poor, what use does the accuracy of our beliefs serve? By shifting our focus from how right we are to what outcomes we want, we are less likely to justify our own behavior and more likely to consider other approaches that have a far greater likelihood of producing the outcomes we really want. The accuracy of our beliefs is far less important than the kind of outcomes we are currently producing. Even if all the world believes that we're right, the only thing that matters is what we are producing, creating, and sustaining by our reactions and choices moment by moment.

This man learned a lesson that few ever come to see—that in spite of how accurate and "right" we may believe we are for whatever reason, the deeper and more important question relates to the nature of the outcomes we are producing. Poor results usually reflect distortions in our mind's eye that cause us to see things in skewed ways, even when we are absolutely certain that we are seeing them correctly.

As our distorted vision clears and we begin to see things more accurately, we become outcome-focused. We become more attentive to creating the kind of outcomes we honestly desire personally and with others and less myopically focused on narrow perspectives that we hold to fervently even while what we really want continues to elude us. It involves seeing things at a new level, a level that is more honest, clear, and true.

Power over Circumstance

The stories in this chapter and throughout this book bring us down to one compelling question regarding choice and circumstance that will never go away. *Do we have power to affect circumstances and shape them in productive ways, or are we governed and controlled by them?* Phrased in this way, the answer seems blatantly obvious. No one would consciously admit that they are victims of circumstance, but many people would then turn around and behave in ways that suggest that they are.

When we are able to produce the outcome we desire, we tend to believe that we had a hand in it all. But when the same circumstances or relationships turn sour for whatever reason, we point to those circumstances and to others as the cause of the problem. Wrenching, difficult circumstances take on a special quality, convincing us not only that we had little to do with what is happening but also that there is little we can do to fix it. From there we begin the inevitable slide into "victimville," where everyone feels "shafted" by something or someone and no one believes that there is any way to turn the situation around.

Actually, it is all a lie, a great untruth that holds us captive and brings upon us the discouragement that always accompanies feeling trapped. It is then, however, that we must ask ourselves how it is that two people can face the very same circumstance, but one can discover in it great opportunity for growth and improvement while the other can find only defeat.

Two men lose their jobs on the same day. One turns this into an opportunity to do what he has wanted to do for years and starts his own business. The other turns inward to despair, self-doubt, and deepening discouragement. The circumstances are identical, but the responses are very different. It is inevitably not what happens to us that dictates our success but how we choose to respond to it. My own life experience verifies this basic truth. The power lies within us to create the kind of world we long for, not on a grand scale, perhaps, where nations come together, but in our own hearts, as we begin to live truthfully, insightfully, and productively.

When I teach my workshops on 20/20 Insight, I always place the following quote on the screen and then ask people to respond to it: *Until we can honestly say and believe that we are where we are, who we are, and what we are today, because of choices and decisions we made yesterday, last month, last year, and so on, we cannot say we can choose otherwise.*

Why is this so, I ask participants? How is it that if we cannot say one, we cannot say the other? Invariably people read that phrase over and over to find the answer to the simple question. Then it pops into someone's head and fills that person with understanding. "Because," someone will blurt out, "if I don't believe it was choice and decision that produced my present circumstances, at least in large measure, then I will not believe that choice and decision can change my present situation." Absolutely true.

Furthermore, if we do not believe that it was our choices and decisions that helped create our present reality, then what else do we ascribe it to? The answers are few—luck, fate, or God. And if we believe that what is currently happening around us is the result of luck, fate, or God, what can we do if these circumstances are not what we would like them to be? Very little, since luck, fate, and God are all things out-side of self and largely outside of our direct control or influence. Hence, if the results we are currently experiencing are not produced by luck, fate, or God, they are the product of choice.

For many, this simple but powerful insight is simply breathtaking. They had always believed in some way that circumstances did have the power to hurt or control them or stand in their way, but they come to see this belief for what it really is and realize that giving their choice away to fate means giving away any opportunity to create meaningful future outcomes. They are sobered by the clarity of the truth, and some for the first time understand the truth of the principles in this chapter.

Understandably, coming to see this insight clearly is liberating and empowering, especially for those who have spent years blaming people and circumstance for their troubles. If we do not believe that we have helped to create our problems, we feel powerless to make any needed change. But when we come to see that we do create our world, that our beliefs do drive our actions, and that those actions pre-dictably and automatically lead to certain outcomes, we are free to choose in ways that we never before imagined. As basic as this may seem to some, many people I have worked with over the years are only now seeing it clearly, free of the distortions and fuzziness that have held them captive for many years. It still may be one of the most important principles we can teach and practice in our own lives as we interface with others and begin to create the kind of outcomes we deeply desire.

Your Assignment: Try to Make a Serious Mess of Things

Even after all that has been said about our power to choose and create change, I suspect that there are still a few skeptics out there who find it hard to accept. For those few, I'd like to offer one final sugges-tion that may bring clarity out of the blur.

Suppose that someone came to you with the following strange proposal. "I'll give you exactly 30 days to make your life and your relationships at work and home a complete and utter mess. If you succeed, I'll pay you $1 million. If, on the other hand, in 30 days things are no worse than they now are, you'll have to pay me."

Think about your current circumstances at work. How hard would it be to create friction between you and your co-workers and boss? Just one nasty comment, a few critical remarks, or calling someone a name or two, and those relationships could be immediately turned in the wrong direction. How hard would it be to ruin the relationship with your spouse? We all know how to do it; we know their soft spots and what would really be offensive. We would be able to cause hurt feelings and provoke resentment in less than a day if we really put our minds to it. How about with our children or neighbors? How difficult would it really be in 30 days to make a complete mess of your personal life and other key relationships? I suspect that it would be a snap, and we would all be $1 million richer.

In this chapter we have been talking about the exact opposite—making things better, more productive, more satisfying, and more effective. For some, it seems too fantastic, too "pie in the sky" and idealistic to talk as we have about creating a world in which we are producing the kinds of outcomes that are most important to us. How ironic it is that we could, with very little conscious effort or forethought, make a complete mess of things, but we cannot see how we could use the same power to produce positive results. We must accept the fact that we can just as easily create positive change.

Many times in this book we have discussed the central and overriding role that our beliefs play in our lives. It is here at the level of basic beliefs and assumptions where everything else gets its start. If those beliefs are flawed, distorted, or fundamentally false, we will be directly affected whether we know it or not. We simply cannot hold false and distorted beliefs and consistently produce productive and successful outcomes. The seeds of false and distorted beliefs will always yield a harvest of ineffective, limiting outcomes as surely as night follows day.

Thus far in this chapter we have discussed the crucial, central role that choice plays in the change process. Embracing the power that we each have to produce positive change is fundamental to identifying and changing false and distorted beliefs. Such beliefs are not set in stone, nor are they as impossible to access as some believe. Like subjects under the spell of a hypnotist, we have been hypnotized to accept false beliefs as if they were true, but we are unaware that this has taken place. We labor under a false set of beliefs without realizing it, and we need to be "dehypnotized" from them so that we can replace them with true and productive beliefs that will enable us to achieve the things that matter most. Dehypnotizing ourselves from false beliefs allows us to see ourselves and others clearly, truthfully, and productively, enabling us to create a different level of effectiveness than we have ever before experienced. It is this dehypnotizing process that we will focus on for the remainder of this chapter.

Recognizing False Beliefs

Because most people are often unaware of the beliefs they hold about the world, they are like hypnotized people; they believe false things to be true and act on them. To some extent, we are all hypnotized—we all hold false and distorted beliefs about ourselves, others, and the world around us that undermine our efforts to succeed.

Even though we hold beliefs unconsciously and assume them to be unchangeable, when we realize that they are beliefs, not hard-and-fast facts, we often see almost immediately the erroneous and self-defeating nature of these beliefs. Breakthroughs occur instantaneously when we come to see ourselves clearly and honestly for the first time and understand where those beliefs are leading. Hence, changing beliefs need not be an arduous, long-lasting, painful process of inquiry and scientific exploration that demands experiment after tedious experiment. Rather it is a matter of laying our beliefs in front of us where we can easily see them and the outcomes they are currently producing. When this happens, our eyes are opened to see ourselves and the beliefs and assumptions we hold in an entirely new light. This is when real breakthroughs begin.

Five Steps to Changing False Beliefs

Although it can be difficult to do, the process of surfacing and changing false and self-limiting beliefs is really quite simple. It generally involves five interlocking steps.

1. Identifying distorted beliefs
2. Establishing meaningful goals
3. Creating an ideal belief window
4. Looking for feedback
5. Finding a coach

Although any one of these steps can be helpful in creating significant improvement, when used together, they sharpen internal vision and enable us to see things as they are and can be. Change can unfold in unimaginable ways once we come to see things clearly and recognize the power we have to change them for greater success and effectiveness. It is not inch-by-inch plodding but leaping forward to new and higher levels of understanding and insight. This is ultimately where 20/20 Insight plays out in day-to-day life.

Step 1: Identifying Distorted Beliefs

Since our beliefs are often so tacit and difficult to observe directly, we must search them out, much as a private investigator searches out the truth by sorting through various kinds of evidence. Fingerprints lead to footprints, which lead to hiding places, which lead to other, more significant facts, tracing back and back until at last we arrive at the beginning. In this case, the beginning is the belief or belief system that serves as the engine for emotion, automatic thoughts, behavior, and ultimately the outcomes we produce. We are less interested in how a particular belief was formed (such as the result of a difficult childhood experience) than we are in how that belief or set of beliefs influences us now. It may be interesting to note, for instance, that my beliefs about myself and my abilities were largely shaped in my early teens as I struggled with blindness. It is more important and significant, however, to see how those beliefs shape my thinking today, for now is the time in which we live.

The exercises that follow are designed to help uncover beliefs that lie beneath other things, such as painful relationships, career frustrations, or personal pain and disappointment. Once they are unearthed, we can go about changing them in ways that will help us achieve that which we desire. To be sure, it is impossible to change something unless we can first see it clearly and understand how it plays out in our everyday lives. Thus, we first detect and note distortions in our beliefs and assumptions and then correct them for greater effectiveness.

Exercise 1: Listen to Language

Often beliefs can be ferreted out by listening to language. Doing the following activities will help provide the raw material for uncovering limiting and distorted beliefs.

1. Write a short paragraph in which you describe yourself to another person. What are you like? Describe your strengths, what you see as the greatest areas in which you need improvement, what you like and dislike about yourself, and so on.

2. Take a moment and reflect on the things that you would really love to do in the next five years if there were really no constraints. Are there some things that you believe you wouldn't do? Why do you feel that way? What would keep you from succeeding? Which of the things do you think you will be able to achieve? Why?

3. Beliefs can also be uncovered by describing your conscious theories of how things work. These are cause-and-effect beliefs that usually come out in language such as "If . . . then." For example, "If I assert myself, I'll feel guilty and still not get what I want." "If I work hard, I will not be rewarded." "If I take a risk, I know I'll fail because I know so many before me who have, and they are smarter than I am." Take a sheet of paper and make a list of your "If . . . then" beliefs. It's often helpful to have someone you know well help you because they have heard you mention your "if . . . then" beliefs or have watched them played out in everyday experiences, so they can often tell you what your notions are.

Create as long a list as you can, then review it carefully. What be-liefs are hiding behind your mini-theories about how things work, and what happens when other things take place? Record these thoughts as well.

4. For this activity, think of a problem situation that you have been attempting to resolve for some time (either personally or an issue with another person). Fix this situation firmly in your mind and then ask, "What does it mean about me that I have not been able to resolve this situation?" Your answer to this question will likely reveal beliefs that you hold about yourself and others that you may not have been completely aware of.

It is also helpful to ask, "What do I want instead of what is now taking place, and what do I believe prevents me from getting it?" Re-view your answers to these questions and look for clues that may point to a certain belief system or pattern.

Exercise 2: Identify Automatic Thoughts

Most people experience life as a series of ups and downs. When things go well, little thought is given to why certain positive outcomes have taken place. When things go badly, on the other hand, these ex-periences serve as warning signals that something is awry. Too often, however, we look in the wrong place for the cause of the negative out-come. We quickly jump to assumptions that it is a situation outside of our control or a person other than ourselves who caused the incident. With negative outcomes, this kind of thinking prevents us from ever exploring other alternatives that could lead to different outcomes the next time. And by not exploring the reasons behind positive outcomes, we fail to empower ourselves with important knowledge that will en-able us to reproduce them. It's little wonder, then, that we begin to think that it is all "luck" that causes certain outcomes.

Automatic thought patterns reveal deeper beliefs and assumptions that cause us to make sense of the raw data of daily experience the way we do. When we have experiences, we *process* those experiences in a particular way, driven by our deeper beliefs, which often go unex-plored. These beliefs determine how we organize perceptions into thoughts, how we set goals and make decisions, and how we understand and come to terms with events in our lives. When these beliefs become too overgeneralized or rigid, they predispose us to see things in consistently distorted ways. But as noted earlier, we rarely recognize these patterns at work since they happen so unconsciously and automatically. The following exercise is designed to identify and change such rigid overgeneralizations and replace them with more productive beliefs.

Exercise 3: Complete an Interpretation Chart

To record your thoughts in response to the questions below, look at the illustration. On a large sheet of paper, draw columns and label them as shown in the illustration. Then fill in the columns based on the instructions that follow.

Event: Think of a recent event that was difficult or frustrating for you, where things did not go as you expected or hoped. It could be a personal situation or something involving another person. In this column, jot down the essence of this experience.

Interpretation: At the time this took place, what automatic thoughts (judgments, conclusions, observations, or opinions, for example) filled your mind? For instance, your boss missed an important meeting at which you were scheduled to make a critical presentation. What were your automatic thoughts about this? "She is always late. I can never count on management's support," "I knew this would happen. My boss doesn't value me," or any of a number of other thoughts may have raced through your mind.

Attitudes: Record the emotions that accompanied this experience and the thoughts just noted. How did you feel while it was happening?

Decision: Think about the ways in which you could deal with the situation. What would be the result of each?

Other possible interpretations: As you reflect on this experience, think about what different interpretations you could have made that you did not. How else could you have chosen to view this event?

Believability: Next to each alternative interpretation, note the degree of believability, from 0 (for an explanation that you cannot

Event	Interpretation	Attitudes	Decision
Co-worker does not keep his commitments. Misses deadlines, etc.	He's lazy and incompetent. Does as little as possible to get by. Is a barrier to my success.	• Anger • Resentment • Deep frustration • Blame	Confront the employee *or* Try to work around him and cope as best I can

Other Possible Interpretations	Believability 0–100%
1. He has not been properly trained to do his job.	10%
2. He is under great pressure from the boss and is doing the best he can.	20%
3. I have not fully shared my expectations. I need to do that.	30%

accept and is completely unbelievable to you) to 100 percent (for an explanation that is totally believable). If you can record other possible interpretations but they strike you as totally unbelievable, this will help reveal deeper insights about the beliefs that guide your actions.

With a completed chart, review the things that you have written, looking carefully for themes in the statements and in the language used. Review specific words or phrases that may provide further insight into underlying beliefs. What do these words or phrases mean to you? Finally, attempt to dig beneath these automatic thoughts to the beliefs that cause them to come about. This may not be easy, since for most of us it is the first time that we have attempted to uncover something that has always remained out of "sight."

Step 2: Establishing Meaningful Goals

In step one, we considered various ways to help uncover and identify current beliefs, being especially on the lookout for false, distorted, and self-defeating beliefs. Certainly not all of our beliefs are self-defeating or distorted, but as we strive to make important changes in our lives and increase our personal effectiveness, understanding the beliefs we hold is critical. It is tantamount to removing the rocks and weeds from the riverbed so the water can flow smoothly to its destination. When we can identify and then remove barriers, we liberate ourselves from limitations from within and free ourselves to pursue those things that we care deeply about.

Setting goals is certainly not a novel idea. It has been around forever in some form. For centuries people have set objectives to aim for and work toward. They focus our attention, direct our efforts, and move us toward something specific. That much we all know. Research on goal-setting and its effectiveness is clear. Those who consistently set goals and work toward them simply achieve more of what they want than those who wander aimlessly in the world of generalities.

What does this suggest about how our minds operate when they are working most effectively and efficiently? Put another way, why is it that setting goals works as it pertains to the manner in which the human mind was designed?

Our understanding of the mind is still in its infancy. There is so much that we don't know about how the brain functions, exactly how memory operates, and precisely how all of the other intricate and complex processes work together to produce reasoning, prediction, and visualization, among other marvels. There is so much left to explore. But we do know some things from our research on the brain. Here is a brief overview of just a few of the human brain's incomparable powers.

- We are born with an instinctive need to progress, solve problems, and always improve ourselves. The mind is one of the complex tools that we draw upon to achieve goals and continually move ahead.

• Like the operating systems that control the functioning of complex computers, our brains are continually at work, even when we sleep, searching for answers to our problems and drawing upon thousands of bits of information that may help us achieve our objectives. The mind literally never sleeps.

• Animals are programmed by instinct or training to pursue certain paths. Human beings have the capacity of self-awareness, which allows us to choose our own goals and to combine instinct with intellect. Woven tightly into the workings of our minds is the amazing capacity of human imagination. Our imaginations have no limits. I can imagine literally anything I want for myself and my family. I can see things in the distant future and visualize them as if they were already here. This capacity is another important element in our efforts to succeed, move forward, and reach for greater effectiveness.

• Our minds work best when they are given goals or targets to aim for and pursue. With no goals, our minds have nothing to aim for, and we wander without direction. With clear goals in mind, our brains go to work to overcome barriers, solve problems, and create solutions that will help us achieve our goals. And even though we may not realize it, our minds are always at work, pressing ahead, searching for answers to problems we present, and helping us move ever closer to our goals.

If only we could comprehend the marvelous power that lies between our ears! Our minds hold within them the ability to see the future and imagine with perfect clarity a life better than that we currently have. They have the ability to resolve our most complex problems if we allow them to do so. They hold within them the solutions to the problems that now hold us back and prevent us from succeeding as we desire. They are ready and willing to help us succeed and achieve greatness, personally and professionally, if we can learn to tap their great power.

In his fascinating book *Beliefs*, Robert Dilts discusses the importance of setting goals and clear outcomes for ourselves: "Once you've helped someone set an outcome, you've already started the change process, because the brain is a cybernetic mechanism. This means that once he is clear about his goal, his brain will organize his unconscious behavior to achieve it."

As Dilts explains, once we set a goal, our brains will automatically begin to provide self-correcting feedback to keep us on course. The implications of this single idea are staggering. Once our minds can focus on a clear goal, they go to work to achieve it. Along the way, they give us corrective feedback when we are not accomplishing whatever we desire personally and professionally.

Our minds have been preprogrammed to help us succeed and to warn us away from failure. It all begins with that clear target or goal that our minds must have in order to move. What better reason could there be for setting goals? If we get out of the way and allow our minds to do what they were designed to do, we will realize our fondest hopes and dreams. It is truly that simple.

For two years I thought about writing a book. I talked in general about it to friends, walked around bookstores, and thought, "I ought to write a book," but never was it set in my sights as a goal to pursue. One day I stood in a large bookstore, looking up and down the aisles at thousands of books, and the question popped into my head, "What is the difference between you and all these authors?" My first thought was, "They are smarter and better writers." I knew that in some cases that was accurate, for in the stacks of books were works by C. S. Lewis, John Grisham, and other well-known and terrific authors. But I also knew that in most cases they were not smarter, for I had known several authors, and I felt that I was as intelligent as they were. Then came the next question, "If they are not smarter, what is the real difference between you and all of them?" It didn't take long for the answer to come: "They did the work. They sat down on their butts, at their computer or with a pencil and paper, and put in the hours and did the work. This is what they have done and you have not." This simple realization was at the same time both discouraging and liberating. As I walked home that afternoon, I made a decision that has affected my life ever since.

Two hours after standing in that bookstore, I outlined *20/20 Insight*. That outline was very different from what you are now reading, but nevertheless, it was the first time I had really decided to write a book. The idea changed from an idle wish or hope to a legitimate objective to achieve. I was absolutely astonished by what started to happen. I started meeting other authors in very unusual places, and they just happened to know publishers and agents. I ran into people who had the very information I needed to complete an idea for a section of the book. When I was most frustrated with what I wanted to say, I would be led to people who had the answers I sought. Doors began to open that I never knew existed as I worked day after day toward my goal. It was as if my entire being was now focused, directed, and aligned to achieve this goal that I had set before me. The miracles continued to happen, as they still do, all designed to help me move in the direction of my dreams and clearly defined objectives.

Commitment to a goal that we care deeply about produces a level of providence and success we could never before have predicted. Why? Because that is how we were designed by our Creator. Our marvelous minds have the power, if carefully focused, to achieve whatever is set before them as a goal. They work tirelessly behind the scenes, resolving issues, clarifying dilemmas, and discovering solutions that move us toward the goal. I have seen it and lived it and am still living it each day as I watch the magic unfold. This is the true power and majesty of our human endowment and the power we each have to accomplish that which we most want, if only we will empower ourselves to achieve it.

The Mind as a Goal-Seeking Instrument

I have always been fascinated and impressed by watching a demonstration of guided missile power and technology. I watch as a missile, designed to hit a very precise target hundreds of miles away, is launched from a ship in the ocean. Although laser technology and other complex processes are way over my head, I watch as this missile guides itself, by means of intricate feedback processes, steadily along its path, corrects itself, and ultimately strikes precisely where it was programmed to hit. It all begins out in the ocean, aiming at a target the engineers can't even see, and through the use of amazing guidance systems, it moves toward and strikes its target nearly every time. What an amazing spectacle this is to observe. What a marvelous achievement to behold! The illustration shows how the missile utilizes critical feedback to make course corrections and ultimately locate its objective with accuracy.

Like a guided missile's on-board navigational systems, our minds provide feedback that tells us when we're not heading toward our goals and are in need of a course correction. There are several elements that are essential for this process to work at all, let alone work well.

1. It all begins with a very specific target or goal. On the ship, an engineer programs very precise coordinates that guide the missile to its final destination—the target.

2. The missile also has very sophisticated laser guidance systems on board that scan various data points to make necessary course corrections. These instruments tell the missile when it is off course or when it needs to modify its path or trajectory to achieve its desired goal.

3. The missile must accept and respond to the input it receives from engineers on the ship and from its own guidance systems. If, for whatever reason, the missile can't recognize or interpret instructions to modify its path, it will fly off course and miss the target.

Of the hundreds of subprocesses and highly complex systems involved, these three elements are at the heart of it all. If any one of these elements is not in place or if the process malfunctions, failure will occur. If there is no specified goal, the missile will fly aimlessly, finally striking something and exploding. If the guidance system fails to work properly, even if the goal was correctly specified, the missile will not seek and find the target. And if the missile is unable to respond accurately to feedback, it will once again move in the wrong direction, unable to self-correct. When these three processes work together, however, success occurs.

But this technical achievement, in all its wonder and wizardry, still

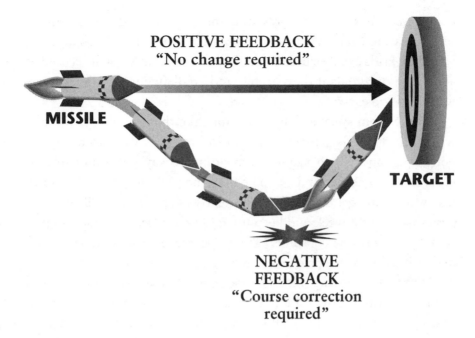

POSITIVE FEEDBACK
"No change required"

MISSILE

TARGET

**NEGATIVE
FEEDBACK**
"Course correction
required"

pales when compared to the complexity and power of the human brain, although the basic processes are much the same.

Much like a guided missile, the human brain needs a target to aim for, a direction in which to focus its power. We give it that direction by establishing clear, specific goals that we deeply desire to achieve. Desire mixed with clarity is power. When we set such goals for ourselves, the mind is designed to help us achieve those goals; in fact, this purpose is its primary role relative to our success and improvement. Even when the answers to our problems may be completely obscured to us, our minds are busily engaged in searching for answers, helping us to recall important information that will help us move toward our goals. They do everything they can to solve our problems—unless we jam the mental processes and prevent our marvelous minds from doing what they have the capacity to do.

Guidelines for Setting Goals

Here are a few specific suggestions for setting effective goals.
Make them realistic. Research shows that the biggest mistake most

people make in setting goals is setting them too high, almost creating a self-defeating cycle. Wanting to turn over a new leaf or change the world by Friday makes little sense. Experts say that we will succeed at achieving our goals if they stretch and challenge us but don't overwhelm us too early.

Make them specific. The other mistake that people often make when setting goals is making them too broad. "I want to become a better person" is too vague. "I'm going to say good morning to everyone in my office and try to be more helpful" is better. "I want to lose weight and get in shape" is not nearly as specific as "I'll go to the gym three days a week and keep my daily fat intake to under 30 percent of the calories I consume." Being specific lends focus to goals and makes it easier to see progress as we move toward our objective.

Write them down. Someone once said that a goal is only a wish until you write it down. I know an author who set a goal to write a bestselling book. On the wall in his office he hung a magnified copy of the *New York Times* bestseller list, then pinned a mockup of his book cover to it and wrote on it "New York Times #1 Bestseller." Every day as he labored over his writing, he looked up at that wall and reminded himself of what he was striving for, where he was going.

This isn't an earthshaking idea, but it illustrates how writing something down that we can review is far better than simply muttering a list of goals to ourselves one day in the shower. Writing a goal down also helps put muscle into a dream, motivating us to do what we have committed to do.

Once goals have been established, the next step in dehypnotizing yourself from false beliefs and developing beliefs that will move you toward your goals is to create your belief window.

Step 3: Creating an Ideal Belief Window

I believe that a person's beliefs provide a window to who they really are. In this sense, they are like windows to the soul. A belief window represents how you look at yourself and the world around

IDEAL BELIEF WINDOW

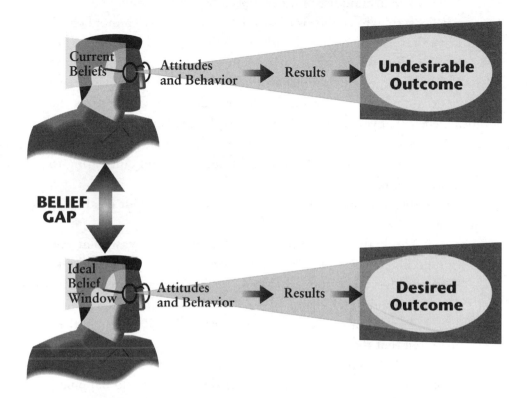

you. It answers the question, "Ideally, what beliefs do I need to incorporate into my life in order to achieve the goals I have set for myself?" Since beliefs drive action, creating a belief window ignites the engine that drives successful goal accomplishment.

For example, let's suppose a person sets a goal such as "I want to own my own business within the next 12 months" under step two. But in reviewing step one, he sees a consistent theme of fear of failure and unwillingness to believe in himself. If deep inside his belief system he doubts his ability and fears the unknown to the extent that he will refuse to take any risk, then a goal like this is likely to flop. This constitutes a "belief gap," a gap between our current beliefs and goals that we have established.

The illustration above shows that often there is a gap between the thing we desire and our current level of belief about ourselves, others, and the world around us. In other words, we do not have the necessary belief system to enable us to succeed. And since we cannot behave in ways that are inconsistent with those deeply held beliefs, we are stymied, feeling the frustration and doubt that comes from wanting more but not knowing how to produce it. When this is the case, we must create what I call an ideal belief window, which captures the ideal beliefs that you need to cultivate in order to achieve what you desire. The ideal belief window lets you answer the question, "In order to achieve my goals, what beliefs would I need to begin cultivating to support my efforts?"

Here are a few questions that may help you fill in your ideal belief window.

1.Think about someone who's succeeding in ways that you would like to succeed. What do you notice about how she thinks and acts? List those points and look for the common threads of belief that run through them.

2. Parents often feel a responsibility to instill beliefs in their children that they feel will serve them well throughout their lives. What beliefs would you want to pass along to those you care about that you feel would encourage their success and happiness in life and relationships?

3. What do you personally believe are your keys to increased effectiveness? Deep down in your gut where your intuition resides, what do you sense about your current beliefs that needs to change?

4. Write a statement of beliefs. If you have ever written a personal statement of purpose or mission, you know a little of what this is about. A statement of beliefs is just what it suggests. It can be a single page or many pages. It can be written in bulleted statements or prose. Format and style don't matter. What does matter is that it reflects your most natural thinking about what you believe or what you want to believe in the future.

The idea that beliefs can be changed is a novel one to many people, but it happens every day as people go through such exercises, as they gradually develop a new set of beliefs and see the results unfold.

Here are some open-ended sentences that you might complete as you write your statement of beliefs.

1. I believe that success and personal achievement are built on . . .
2. The difference between those who achieve what they want and those who do not usually boils down to . . .
3. The luckiest people I know believe that . . .
4. People I know who are at the greatest peace with themselves seem to believe . . .
5. Someday I hope that I can honestly say that I believe that . . .
6. If I had the power, with the wave of a magic wand, I would change the way I believe about myself from (current image) to (desired image).

Now take your completed sentences and convert them into a statement of beliefs that best describes the things you care most about and the kinds of beliefs you want to cultivate more deeply in your life. As we replace false and distorted beliefs with realistic, productive ideas and beliefs, we unleash the power that lies within to accomplish far more than we ever imagined. It is rarely our lack of ability or conscious motivation that holds us back. Rather it is our unconscious beliefs that stand in our way. Once we remove this barrier through the process of dehypnotizing that we have discussed, we remove the limits to our effectiveness and are free to move forward with astonishing speed.

Step 4: Looking for Feedback

In the guided missile example used earlier, we noted that a missile moving toward a designated target relies continually on feedback, both from internal sources on board the missile and from external sources such as technicians at mission control or on the ship from which the missile was launched. If the missile does not recognize these signals, it will likely miss its target, since these vital forms of feedback tell the missile whether it is on or off course.

Whether we are referring to sophisticated guided missiles or human beings moving toward designated goals, the general processes are very similar. In both cases there are two kinds of feedback in operation at all times—positive and negative.

These processes of feedback and course correction have direct application to us as we set goals and strive to achieve them. Both positive and negative feedback are being sent to us constantly as we move toward our goals, but we must be able to recognize and correctly interpret the signals when they arrive. Ironically, we humans tend to pay far more attention to negative input than to positive. Those who are consumed by doubt and negative beliefs about their ability to succeed often "hear" negative feedback that is never sent or create it in their minds. Positive signals find it hard to penetrate the skeptical, often cynical individual who is held down by old habit patterns and self-defeating beliefs. Thus, learning how to recognize positive feedback is vital to our ongoing effectiveness.

In the guided missile example, both kinds of feedback are critical for the missile to hit its prescribed target. As it flies toward the target, positive feedback essentially says, "Everything is going as planned. The selected target is in view. The course we are currently on is exactly the right course for hitting this target. Make no changes at this point. Proceed as you are currently." This input is critical for the missile's guidance systems, which now know that everything is as desired and that no significant changes or course corrections are needed. Positive feedback to the missile is critical information for achieving the specified goal. Where negative feedback tells the missile that a change is needed, positive feedback reinforces the current path and says in effect, "All systems go!"

Negative feedback also provides essential input as the missile moves toward its target. Negative input says, in effect, "Given the target that has been selected, you are moving in the wrong direction and need to correct your current course. You can still hit the target, but not without making some changes now." Negative input does not imply that the missile is faulty, that the mission never should have been started, or that the target that was selected is wrong. It simply communicates with the missile to let it know what needs to happen to attain the goal. Hence, both positive and negative input are essential for the missile to reach its desired destination.

We all have "sensors" that pick up signals from all around us, telling us we are either on track or off course in some way. Recognizing various kinds of input for what they are and making needed corrections is essential for success. Ignoring positive and negative input is a recipe for disaster. We simply cannot afford to set off on a journey and ignore the input we receive from various sources that help us know when we are moving toward our desired destination and when we are not.

Personal Negative Feedback

As you drive down a highway, you think very little about the intricacies of your car's engine and its many operations under the hood. But on your dashboard are several indicators to warn you if something needs attention. If your oil light comes on, that tells you that unless you do something (in this case, add more oil), you will eventually have serious problems. Pressure gauges and signals such as those that alert you that a door is open perform similar functions. These signals are negative feedback, input that tells us that things are not what they should be and that we will be unable to accomplish our goal unless a course correction is made.

The human body also has some fascinating built-in warning signals that alert us to potential trouble. Perhaps the most amazing warning signal we have is pain. In his fascinating little book, *Where Is God When It Hurts?*, Philip Yens writes about the role that pain plays in our physical bodies.

> *Pain sensors in the body warn me of impending danger.*
> *The feeling of pain forces my body to concentrate on a*
> *problem area and respond to it. Sometimes the reaction*
> *is almost subconscious. For example, when I go to the*
> *doctor for a checkup and he taps my knee with a rubber*

hammer, my leg straightens violently. The automatic reaction occurs because the doctor's stimulus gives the knee the impression that it is bending. His hammer hits the same nerves that would be affected if my knee would suddenly buckle while walking. My body rushes to compensate, lest I stumble and experience greater pain. The reaction is too spontaneous and lightning-quick to allow the brain time to reason that I'm seated on a table, not standing, and there is really no danger of falling.

The body and its functions form a perfect model of how feedback, positive and negative, works. And there are other examples around us everywhere. Dead-end signs on a street tell us, in effect, "Don't go down this street. It won't take you where you want to go," so we turn around and choose another course. There are also warning signs in relationships, telling us that adjustments need to be made in order for us to have a positive, resonant relationship. Organizations must attend to numerous signals to stay in business. The question in all of these examples is whether we recognize and respond appropriately to the signals we receive.

This book is about how we can achieve the things that we desire in more productive ways and how we can more clearly see things as they really are. For us to do this, we must be able to recognize the personal negative feedback that we receive and respond accordingly. There is a variety of signals that we receive to indicate that our vision is blurred, distorted, and limiting. These signs tell us that something must change for us to move in the direction of the targets we have selected.

Five Kinds of Negative Feedback

In my experience, there are at least five kinds of negative feedback that can serve as important input for us in all that we engage in.

1. Frustration
2. Fear and uncertainty
3. Loneliness
4. Depression
5. Resentment

These forms of feedback operate much like the mechanical warning signals in a car to help us know that something may be awry and needs to be changed.

I say "may be awry" because the existence of these warning signals doesn't necessarily mean that something is wrong. Initially, early in a project or a relationship, we may experience some of these forms of feedback. Starting a new job, for example, usually has a high degree of ambiguity and newness connected with it; we often feel frustrated, useless, and maybe even lonely as we strive to learn the new job, get to know people, and become part of their lives. These kinds of reactions are to be expected; they are temporary, and they are not the type of feedback that I'm referring to in this section.

I am speaking more about experiencing these kinds of feedback on a regular, sustained basis. For people in this situation, frustration, pain, and fear become a way of life, not just a temporary challenge. When these conditions become a natural way of life, they are strong signals to us that something is wrong and in need of careful examination. As the saying goes, "If you always do what you've always done, you'll always get what you've always gotten." This is surely true when it comes to responding to consistent negative feedback. In order to respond appropriately, we must learn to recognize these signals when they occur and be able to distinguish whether they are normal and temporary or long-standing and unsatisfactory.

Frustration. This is the most reliable and consistent form of negative feedback we have. The dictionary defines frustration as "disappointment, a deep chronic sense or state of insecurity and dissatisfaction arising from unresolved problems or unfulfilled needs." Who has not experienced frustration at one time or another? The difference between those who recognize it as negative feedback and those who accept it as a way of life is dramatic. I know people who have been frustrated for so long that they believe it is simply the way things must be and that there's nothing much they can do about it. They fail to see frustration for what it is: negative input, telling us that we must do something different to get what we desire. If we don't, we will be mired in deep, chronic stress and disappointment. No one wants to feel this for 10 minutes, let alone a lifetime.

Frustration, therefore, is a useful warning signal to us, an indicator that we are off course and that we need to self-correct, make some adjustments, and try again. It does not suggest that we are failures, but it does indicate that we are failing—in other words, that we are not moving in the direction of our deepest desires. If we were, we would not feel the frustration that comes when we are off course.

I know a man who was fired from three jobs in four years. In each case, he had various reasons to explain why things didn't turn out as he hoped; usually those reasons didn't involve him, such as "My boss didn't appreciate what I was doing for the company" or "The business just didn't know where it was going" or "I was too much of a threat to those who were in charge. They couldn't handle it, so they let me go." But as you read his explanations, you also can see a very frustrated person. Like a red light on the dashboard that says, "Check Oil," his frustrations should provide similar input for him. Frustration is a reliable indicator that he is moving away from his goals, away from what he really wants. It doesn't mean that he is not worthwhile, that his jobs have been bad, or that he is bad. It simply indicates that something is off course and needs to be examined carefully and modified before he can succeed.

I firmly believe that we are all engineered for success. Frustration merely reminds us that we are headed in a direction inconsistent with our basic engineering and desires. If we can recognize it for what it is, we can move back on course and proceed confidently in the direction of our dreams.

Fear and uncertainty. When our target is clear and we are moving toward it, we feel confident and assured. We are enthusiastic about what we are doing because we can see that it is moving us forward toward a goal we honestly want. Of course, we all experience moments of fear and uncertainty in our lives, but for too many, anxiety is their only way of life. They are afraid to reach out, to dig in, and to move. They are completely nailed down by the fears they experience. Frustration, fear, and uncertainty are simply indications that something is not right and needs some attention.

It is impossible to experience fear and uncertainty when the following two realities are in place. First, our goals are clear in our minds and they are what we truly want, and second, we are willing to do what it takes to achieve them. If we are experiencing failure, it is usually because we are not willing to do what is required to succeed. Most often we have the ability or capacity to do what it takes, but our willingness falls short. It is will, not ability, that moves one person to achieve what she desires and leaves another one coming up short.

In his insightful essay, "The Common Denominator of Success," E. M. Grey describes the one common factor that seems to separate people who succeed from those who do not. Hard work, good interpersonal skills, and talents are all useful, but the thing that he discovered has to do with our will to accomplish that which we desire. "The successful person has a habit of doing things failures don't like to do," he observed. Then, speaking of those who consistently succeed, he says, "They don't like to do them either, necessarily. But their disliking is subordinated to the strength of their purpose."

Having strength of purpose means that we strongly desire to bring about that which we seek; we will do anything it takes to accomplish it. Some people set nebulous, vague goals for themselves. They don't have a great deal of emotion invested in such vague goals, and consequently, their will is weak. We will almost always experience failure in such circumstances, but not due to any lack of skill. If we are truly willing to do what it takes, to see differently and make needed changes, we will find ourselves moving confidently in the direction of our dreams. If our will is lacking, we will continue to experience the frustration that always accompanies hollow effort devoid of deep commitment and desire.

We must have a clear goal that we desire to accomplish and the will to pursue it with gusto. When these two conditions are in place, fear and uncertainty melt away like the dew before the summer sun. Moving confidently in the direction of our dreams is more than a trite phrase. It is the assurance felt by people who know what they want and are working to achieve their goals on a regular basis. They also know that when they experience fear and uncertainty, something is wrong—but not with them. A change in course is necessary for them to achieve what they have set out to achieve.

Loneliness. Another sobering indicator that we are not moving in the direction of our target is loneliness. As I visited with a college-graduate friend who was looking for work, he had loneliness written all over his saddened face. It seemed that everywhere Joe turned, the answer was "No, thank you." Every effort that he made to get an interview met with closed doors. His feeling of having to do this all by himself was almost overwhelming. He was mailing out résumés and no one was calling. He read the paper each night, praying for attractive jobs that he could go after, but they never appeared. He sat and waited for the phone to ring, but it was silent. While Joe's friends were out working and moving ahead with their careers, he sat motionless, lonely, and going nowhere. He was frustrated, afraid, and filled with deep uncertainty about whether he would ever find a job.

Such feelings almost always spawn personal loneliness and, in the worst case, depression. Obviously, this condition is counterproductive as well and comes back to haunt us when we are trapped in the labyrinth of loneliness.

I had another friend who lost his job, and when he went to interviews, people wondered what his problem was. One day someone who had just interviewed him called one of his references. "What's wrong with Jim?" he asked. "He acts like someone just died." Jim's personal sense of loss, depression, and loneliness was creating new challenges for him as he tried to find work again. These feelings were now self-defeating and prevented him from moving ahead with confidence.

The conclusions that Jim drew from the layoff were negative and destructive. "I'm no good or they wouldn't have laid me off. I'll never find work again. Who would want me? Who would hire a guy who just got laid off?" His head was full of negative thoughts, spawned by dark and lonely pictures of life after a layoff. This mental and emotional state became the reason that it took him nearly three years to find work again. He had the same skills and talent as anyone else who interviewed, but his melancholy state did him in. Sadly, when rejection became so common, it reinforced what he feared all along: "I'm no good and no one wants me." He is a perfect example of someone with wonderful abilities who shoots himself in the foot and then looks around and wonders who pulled the trigger.

Like the other forms of negative feedback we have discussed, loneliness need not be disabling. It is nothing more than another signal that we are off track and something must change. The way we look at the situation or ourselves is distorted, blurred, and ineffective. Loneliness helps point our attention in the direction of the problem so that we can self-correct and move back on course toward what we really want.

Depression. Another alarming signal that things are awry is the depression that sets in, discouraging us and leaving us with a futile feeling of "Why try?" I'm not speaking of clinical depression, which is often caused by chemical imbalances. This form of depression requires medical treatment and is often chronic. What I'm talking about may be characterized as "feeling low" or "the blues."

Many people struggle with depression on a regular basis. They are not clinically depressed or in need of therapy; they simply feel low and down on themselves and the situations they are in. Interpreted correctly, depression indicates that changes are appropriate. Not trying anything new is pointless if what we are currently doing isn't working. Depression indicates, whether consciously or not, that we are not moving in a direction that is meaningful to us. Our hearts and emotions are out of alignment with our direction or circumstances.

When this is the case, depression rears up like a dead-end sign on a deserted country road, telling us to turn around. It tells us that we should take stock and make some changes in the way we are looking at the situation or in our direction. It is unnatural to be depressed for long. Brief moments of discouragement are normal and we all experience them; when we become clear and committed to something important to us that honors our deepest values, however, these times of discouragement come less frequently and are succeeded by the optimism and hope that comes through strength of purpose.

Resentment. Resentment is the crust on the bread of frustration. In nearly every circumstance where people are frustrated, they look outside themselves for reasons, for someone else to blame for their circumstances.

Resentment is little more than resurrecting instances in the past where we have been wronged and dragging them into the future to mull over, talk about, relive, and become angry over one more time. It is also one of the most useless emotions that we experience. Reliving something that has already happened is fruitless, since nothing fundamentally changes, no matter how long we complain or talk or worry. Moreover, our hearts become increasingly harder as we relive something that was painful to begin with. In many cases the initial experience was painful, but reliving it is much worse as we drag it out for all to see, painstakingly walking through every last detail, attempting to exonerate ourselves and blame others.

In the midst of all the blaming and resentment, we lose sight of what really needs to happen to make the situation better. It is as though we move into a fog bank where our vision is limited to things at our feet. We become very myopic and are unable to stand back and see things as they really are. We cannot see clearly enough to make necessary changes. If all this isn't bad enough, resentment is a two-edged sword, cutting us as much as it cuts those we blame and resent. Poison fills our souls as we engage in resentment of others, and we become alienated from them.

Of all the indicators that a course correction is needed, resentment may be the most clarion of all calls. The emotions that accompany resentment—namely, blame, anger, self-pity, rationalization, and self-justification—poison our hearts and are clear evidence to us that something we are doing is wrong. Resentment is reliable negative feedback. It reminds us that we are off track and that we can never achieve what we really desire while we are filled with bitterness and blame.

Whenever I find myself in a situation where I sense myself blaming and resenting someone else, I know that I am headed down a path with a grizzly bear at the end. It is self-destruction in slow motion, and the results are as predictable as night following day. If we see it for what it is, resentment can be a flashing light, a sharp pain that tells us something is dreadfully wrong and needs correcting. If we fail to heed this important warning sign, we will find ourselves veering farther off track and slamming into a brick wall. Hence, recognizing resentment and taking steps to root it out of our hearts is essential to achieving the important goals that we set for ourselves.

Each one of these five basic forms of negative feedback acts like a sign on the highway telling us that we ought to turn around. If we ignore the warning signals and become consumed by negative emotions, we enter a cycle of self-defeat that is hard to get out of. But if we listen to and recognize these signals for what they are, we can begin to reshape our future and achieve the success and happiness we really want.

Step 5: Finding a Coach

A final way to help dehypnotize yourself is to find a coach. It is difficult to know what untrue, untested beliefs we hold until someone comes along and challenges our thinking. We can sometimes hang on to ideas that are basically flawed and have no factual basis at all but which nevertheless have a powerful influence on our lives and the choices we make.

I have a good friend, Jacques, who teaches me something every time we are together by challenging some beliefs I've clutched for years. He was born in another part of the world than I—Haiti. From the first time I met him, I could tell that he was vastly different from me. He saw the world in terms that were radically different from my views.

I recall a conversation with him that changed my thinking in significant ways. I was trying to make a difficult decision about starting my own company and leaving the one I was currently with. Here's a portion of this conversation. As you read my words and his, look carefully at the ideas each of us holds, the beliefs behind the conversation that each one draws from.

RANDY: I think I'd really like to start my own company, but I'm not sure if I can make it.

JACQUES: Why do you think that?

RANDY: Well, I'm not sure if I have everything it takes to make a new business successful.

JACQUES: Have you ever done this before? If not, how would you know if you have what it takes or not?

RANDY: Well, I can't just leave my old company without another job.

JACQUES: Why not? What's the worst that can happen?

RANDY: Well, I could fail, fall flat on my face, and put myself in financial ruin! (I thought he was crazy for even suggesting such a thing.)

JACQUES: What reason do you have for thinking you would fail? You've always succeeded at everything you have done. Why wouldn't you succeed if you started your own firm?

RANDY: Well, I don't know if I could get clients fast enough.

JACQUES: Why couldn't you?

RANDY: (I paused, not having an immediate answer.) Well, I don't have the materials written to show to potential clients. I would need something to show them what I do.

JACQUES: Yes, that sounds right. So why don't you write them? Could you do this in the next few weeks?

RANDY: (I paused again; I really didn't have an answer.) Yes, I suppose I could. But I don't know if clients would hire a one-man show when they are used to working with a big consulting company.

JACQUES: Why wouldn't they?

RANDY: (I paused, then shot back a retort.) They might think that one person wasn't a real company and couldn't provide them with good service. (This was like intellectual volleyball, and I had him on this one.)

JACQUES: Is that true? Is it true that you couldn't supply them with high-quality service?

RANDY: No, it's not true. I think I could really do some things that a large, slow-moving firm could not do.

JACQUES: Then tell them that, sell them on it. Sure, there will be some who won't hire you, but no firm has everyone as customers. Get the ones you can who want high-quality service and a real relationship that others can't provide.

RANDY: I don't know if I have the financial means to hold me until I start making money.

JACQUES: Why not? Why can't you start making money immediately once you know what you will provide and sell people on it?

RANDY: (I was thinking that he just didn't understand the business of business here in the States. I was going to have to educate him here.) You see, these clients take a long time to make a decision, so it would be a year before I would have any income from them.

JACQUES: Why do you think a year? What can you do to shrink that amount of time? Do you have any ideas?

And so it went for about three hours. My language was riddled with phrases like "I can't," "I shouldn't," "I have concerns that," "What if I don't," "I'm unable to do thus and so," and "They won't want me to do such and such." A hundred negative ideas rolled out of my mouth. Each time I lobbed one at him, feeling that I was letting him in on how the world really operates, he came back with a question that came from a different paradigm, from a different set of beliefs. He saw the world as an unlimited opportunity. I saw it as risky, dangerous, and potentially disastrous. His last volley really got me, and I went home to rest after this one.

"Randy," he said, "you have a lot of talent and seem to know what you really would like to do. America is a country that will allow you to do it. The very worst thing that can happen is that you may not succeed and will have to go get a job with a big company. You won't die, or be shot, or have heart failure, or anything else really tragic. If you never try, you'll never know, and the consequences of failing are not very severe."

What could I say? I had painted a picture of disaster that was so bad, so terrifying, that no one would attempt what I was thinking of. No matter what rebuttal I had for him, in the form of "I can't" or "I shouldn't" or "I'd better not," he would ask "Why not?" "Give me a reason for your thinking" he said numerous times. "Prove to me that what you are saying is really true and not simply a belief you have that is untrue but controlling your behavior."

When I went home after this conversation, I was thinking more about my thinking than I was my new business. Why, I wondered, did we see things so differently? He grew up outside of my country and came to it with a different set of assumptions about how the world operates. He had run several businesses and succeeded. People who knew him thought he was a little eccentric and unusual, as indeed he was. His beliefs were 180 degrees different from mine, and as we compared notes on what we believed was true, my mind was flooded with insights that ultimately led me to do what I had always wanted to do.

The differences between us were in the beliefs and assumptions we both held about the world, business, my own talents, and how to succeed. He believed one thing and I believed another. We both got just what we believed we would.

Now, two years later, I'll lean over the back fence and say, "Hey, Jacques, I have a problem and need a different way of looking at it." He will walk over with a broad smile, knowing that he has another opportunity to ask me questions that I have never asked myself, questions that will send me into my house with a head cramp but filled with ideas that I've never before considered. As my beliefs are exposed to his view, I sometimes feel as though I'm talking with someone from another planet because he sees life so differently, but that difference shows me how I tend to see the world and believe it operates. Thinking is the starting place for accessing all of our talents.

The idea of having a personal coach, formally or informally, is really catching on. Executives in large organizations are finding it helpful to locate a trusted, competent individual with whom they can discuss ideas and talk openly about their deepest fears and aspirations. Finding a coach who works well with you is a challenge, but the first step is knowing what to look for. Here are a few suggestions.

Find someone you can trust. Even more important than brilliance is comfort, the feeling that you can really be open with your coach.

Often a good friend or close work colleague can fill this role. You need to feel that this person accepts you and has no need to judge you in any way, otherwise you will hold back when you need to be open and honest. It matters less what your coach does than how comfortable you feel in the relationship. People are more open than ever before to having a trusted friend or colleague assist them as they strive to make needed improvements or break out of old patterns. I've found that most people react so positively to the idea of coaching that they may want a reciprocal deal in which you coach each other. Trust is a critical component in this process.

Look for complementary skills. It's of little use to find a coach who thinks and believes much as you do. Try to find someone whose background is very different from yours or who perhaps has a much different set of skills. That person will see things you will not see and think of ideas you may never come up with, much like Jacques and myself. We are inclined to find people to whom we can easily relate. But once you know whom you feel you can trust, select people from that group who can provide a much wider and different viewpoint. As they say, "If two people think and act the same, only one is necessary."

Create a schedule. Often people establish a coaching relationship and keep it so informal that years pass and then one day, they realize that they haven't talked. Life is too hectic to expect this kind of relationship to just happen. It needs to be part of a schedule. I'd suggest that you meet once a month at first to talk about projects, thoughts, and concerns. Record your conversations, if necessary, to capture the salient aspects. It helps you listen better and capture more in the long run. Don't leave this kind of relationship to chance: Make it a priority as part of your weekly or monthly schedule, and don't let it slip.

If you have trouble locating a coach who fits well with you, I have two suggestions. First, start reading biographies and autobiographies of people you admire. Even though Lee Iacocca may not be sitting in your family room talking with you about your career, his intriguing life story can reveal great insights that may be useful as you think through your challenges. You'll also find that these noteworthy people have dealt with some of the same struggles and reservations that you and I have, which is always reassuring. Second, there are professional organizations dedicated to professional performance coaching. Call a business school at a local college and ask about finding a coach.

Our world has become far too fast-paced and complicated to go it alone. How much easier it is when you can get together on a regular basis with a trusted, competent friend or colleague and talk through the things that matter most to you. Good coaches have few boundaries. They can be helpful in talking through tough issues in the family as well as complicated business projects. A coach is not meant to be a highly trained specialist as much as a person who can lend support, help generate new ideas, and provide a sounding board for existing ideas. Change is never easy, but it is much more doable when you have another person walking with you down the road.

Seeing the Patterns

In the first three lenses of 20/20 Insight, our internal vision of self comes into great focus. We begin to see the connections among things that we never saw before. The roles of beliefs as they play out in everyday life open up greater understanding about behavior and human emotion, both of which flow directly from beliefs, assumptions, and automatic thoughts. There is great kinship among these various factors as well. It is impossible to talk abut beliefs independent of where they lead and what they cause us to think, feel, and do. Similarly, we cannot effectively discuss change without first understanding how it begins and the foundation upon which all change is built. Until we can come to see these patterns unfolding and flowing in our life, we will continue to see things in a superficial manner.

In my experience, most people and organizations can easily recognize that change needs to take place but are often stumped as to why they cannot produce it. In most cases, their dilemma is a reflection of their inability to see and understand things as they really are and really can be. The clarity that comes to us when our internal vision clears and we can see with 20/20 Insight reveals patterns of cause and effect that were hidden from our view until now. It also reflects my belief that significant change can take place quickly as the darkness in our eyes is taken away, vision clears, and we see for the first time the patterns before us.

The great secret to change lies in the clarity of our vision, not in the complexity of the process. Hence change is revealed and discovered, not engineered, created, or planned. We cannot set a goal to have deep internal insight. It comes upon us as we learn to see without distortion and blurring. It always has been and will continue to be a highly adventurous journey of discovery.

Interlude
Within Us
and between Us

Before moving into the second half of the book and discussing interpersonal effectiveness, we need to pause and review. As we look back over the terrain of personal vision and then look ahead to where we are going, we will see that we could only have come this far by going the way we did. Our ability to create and sustain effective relationships with others is built upon the foundation of clear, undistorted inner vision. If the way we see ourselves is flawed and the lenses through which we see are blurred, it is nearly impossible to develop effective, satisfying relationships with other people.

Over the years I have asked people in my workshops two questions that have always yielded fascinating responses. "How many of you think that you are a difficult person to get along with?" I ask first. In more than 15 years of asking that question, I have had only two people raise their hands, and in both cases, they misunderstood the question. When we view ourselves in relation to others, we generally see ourselves as not difficult for others to be around.

Then I ask the second question. "What kinds of things really bother you and get under your skin, even make you nuts?" Here's a short sampling of the kinds of things I hear.

- "It really bugs me when I'm standing in line at the bank or a restaurant and some jerk comes and butts in line like he owns the place."
- "When I meet someone who thinks he knows everything but really knows nothing, it really irritates me and I want to leave."
- "When I have a boss who thinks I'm his little slave and expects me to do all his dirty work, that ticks me off."
- "At work when people are offended by something they think you did, but they won't come out and tell you. They tell everyone else but you."
- "When I tell my kids to do something like clean up their rooms or take out the trash and they ignore me. That really gets me steamed."
- "When I have something important to share with my mate and they won't listen. I guess they don't think it's very important. That really hurts."

Well, I think you get the drift: None of us believes that we are difficult. Rather, we believe that almost all of our frustrations in life are caused by others: managers, husbands or wives, children, colleagues, neighbors, extended family, you name it. We seem to think that if it were not for all of these people that we have to interact with, life would be a bed of roses. It's like the business owner who says in frustration, "If it weren't for these ornery and demanding customers, this would be a great job," or the parent who complains, "You know, parenting wouldn't be all that bad if you could do it without having kids." In essence, most people feel that the world would be a pretty nice place to be if it weren't for all the rude, inconsiderate, insensitive, demanding, frustrating, ignorant, offensive, and unkind people that they have to deal with day after day.

Two Types of Internal Vision

In the first part of this book, we focused as much as possible on the processes inside us—the lenses of personal vision. I asked you to go inside and think about your thinking, search your mind and heart for the beliefs that stand in your way, examine the way you make sense of everyday events, and choose a different way of being. So far, the focus has primarily been on forces inside us to which we respond on a moment-to-moment basis. Increasing personal effectiveness through clearer internal vision was our fundamental objective.

Just as we cannot easily separate internal variables such as beliefs, thoughts, interpretations, and assumptions from external factors such as our behavior and the outcomes we produce, we can hardly separate personal vision from interpersonal vision. In fact, that is the last thing we want, as it distances us from the very nurturing that makes us human. When we focus too narrowly on self, we exclude the relationships that we have with others and cut ourselves off from the life force. We create an arbitrary distinction that does not really exist, simply to make it easier to examine.

In reality, the line between personal vision and interpersonal vision is not a line at all. It is more like two sides of the same coin. They are as connected as our very physical eyes. We have two, but they work in tandem to produce clear binocular vision. They overlap and influence each other to produce our field of vision. To separate them would be to destroy the balance and symmetry of both. The interplay between personal vision and interpersonal vision is just as constant and dynamic.

Can we become truly effective without the involvement, cooperation, and interest of others? Can we be highly effective in our relationships with others if our internal beliefs are distorted and our personal views of the world are skewed and dim? Is it possible to be effective in one arena without also being effective in the other? No. These are interlocking systems that flow back and forth into one another like two rivers that run together. It is hard to accurately tell where one river ends and the other begins.

As simple and obvious as this truth may be to most, it eludes many. People I've met over the years who are wrestling with interpersonal problems in their families or workplace fail to see the roles they play in creating those problems. Their own beliefs, motivations, and conclusions are not factored into the problem, and they talk as if they had nothing to do with the mess that overwhelms them. Similarly, I have met people who are struggling in their personal lives because they have created and are sustaining deep interpersonal pain and anguish. When we fail to meet the needs of others, our own needs are automatically affected. If we hurt others, we hurt ourselves, because we are all connected. When we come to see the relationship that by design exists within us and between us, our vision is raised to the dimension of 20/20 Insight. We are then able to see not only the connection between ourselves and others but also new ways to create harmony between us and within ourselves.

In part two we discussed the three lenses of personal vision and the many ways that they play off one another to produce 20/20 Insight. The context for personal vision was built upon the one fundamental truth that our heads create our world. Within that framework, we discussed how beliefs, interpretations, and choice interact and produce personal vision. To this we will now add the three lenses of interpersonal vision. Lenses four through six provide the viewpoint through which a change of heart can come about.

Although I have divided this book into two sections, personal vision and interpersonal vision, such a separation cannot be made in real life. Yes, we are all individuals, with individual capacities to choose and act for ourselves, but we are so deeply influenced by the situations around us and the people with whom we live and work that it is impossible to completely separate ourselves from others. When we try to separate ourselves too much, we find that our deepest needs for love, support, and caring go unmet, and we begin to feel the effects of loneliness, meaninglessness, and depression.

We are meant to be with others, to work with others and to live in families. It is essential for us to figure out how to be together in ways that bring us joy, peace, and support from others rather than frustration, resentment, and alienation. We live in a time when far too many people stand apart, trying to make it on their own and attempting to live independent lives. These people constantly struggle to fit in because they are trying so hard to pull themselves away. They behave independently in a very interdependent world. They are playing by rules that simply don't apply to the game of life—at least not if we want to play it successfully, joyously, and productively.

I close this small connecting chapter with the words of one of my favorite authors, C. S. Lewis. He describes this interplay between our own behavior and our interaction with others in a way that succinctly captures what I have described.

> *There is an inextricable relationship between who we are inside and how we behave with others around us. But unless we begin first with the tidying up inside each human being, we are deceiving ourselves. What is the good of drawing up rules of social behavior if we know in fact that our greed, cowardice, ill temper, and self-conceit are going to prevent us from keeping them? Nothing but the courage and unselfishness of many individuals will ever make a system work properly.*

Part III
Interpersonal Vision

Lens Four
The Dance of Doom—Getting In

Progress means getting nearer to the place you want to be. And if you have taken a wrong turn, to go forward doesn't get you any nearer. If you are on the wrong road, progress means doing an about turn and walking back to the right road. And in that case, the man who turns back soonest is the most progressive man. Going back is the quickest way on.

—C. S. Lewis, English author and critic

After I had worked for a large electronics company in the Northwest for several years, my wife and I decided it was time to move east. I interviewed for and accepted a promising new position with a large food company. I had met my boss-to-be at the first interview, and he had seemed nice enough, the position was interesting, and we were excited about experiencing life in a new city.

My first day on the job was one I'll never forget. I expected my boss to meet me and show me around, perhaps to sit down for a bit, chat about the job, and talk with me about what kinds of things I would do in the days ahead. That didn't happen. When I arrived, Bob, my new boss, was behind his closed office door, and he stayed there for the rest of the day. I was shown to my new office, and I did the best I could to busy myself, not knowing what else to do. "He must have a lot going on," I thought.

On day two I arrived at work a little early, hoping to catch Bob before he shut himself in his office, but I was too late. Three more hours of boredom passed before I accidentally bumped into him in the copy machine room. I said hello and he shook my hand coolly, without making eye contact. Then he shuffled off to his office and shut the door. He seemed angry about something, but I had a hard time believing it was me, since I was the new guy in the office. "Maybe he's having a bad week or something," I thought. I remember wondering what this job was going to be like if during my first week my boss barely talked to me, but I hung in there, trying to busy myself with getting to know some of the other people who worked near my office.

The first real talk Bob and I had was equally memorable. I had taken a short business trip to the East Coast for a three-day meeting with some of my new colleagues. During the last half of the third day, several of us left the meetings and went shopping at a nearby mall. It seemed innocent enough, since we had attended all the previous meetings that pertained to us. It turned out, however, that several people from headquarters saw us leave and phoned our bosses to let them know.

When I arrived at work Monday morning, Bob came to my office and asked me to come into his. We sat down, and he jumped right into it. "Why did you skip the meeting last week?" he began. I tried to explain, but it seemed that the more I explained, the more feeble it sounded to him.

"Don't you realize that these meetings are to be attended?" he demanded angrily. "That is why you went, and you were not supposed to be off messing around." He was angry, and for the next 15 minutes or so I got "taken behind the woodshed."

I felt truly chastened by my new boss, and all my attempts to apologize only seemed to make him more upset. I felt defensive, upset, and frankly, scared. He threatened me with the loss of my job if I ever did anything like that again, and I could tell he was very serious. I had embarrassed him and made him look bad to his colleagues at the meeting, and he didn't like being embarrassed.

As I left his office that day and walked back to mine, I didn't realize that Bob and I had initiated a frustrating and ineffective pattern of working together that was to last several months. After I walked home that night and told my wife, both of us grew angry at how he had treated me. "What gives him the right to treat me like a little kid?" I groaned. "I have never been treated like that in all my life."

My anger deepened over the next few weeks as he continued to mistreat me. He was critical, blaming, belittling, and harsh. It wasn't long before I developed some pretty deep-seated resentment of Bob and his harsh behavior. Little did I realize then that we had started to dance a dance of doom. From my perspective, I had been standing around minding my own business when boom!—Bob began attacking me. In my mind, I had done nothing to deserve such mistreatment. Yes, I had missed the meeting, and I shouldn't have done it, but that didn't give him the right to humiliate me and threaten me as he had.

I had been on the job less than two weeks, but I seriously wondered if I would have a job two weeks later. I even called a close friend to talk it over. He listened carefully and then reminded me that I had just moved halfway across the country and that bailing out now would look horrible on my résumé and be devastating to my family. Leaving was not what I wanted to do, but already I wondered if I could tolerate working for this kind of person. He was a nasty tyrant, and I felt trapped in a losing situation.

I have come to realize that the patterns that Bob and I created between us were very much like a dance. One person leads by acting in a particular way, and it provokes the other to follow. Bob's mistreatment of me provoked an angry, resentful response, and my reaction only added fuel to his fire. Because this dance has no elements of enjoyment, I call it a dance of doom. This is how our painful relationship looked and felt to me in those early days of my dance with Bob.

Whenever I tell this story to people, I am always amused at how quickly they can relate to this experience and how strongly they sympathize with my plight. It seems that almost everyone has been in a relationship like this one, either with a boss or colleague at work, a husband or wife, or even a friend or child. In my case, I felt as if I just showed up at work one day and before I realized it, Bob and I were dancing the dance of doom. We were engaged in a way of interaction that was confusing and deeply frustrating.

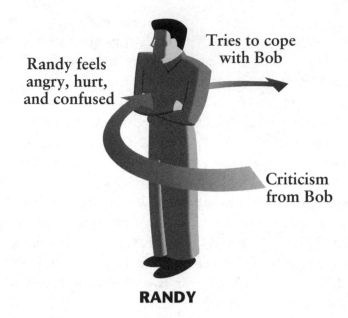

Randy feels angry, hurt, and confused

Tries to cope with Bob

Criticism from Bob

RANDY

In most cases, as I listened to other people's experiences, it became clear to me that they weren't sure how they got into such painful patterns either. As at a dance, it seems that we are just standing against the wall listening to the band when all of a sudden someone jerks us out onto the dance floor. We are forced to dance, and we don't like the experience one bit. This was certainly the case with Bob and me. I felt as if I had simply started a new job and within just a few days, I was swept away by Bob in a manner that I hardly even recognized, let alone understood.

You have heard my side of the story, but as with every dance, there is always one other person dancing. Months after Bob and I first began our dance of doom, we finally stopped and started a new dance, one that was satisfying, workable, and productive. (I will explain how we resolved our problems in the following chapters.) I then learned how this appeared from Bob's side of the relationship. The illustration on the opposite page shows how it looked from where Bob sat.

Bob felt that given a couple of things that had transpired between us, he needed to coach me, tell me what I was doing wrong, and ride me more than he did some of his more experienced managers. Unfor-

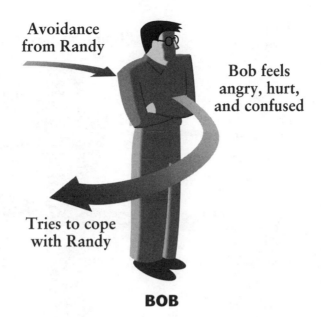

BOB

tunately, his "coaching" came across to me as criticism and judgment, which I resented. Feeling that resentment, he saw me pulling away by avoiding him and trying to stay out of his line of fire. He experienced that as resistance, avoidance, and a desire to act independently of him. Hence, the more I avoided Bob, the more he pulled me in, and the more he tried to pull me in, the more I resisted. If you put both sides of this dance together, you get just what you always get when you have people engaged in a dance of doom, as illustrated on page 152.

This shows just how much like a dance these kinds of relationship challenges really are. One person does one thing, which causes the other person to do another, and so on. Without realizing it, I was doing the very thing that led to Bob's mistreatment of me, as I saw it, and he was doing the very thing that increased my desire to avoid him. Did he want me to run away every time I saw him? Of course not. Did he want me to avoid him, resent him, blame him, and dislike him as I did? Definitely not. Did I want him to criticize me, mistreat me, and cause me untold consternation over my job and my future with the company? Never. Did I enjoy our little chats in which he raked me over the coals for not doing what he wanted done in the way he

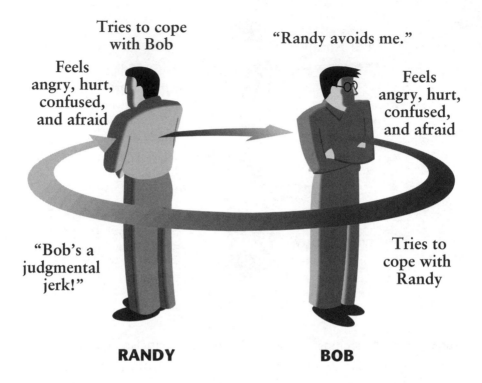

Tries to cope
with Bob

"Randy avoids me."

Feels
angry, hurt,
confused,
and afraid

Feels
angry, hurt,
confused,
and afraid

"Bob's a
judgmental
jerk!"

Tries to
cope with
Randy

RANDY

BOB

wanted it done? No, I bristled and felt angry. Can you imagine two
people more entangled in destructive irony than Bob and me? There
we were, two grown men, engaging in behavior that created in each
other the very mistreatment that we most complained about. We had
begun to dance and had no idea how it had started, although each of
us was certain that we had not been the one to "throw the first
punch." So we labored under false, distorted ideas of what was really
taking place, failing to see our own part in the painful dance we were
dancing together.

10 Basic Dance Steps

Regardless of who is involved or how they get into it, the dance of
doom has several peculiar characteristics. I call them dance steps, and
they form a pattern of behavior with the following features.

1. The dance pattern that people become engulfed in is not readily apparent or obvious to those on the dance floor. Even though Bob and I were definitely dancing and stepping on one another's toes, neither of us was able to see the pattern that we were creating together. This is true in nearly all negative relationship challenges.

2. The steps are self-sealing in that each party does the very thing that makes certain the dancing continues. For example, a nagging wife, by her nagging, creates a lazy husband who resists her efforts to motivate him. Thus, he resists because she nags and she nags because he resists. They each do the very thing that creates a problem for the other party, thus keeping the dancing alive over time.

3. Patterns like this are very predictable. Once you see the first stages of the dance, you can predict with amazing accuracy where it is going. How hard is it, for example, to predict what would happen to Bob and me after knowing how we started to dance? Unless something significant changed and one of us danced a different dance, the pattern was set.

4. Patterns usually become entrenched over time, ultimately turning into "the way things are." Hence, neither party believes that anything can be done to stop the pattern, since neither party believes he had anything to do with its creation. As a result, people continue to do what they feel they must do to cope with the other party, not realizing that by so doing, they ensure that the dancing persists.

5. Once entrenched, those involved honestly see no other way to behave than the way they are presently behaving. They falsely believe that if they do not persist in their present behavior, things will get worse. The manager who feels that his people are lazy and need to be micro-managed believes that if he doesn't hover over them, they will slack off. He earnestly believes that if it were not for his micro-managing (although he claims to dislike it), things would "go to hell in a hand-basket."

6. You can never dance alone. I suppose that there are people who can fight with themselves, but it is quite rare. Usually, we

dance with another person or persons. What's more, we "need" them in order to stay on the dance floor. If the other party leaves or stops dancing with us, we can no longer dance as we have been. It is the mutual collusion that we engage in with another that gives life to the dance. We need them to dance the fox trot so that we can do the same. The minute the other person starts to waltz, the entire fox trot pattern is messed up and the dance is over.

7. The dance of doom also carries with it predictable emotions. People almost always feel angry and resentful of what is being done to them by their dance partner, and this is expressed by blaming the other and feeling victimized. When I feel another person is doing something to cause me pain, I feel that I am his victim, and I resent it. I am blind to my own complicity in the dance and the self-inflicted pain I am helping to create.

8. Within every individual dance, there are certain styles of dancing. For example, an intimidator needs a submissive partner— someone who will submit and buckle under his bullying—in order to keep intimidating. The moment this tit-for-tat arrangement changes, the dance cannot continue. In any relationship that is not working well, there are two different interlocking styles that reinforce and feed the other. You can see it in every dance of doom, no matter who the individual players may be.

9. In any dance, both parties feel innocent of any wrongdoing and, as such, feel powerless to stop dancing. The logic is simple. "If I have done nothing to produce this frustrating situation, I can surely do little to change it." We fail to see our own involvement, and because of our twisted logic, the dance can roll on for years while both people feel trapped into responding in the only way they know. And so it continues.

10. From a particular point of view, as seen through the eyes of a person afflicted with distorted internal vision, any solution will fail. When we are in the dance, our emotions, which are almost always negative, cause us to invent solutions that lead to even greater problems. We become prisoners of our own fuzzy thinking, and in that sense, we really are trapped. Everything I thought of in

my relationship with Bob was created out of my anger and resentment toward him. Consequently, even though I felt I was trying to do the best I could, my feelings were leading me to do the very things that reinforced Bob's perception of me.

Think of any difficult relationship that you have had or are now engulfed by and you will likely see traces of most of these dance steps. It is what happens between us that determines the quality of our interactions with others, and yet it is this "betweenness" that eludes us when we are in the midst of a painful dance of doom. The most telltale sign that we are dancing with another person is the way we feel. With Bob, I felt that he was treating me unfairly, accusing me of things I had not done, and twisting my intentions to make them appear nasty. I felt trapped by him, as if I were his victim and he my victimizer, doing things to me that I did not like or deserve. When we feel these kinds of emotions, we can rest assured that we are dancing the dance of doom, and unless we come to see it for what it really is, we will continue dancing indefinitely.

Examples of the Dance

If my experience with Bob is not one that you can easily relate to, let me provide a few more examples of people I have met who were dancing the dance of doom and didn't know how to stop.

Rich and Andrea have been married for three years. Things started out okay, but Rich has started to get on Andrea's nerves.

"He's lazy and won't do anything around the house," she complains.

"What do you do?" I ask her.

"I remind him of it as much as I can," she says, "because if I don't, he won't do anything."

Rich has a different story. "Andrea is always nagging me to do things, and I'm tired when I get home from work. If she would just leave me alone, maybe I'd do it."

Andrea "nags," as Rich sees it, but she nags with the best of intentions—to get Rich off his butt to do something! Rich holds back because he doesn't like to be nagged by his wife. So the more she nags, the more he withholds his assistance, and the more he holds back, the more she feels she must nag. Each is blind to the other person's side of the relationship and the story they are weaving.

WIFE SEES...

"He won't help. He's lazy."

HUSBAND SEES...

"She always nags me."

Andrea sees her side of the problem with crystal-clear perspective: She has a lazy husband who will do nothing, so she feels the need to light a fire under him or nothing will happen. Rich sees his side perfectly clearly as well. He hates to be nagged; he asks Andrea to leave him alone since he'll do it when he can. And the more he does this, the more she nags; thus, he experiences her as a nagging, insensitive wife. The following pattern is one they created together, and they keep it going by doing the very thing that feeds the other person's viewpoint (see illustration on opposite page).

The parents of a 16-year-old are fit to be tied. In spite of their best efforts, their daughter is failing at school. The more they try to help her, the worse things seem to get. "We have talked and talked with her until we have nothing left to say, and still things get no better," they

WHAT NEITHER CAN SEE

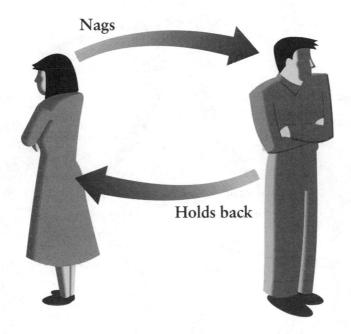

Nags

Holds back

complain. These parents have, as they see it, a lazy, uncooperative teenager who is defiant and unwilling to do what she should do. But what about their daughter? Talking with her is a different story: Her parents are always on her back, judging her, criticizing her, and trying to run her life. "If they would just back off, I might do something, but not until then," she says.

Both can see their own narrow side of the relationship and neither can see what they are creating together. And in my experience, even if they could, they would have no idea how to stop the dance they are dancing. They are doing the best they know how in a very difficult situation. Options other than those they are using seem ridiculous or are solutions that they have already tried. They are locked in a dance of doom that none of them likes, but they have no power to stop.

Think of how incredible all of this is. Party A makes efforts to solve a problem, while Party B is absolutely certain that Party A's ef-

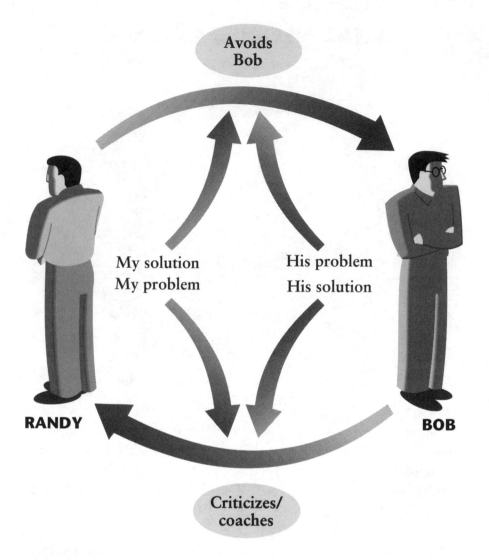

forts *are* the problem. And while B tries to cope with the problem, A sees his coping as more of the problem that A is attempting to resolve. Thus, the more I avoided my boss, the more of an avoidance problem Bob had to resolve, and the more he criticized. All that I did in an effort to solve the problem was fuel the fire, increasing the size of the problem. And so the dance of doom goes on, deepening, intensifying, and alienating people from one another in painful and destructive ways. When we are in it, we cannot see our way out, and yet, like a person locked in a prison of his own designing, we hold the key in our own pockets, all the while pounding angrily on the door for someone else to set us free.

Reviewing only a few examples illustrates just how widespread the dance of doom is in families, in the workplace, and in society in general. People are caught in patterns of interaction that they cannot fully understand and are unable to stop. As the dance rolls on, the pain intensifies and leads to deeper and deeper frustration, resentment, and blame of another. It leads us to three critical questions that will be answered in this and the following two chapters.

1. How do we get caught in such destructive patterns in the first place? What do we do that starts the dance? How do we move from standing against the wall listening to the music, as it were, to being caught out on the dance floor in the dance of doom?

2. Once the dance begins, what keeps it going? Why do we continue to dance with others this way, often for years at a time, living in pain, frustration, and interpersonal malaise? Why don't we just stop dancing once we realize that it is not getting us where we want to go?

3. Finally, and most important, how do we stop the dance of doom and begin a new dance, one that is productive, effective, and satisfying? What is required in order for us to dance a new dance?

The question of how we get into frustrating and painful patterns in the first place is not insignificant, for how we answer it places our feet and hearts on a specific path leading to certain kinds of solutions. A wrong answer is the equivalent of a turn down the wrong street. It won't lead us to where we honestly want to go.

Conventional wisdom on the subject is diverse. Some believe that conflicts such as the kind we have been discussing are a normal part of life and should be expected: "You will simply come across some people with whom you cannot get along," the theory says.

This answer assumes that the problem lies within the person and not *between* people or groups. Some individuals are defective in some ways, and when you come across them, it is your sad lot to have to deal with them as best you can. The critical problem with this view is the solutions that it leads us to invent. If it is the other person's defects or personality traits that are "the problem," then you have two choices. Either you can try to make that person better somehow or you can admit that personalities don't easily change and simply cope with the perceived defects. But if the problems were really caused by the weaknesses or defective characteristics of that person, wouldn't she have similar problems with everyone she came across?

Take Bob, for instance. I had begun to see him as nasty, uncaring, critical, and manipulative. But the man had friends, a wife, and four nice children, and he was very successful in his role as vice-president. If he really were all these terrible things, it would make sense that such dark and nasty traits would follow him everywhere, and others would feel toward him just as I did.

There are also interesting but ineffective theories of human nego-tiation that suggest that the problem lies between people but the an-swer is negotiating roles or using conflict resolution skills. In my experience this often leads people to hold the same negative feelings they always did toward the other person, but it has them strategizing about the best ways to work with them. Sometimes such tactical and strategic moves are better than what has been happening, but they usually just shift the dance from the fox trot to the waltz. Basically, the individuals are still dancing.

We get into such negative patterns with others because of our own internal and interpersonal vision. It has to do with how we respond to our internal sense of right and wrong. It is wrapped up in the way we choose to see others and the manner in which we respond to what others need from us.

Internal Vision and the Law of Human Nature

The renowned Spanish cellist Pablo Casals once said of the inter-connectedness that we have with others that "we ought to think of ourselves as one of the leaves on a tree, and the tree is all humanity. We can't live without the others, without the tree." What is it that ties us together? What is the common bond that we have with all human beings that makes us the "human race"?

In addition to the obvious physical similarities that we share with all other people, there is something much deeper that everyone possesses that comes "wired in from the manufacturer." It is real and deep and profound and cannot easily be ignored. It expresses itself in our conscience in many ways but most often as an inner sense of what is right and what is wrong. It "talks" to us in ways that are often quiet and almost imperceptible yet are very real in the form of impressions or a summons that we ought or ought not to do something about a particular thing. Regardless of culture or ideological background, it is one thing that all humans have in common, and it is this fundamental law of life that has the power to bring us together, if we will but listen to and obey its whisperings.

Understanding this internal voice lies at the very center of greater insight about how we get into the kinds of interpersonal problems we encounter. As with so many answers in this book, however, looking inside is typically the last thing we do when we are having problems with someone else. We are like the man who has lost his wallet somewhere in his house, but the police find him wandering around outside under a street lamp.

"What are you doing out here?" the police officer asks, a bit confused.

"Well, sir, I lost my wallet and I'm trying to find it," the man answers.

"Did you lose it out here?" asks the policeman.

"No," says the man. "I lost it inside, but I've found that the light is much better out here." When we're trying to find answers to important interpersonal struggles, the light may be "much better" outside ourselves, but the real answers lie inside.

C. S. Lewis has written insightfully of this "law" that we all share. He calls it the law of human nature.

> *Everyone has heard people quarreling. I believe we can
> learn something very important from listening to the*

kinds of things people say. They say things like this, "How'd you like it if anyone did the same to you? That's my seat, I was there first. Leave him alone; he isn't doing you any harm! Why should you shove him first? Give me a bit of your orange, I gave you a bit of mine. Come on, you promised!" People say things like that every day. Educated people as well as uneducated. Children as well as grownups. Now what interests me about all these remarks is that the man who makes them is not merely saying that the other man's behavior does not happen to please him. He is appealing to some standard of behavior which he expects the other man to know about. And the other man very seldom replies, "To hell with your standard!" Nearly always he tries to make out that what he has been doing does not really go against the standard, or if it does, there is some special excuse. He pretends that there is some special reason in this particular case why the person who took the seat first should not keep it, or that things were quite different when he was given the bit of orange or that something has turned off which lets him off keeping his promise. It looks as if both parties had in mind some kind of law or rule of fair play or of decent behavior about which they really agreed. And they have. Quarreling means trying to show that the other man is in the wrong and there would be no sense in trying to do that unless you and he had some sort of agreement about what right and wrong are.

The law of human nature that Lewis refers to is different from natural laws such as the law of gravity in one critical way. Gravity is a law that we cannot choose to disobey. It operates independently of us; whether or not we like it or believe it or feel it is convenient does not change the fact that it is a natural law to which we must adhere. The law of human nature, on the other hand, is a law that we can choose to obey or disobey. As with every other law, however, disobeying the law of human nature carries with it certain predictable consequences.

Anyone who cares to study different cultures and civilizations will discover that amidst many differences in perspective, there lies a common ground about basic goodness, about fair and decent behavior, and it exists among people around the world as a law that they *ought* to obey. No matter where you go, it is always agreed that it is wrong to put yourself first. "Selfishness," says Lewis, "has never been admired."

The greatest evidence we have that there is a basic internal law of right and wrong that we feel compelled to obey is what happens when we break it in any way. Here's a small list of the kinds of excuses we invent to rationalize doing the wrong thing or in some way breaking the law of human nature.

- "I know I was mean to the children, but they drive me crazy and never do what I tell them to do."
- "Yes, I know I ought to let this person have my parking space because she is old and has been driving around longer than I have, but no one does that for me."
- "I realize that I should do my homework, Dad, but my teacher is an idiot. She doesn't even know what she is teaching. It is a waste of my time."
- "I know I should apologize for how I treated my secretary, but I have told her a million times what she is supposed to do and she continues to screw up."
- "What our marriage has turned into is not good, and I realize that we need to sit down and talk it over. But every time we do, she just blows up and things get worse than ever."

If we do not believe in a law of decent behavior and know in our hearts what we should do, why do we expend so much energy creating excuses for not having done what we know we should? If we didn't feel so strongly compelled to do a certain thing, we would have no reason to excuse ourselves for not doing it. Thus, in order to go against our sense of right and wrong, we must have a way to justify our actions. It is this rationalization and justification that provide solid evidence that we feel the law pressing on us always, gently prompting us to do such and such. And it is this internal sense of right and wrong that leads us, if we follow it, to do right by others, for it is this voice that ties us to others. We all hear a similar voice, and it has a familiar sound. We do know what we should and should not do in most situations if we but consult our internal director and then follow it. When we do not, justification and rationalization immediately set in, excusing us for not doing what we know we should have done.

Justification

When a contractor justifies a crooked wall, he does something to make that wall appear straight. When you justify words on a page with a computer, you space the words in each line so that the margin is even. And when we go against our own senses of right and wrong, we must justify it somehow. We know what is right, and the only way that we can know right and simultaneously do wrong is to justify ourselves by making the crooked things we are doing appear straight. Thus, if I blow up at my son and don't apologize, even though I know that I should, I immediately conjure up a lot of reasons, rationalizations and justifications aplenty that make me feel okay about doing wrong. As Lewis so eloquently puts it, "The truth is, we believe in decency so much, we feel the rule or law pressing on us so, that we cannot bear to face the fact that we are breaking it. And consequently we try to shift the responsibility." We shift responsibility from ourselves to others through justification and rationalization. "I would have done right but . . ." In essence we say, "I would have done the right thing, *but* someone else prevented me from doing so."

It is at this critical intersection between doing right and doing wrong that rationalization and justification come rushing in. If we do what we feel is right, they are not needed, for we have nothing to explain away. But if we turn against what we know is right, they rush out hastily, ready to reassure us that even though we feel bad, it wasn't our fault but the other person's. "You would have done the right thing if you'd had half a chance," they whisper in our ears as we are carried off down the path of self-deception. In all of this, our vision is clouded by deep scales of justification that prevent us from seeing others clearly or recognizing what they really need from us. In so many situations, interpersonal conflict has its roots in our individual unwillingness to follow the path we know is right. And because the voice we turn away from is the same voice that others hear, we are really turning away from others and their needs, thus bringing upon ourselves all kinds of trouble.

This story shows how quickly justification sets in when we fail to do what we feel is right. It was told by a senior vice-president of marketing following a critical meeting with the director of research.

> *John (the R&D director) and I had experienced major differences in the past, but we were getting more and more pressure to identify the new products for next year. We scheduled a meeting to talk through the issues and make a plan, but at the meeting we got distracted by problems taking place in both our organizations that were causing one another problems. He pointed the finger at me and I at him, and before long we were nearly yelling at each other. The more he yelled and accused me, the more I got upset and the further we got from what we had come together to accomplish. Finally, I got up and said, "This meeting is through right now. If all you can do is scream and yell and accuse me of screwing up your work, then I want no part of it." And I walked out, slamming the door behind me.*
>
> *The rest of the day I was angry at what had happened, but I also knew what I should do. I needed to go to him and apologize for getting angry. There was no way we could leave things where we had left them after the meeting. But I didn't go to him and apologize.*

The voice of conscience and turning away from what we feel we should do happens in split seconds. This individual knew that what had happened was wrong, and his own conscience called him on his wrong behavior. The call came not from another person but from within, and it was something he knew he should do. But in that split second between following the impression and turning away, something significant takes place. We first go against ourselves and what we feel we should do. On a different occasion this manager might not have felt that he should apologize, but on this occasion he did. As noted earlier, the only way we can do the wrong thing and feel good about it is to rationalize it somehow to make it appear that the wrong thing is right, or at least that it is a decision over which we feel we have very little control. Here is how it looks.

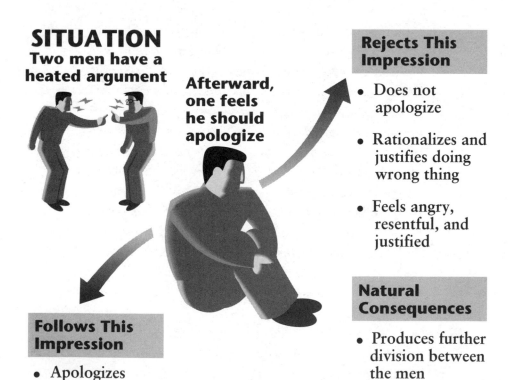

SITUATION
Two men have a heated argument

Afterward, one feels he should apologize

Rejects This Impression

- Does not apologize

- Rationalizes and justifies doing wrong thing

- Feels angry, resentful, and justified

Natural Consequences

- Produces further division between the men

Follows This Impression

- Apologizes

When we go against our own sense of what we should do, several things happen. First, we fail to do what is right. A simple, although difficult, apology might have been all that was needed in this situation. It might not have taken care of every problem between the two men, but it would likely have gone a long way toward resolving the pain caused by the immediate blowup. However, when we reject what we feel is right, the action must be justified, since we are in effect saying no to our internal sense of right and wrong. Because this sense is so tightly woven into who we are, we are essentially going back on ourselves, a process that is sometimes referred to as self-betrayal. We are not betraying some social rule or some cultural sanction that we feel legally bound to obey. We are literally going against ourselves and what we feel is right for us in the immediate situation.

When such self-betrayal occurs, we cannot expect it to happen without serious internal and interpersonal consequences. In this example, the apology is never offered. Where might this lead? To further divisions between these two men, to cool superficial conversation and an inability to talk openly and honestly with one another. Maybe they even begin to avoid each other after a time, and what was once a cordial, open relationship turns into one of casual "hellos" in the hallway. Real work never gets done, as each man feels justified in holding his position; after all, each could correctly say, "Look what he is doing!" In every example where people violate the common laws of life or the laws of human nature, they cannot do so without suffering a predictable and significant series of consequences that leave pain and conflict in their wake.

Living Truthfully

The difference between living truthfully and living a lie is colossal yet subtle. On many occasions we get into the dance of doom by living untruthfully, but justification makes our lies appear truthful. Consider the following experience between my son and me.

I volunteered to coach my son's baseball team one summer for many reasons, but mainly so that he would have the opportunity to play on a good team under a fair coach. Our team started off strong but soon slipped into a losing pattern. I noticed that as the season went along, Shawn's interest in playing and coming to practice started to slip as well. One afternoon our team was scheduled to practice; it was the day before a game. Shawn came into my office where I was working and announced flatly, "I don't think we should have practice. No one will come."

The first thought that shot through my mind was "He doesn't want to practice. He wants to go off and play with his friends and not go to practice. He's telling me that we should cancel the practice because *he* doesn't want to practice, not the other players. He's not being fully honest about this." That thought led to my first question. "Why, what do you want to do?" I asked him.

This caught him off-guard, and he immediately grew defensive. "I don't want to do anything. I just don't think anyone is coming to practice. Why, do you think I don't want to come to practice?" he said.

That is exactly what I thought, but I didn't admit it. "No, I just wondered why you don't want to practice."

This made him even angrier. "I didn't say I didn't want to come to practice. I just said that nobody else will be there." He was really heated, and his tone of voice was growing ugly. It was my job to let him know this.

"Listen, Shawn, when you walk in my office and talk to me this way, I don't want to listen. Now why don't you leave and get control of yourself and come back when you've settled down," I told him.

Like everything else I had said, this made him angry, and he left very upset at me. I was also angry as I sat at my computer with a tight chest and an increased heart rate. "Can you believe that smart-mouthed kid?" I grunted to myself. "I know what he's up to, and he comes in here trying to get me to cancel practice so he can go mess around with his friends."

Before I tell the rest of the story, there are some questions that need to be asked. Was I living truthfully in this story? Was I doing the right thing by my son and seeing him honestly and clearly? Was I being completely honest with myself about what was happening? Most people who hear this story recognize intuitively that I was not being fully honest with myself or with Shawn. And where did it lead? Predictably, it created defensiveness in both of us, and as he left my office, slamming the door behind him, it was clear that I had helped create distance between us. He was upset at me, and I was upset and angry with him. He felt that I was accusing him, and I felt that he was being dishonest with me. The dance of doom had begun with me and my precious son, and it was not Shawn but me who had caused it.

After Shawn left, I turned back to my computer to write about, of all things, justification and rationalization and living truthfully with others. As I sat there still grimacing over what had just happened with Shawn, the full truth came into focus. The story that I was telling to myself about Shawn was a lie, and it revealed itself to me in living color as I sat pondering the experience. I had accused him of coming to me with a hidden agenda and of not being fully honest with me about what he wanted. But I realized that this was exactly what I had done. In my heart, I believed that he wanted to skip practice to be with his friends, but that is not what I said. I disguised my assumption in the form of a question, which he picked up on immediately. And when he did, when he saw through to what I was really saying, I became angry, as if he had found me out.

The rest of the story is one great lie that I invented to cover up my own dishonesty. I had done wrong, and in that moment I realized how it had happened and what it had produced between Shawn and me. He had done nothing other than come into my office and ask me a simple question. The rest of the incident, as I tell it, was something that I helped create, and it was built on a lie. "Oh, what a tangled web we weave, when first we practice to deceive," as British novelist Sir Walter Scott so aptly put it.

When we go against what we know is right, we immediately enter an untruthful stand with others. We begin to see "through a glass darkly," preventing us from seeing ourselves, others, and the situation we are in clearly and without distortion. Going against the truth we know sets us on an untruthful path that leads every time to sad and predictable consequences with others. It is impossible for us to live a lie and behave truthfully, as my experience with Shawn illustrates.

As this experience began to come clear before my eyes, I called Shawn back to my office. "I'm sorry, son," I said. "You came into my office to ask a simple question, and I judged you unfairly. I apologize. This was my mistake, and you did nothing. Now, can we start all over and talk about the baseball game?" Luckily, Shawn is kind and forgiving; he allowed me to apologize and we embraced after we had made a decision about practice. This was such a simple experience, but it carried so many profound and important lessons about being fully truthful with ourselves and others.

Following a Script

The most common response that I receive from people about getting into the dance is this: "I don't ever recall a moment where I went against my conscience. I don't even know the precise moment when the relationship started to turn sour. All I know is that we didn't get along, and it got worse over time." This was true for me and my boss, Bob. I can recall specific incidents that took place early in our relationship, such as the first time he criticized me and how that felt. But I cannot recall any time when I knowingly went against what I knew was right nor a time when I engaged in behavior that I knew was wrong. So caught are we all in the dynamics of the dance that we lose track of such details as if they never took place.

What's interesting is how the dance looks in retrospect after months or years have passed. "Did you know then that you were behaving badly toward Bob?" some have asked. The answer is no. When I look back on what happened in that relationship and how I felt and how I responded to him, I realize now that it was inappropriate, and I hope I never do that again. At the time, however, I had no such understanding. I simply followed a natural course of events and went with it. This is what is known as following a script.

A script, simply stated, is a routine, automatic way of responding that takes on a specific course that is predictable. Actors are given scripts and they act out the parts, playing their roles; the better they play their roles and the more realistic they can make them, the better.

It turns out that there are all kinds of scripts in life for so many different things. Watch parents and children interact, and you'll see a parent/child script that nearly all parents follow almost without thinking, and their children act in response. Scripts are like "rules" that we follow, usually without thinking, such as the way we behave on the highway or in a supermarket or when we're under stress or perceive a threat. With little forethought, we fall into a patterned response to the situation that leads us to behave in predictable ways.

Not long ago I witnessed a script play itself out on a dangerous freeway. It began when one driver cut off another car; instantly the dance began. The driver of the first car sped up and started flashing his lights, shaking his fist out his window. He swerved to get around the other car, but the second driver wouldn't let him in. In a split second a high-speed cat-and-mouse game was under way, and both drivers were acting out a negative and dangerous script. Once a primitive response kicks in as it did with these two drivers, a belligerent script takes over. The drivers were acting on impulse, not thinking about the danger they were creating for so many others as well as themselves as they played their highway game. But we can always override a negative script if we stop long enough to get our wits about us and do the right thing. In this case, such an override never took place and the two cars ended up turned upside down in the middle of the freeway, and several people were seriously injured.

Under pressure, threat, or fear of embarrassment, negative scripts like this take over and we follow them to a tee. What's interesting is that anyone who is not part of the script can describe it perfectly, for we see it played out in some way all the time.

The script leading to the dance of doom is just as powerful and predictable. Someone says or does something that we feel is wrong or unfair or mean or deliberately manipulative or a hundred other things. When this occurs, we follow our scripts, which tell us to take defensive positions because we feel threatened by another. When we do, the other person feels our defensiveness and responds similarly, feeling that he did nothing wrong to begin with. Once it goes this far, if nothing else changes, we can predict with 100 percent accuracy where it will lead. Such is the power and predictability of scripts.

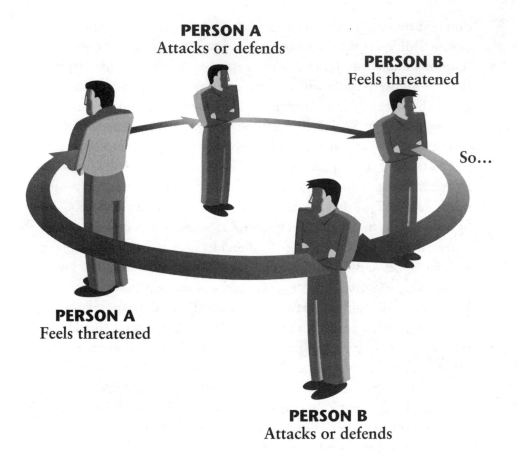

PERSON A
Attacks or defends

PERSON B
Feels threatened

So...

PERSON A
Feels threatened

PERSON B
Attacks or defends

Even in relation to scripts, the law of human nature lies underneath everything. When we feel that someone else has done something wrong, we are referring to a standard of decent conduct that we feel the other person has violated. Even when others may not feel that they have done anything wrong, we spot it a mile away and feel a need to protect ourselves from their wrongdoing. We judge their motives negatively, believing in most cases that they consciously intended to mistreat us. And this is all part of the script.

At any point in this scripted pattern, either party can override the script and do what she knows is right. The first time Bob criticized me, I could have gone back into his office at a better time and talked it over, working out a solution. Instead we both fell deeply into the dance of doom script, with each of us giving tit for tat, me avoiding and Bob criticizing and accusing. This script always leads to the dance of doom, producing very predictable results. Others can see our folly and where the script is leading, but when we are "on stage," reading our scripts and playing our roles, much of the interaction we are helping to create is invisible to us.

Whether we knowingly reject a prompting or merely fall routinely into negative scripts, the consequences are serious and also predictable. We simply cannot violate the laws of life, the moral laws of human nature, without paying a heavy price. And no matter who we are or how our particular relationships play out, the consequences are always identical. That is what makes a script a script rather than a random occurrence. The behavior of both parties follows a set pattern and the consequences that are created are patterned as well.

As the Dance Begins: Painful Consequences

The consequences of failing to do what we know is right and not living truthfully are not insignificant. My own story with my boss provides ample evidence of just what happens to us and between us when we start to dance with another individual. Some of these consequences happen inside us as we pay the price for going back on ourselves. If we didn't feel so deeply compelled to act in a certain way, we wouldn't make such a fuss when we fail to do so. If we didn't care, we wouldn't spend so much effort and energy convincing ourselves and others that we had so many reasons for acting the way we do. The length and breadth of our justification reveal just how much we do care and that we know what we should have done.

There are several predictable and automatic consequences of failing to do what we feel is right, as illustrated in the following example. This story was told by Bill, a friend of mine, after his young son broke his arm in a skiing accident. Notice the many ways in which he is "crooked" and the price he pays for not being fully honest with himself and the situation.

My wife and I have always shared parenting responsibili-
ties more or less equally. But then my work began taking
me out of town a great deal, and late nights at the office
left me exhausted when I got home from work. One
weekend we went skiing as a family, and while on the
slopes my three-year-old son fell and broke his arm. He
was in great pain and needed to be held by his mother for
most of the day while I was at work. It was difficult for
all involved.

One night as I was lying in bed asleep, I was awak-
ened by his cries. Since his accident he woke up often and
cried out. This time he called for his mommy. I looked
over at the clock; it was 4:35 A.M. My wife, Kathy, didn't
stir, and I rolled back over, hoping Seth would quiet
down, but he continued to cry out. For a split second I
felt that I ought to get up and take care of him before he
woke anyone else, especially Kathy. If I got up quickly
and took care of him, she wouldn't have to wake up. But
I didn't get up.

This simple story is everyone's story in some way. We have all been
in situations where something happens and we feel prompted to do
something that we know is the right thing at that moment. But for
whatever reason, we fail to heed the call and turn away from it, rejecting our own promptings. But this isn't where the story ends. As
noted earlier, the only way that we can do wrong and at the same time
feel we are doing right is to serve up a list of reasons why doing the
right thing is not applicable in this case. We say, in essence, "I know
what I should do, but I didn't and I have my reasons."

Here is what happened to Bill when he failed to get up as he felt
he should.

I didn't get up, but I couldn't go back to sleep, either. I
kept waiting for my wife to wake up and help him, but
she never budged. "How long does he have to cry before

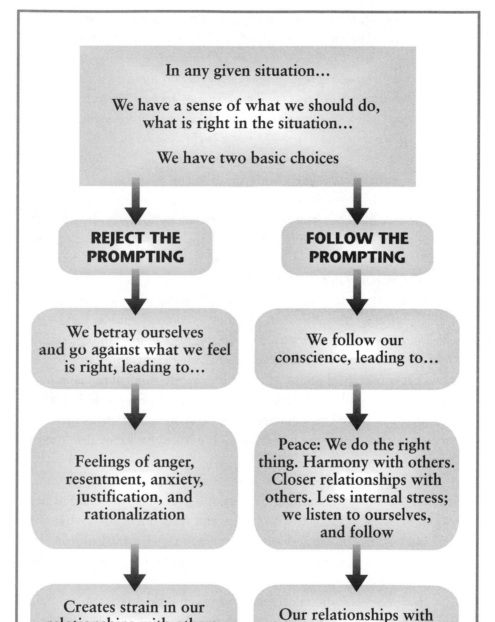

In any given situation...

We have a sense of what we should do, what is right in the situation...

We have two basic choices

REJECT THE PROMPTING

FOLLOW THE PROMPTING

We betray ourselves and go against what we feel is right, leading to...

We follow our conscience, leading to...

Feelings of anger, resentment, anxiety, justification, and rationalization

Peace: We do the right thing. Harmony with others. Closer relationships with others. Less internal stress; we listen to ourselves, and follow

Creates strain in our relationships with others; it isn't really present until we invent it

Our relationships with others are strengthened; harmony increases

she'll get up?" I asked myself, feeling irritated by what
was happening. "She can take care of him better than I
can anyway. Besides, I have an early-morning meeting at
work and need my rest. She has the day off tomorrow, so
she can sleep in." As I lay there trying to get back to sleep,
I got angrier and angrier at her and at my son for being
such a whining baby. "The boy is three years old, why
does he have to wake up in the middle of the night
anyway?" I thought.

When we elect not to follow our consciences honestly, the excuses for not doing so immediately pile up. It is the only way that we can do the wrong thing, as this man did, and yet convince ourselves that it is okay and certainly not our fault.

What was the fallout of this seemingly innocent act? On a practical level, Bill woke up the next morning tired and irritable. Inside, he was still irritated and angry at his wife and his son for ruining a good night's rest. At the breakfast table, he ate his Cheerios through a scowl while his wife moved about as she did any other morning. This personal irritation and the distance that was created between Bill and his wife are the type of consequences that everyone experiences in some way when they break the law of human nature. And they don't stop there.

While he waited for his wife's apology (which would never come because she had done nothing wrong), Bill grew more irritated at her insensitivity. He was filled with blame and resentment for "what she did" last night. And what did his blame and resentment lead to? His wife was annoyed because he seemed so distant and grouchy, but she had no idea what brought it on.

How many times in relationships do such little things lead to "big things" down the road? I've met with people who have been feuding for years and cannot remember what it was that started the disagreement. As time moves along, the resentment builds, the blame intensifies, and the dance that began years ago becomes so deeply entrenched that people don't even realize how painful it has become. For this man and his wife, one night of self-deception, in which he felt that he should do something but did not, led to other problems that he never would have predicted.

Anger and Fear: The Red Lights of Self-Betrayal

People often ask me how they can know when they are in the middle of violating their conscience. "I find that I'm just in the middle of something ugly and unwanted with another person and I don't know how I got there," they say. They cannot retrace their steps to a point in time when they felt they should do one thing but did another. I have found this often to be the case. Most acts of self-betrayal go unnoticed by us, partly because we are unaccustomed to looking for them. Also, we are blind to the warning signs that we are doing wrong. So quickly do the justification and rationalization set in that we don't take the time to rethink what has happened and our part in it.

One of the most reliable indicators that we have violated our own sense of right and wrong is anger. Anger is the flashing light on the dashboard, the red light at the intersection, the warning signal to us that self-betrayal is under way, whether we realize it or not. When anger is present and we allow it to drive our actions, what follows will always be ineffective, particularly in interpersonal relationships. There are times when people are violated and anger is an appropriate reaction. I'm talking instead of the relationships that we have with family or colleagues that take on an angry posture. We may have clever adult ways of disguising our anger, but in the end it can't be hidden. If we pay attention, anger can signal us that we are in the process of doing wrong, of going against what we know is right. The fact that some person or situation creates so much anger in us proves how deeply we care.

Jacques Lusseyran, author of *And Then There Was Light*, was born in France and was blinded at an early age by a tragic accident. Blindness became a great teacher for him as he learned to appreciate a great power of light that surrounded him as long as he remained true to that light. Light, as he writes, is synonymous in many ways with our conscience or the light within us that we must follow or pay severe consequences.

> *The substance of the universe drew together, redefined and propelled itself anew. I was aware of a presence emanating from a place I knew nothing about, a place which might as well have been outside, as from within. But radiance was there, or to put it more precisely, light. It was a fact, for light was there. I felt indescribable relief, and happiness so great it almost made me laugh. Confidence and gratitude came as if a prayer had been answered. I found light and joy at the same moment, and I can say without hesitation that from that time on light and joy have never been separated in my experience. I have had the most of them together.*

For Lusseyran, the light he felt within was deeply connected with the joy he longed for as a young blind boy. As we have talked of listening to the voice of conscience, we could just as easily have called it light or understanding from within, for that is exactly what it is.

Lusseyran goes on to explain how, when he became afraid, the light would grow dim and he would once again be trapped in darkness.

> *There were times when the light faded almost to the point of disappearing. It happened every time I was afraid. If instead of letting myself be carried along by confidence and throwing myself into things, I hesitated, calculated, thought about the wall, the half-opened door, the key in the lock: If I said to myself that all these things were hostile and about to strike. When I was playing with my small companions, when I suddenly grew anxious to win, to be first at all costs, then all at once I could see nothing. Literally I went into fog or smoke. I could no longer afford to be jealous or unfriendly, because, as soon as I was,*

a bandage came down over my eyes, and I was bound hand and foot and cast aside. All at once a black hole opened and I was helpless inside it. But when I was happy and serene, approached people with confidence and thought well of them, I was rewarded with light. So is it surprising that I loved friendship and harmony when I was very young?

Armed with such a tool, why should I need a moral code? For me this tool took the place of red and green lights. I always knew where the road was open and where it was closed. I had only to look at the bright signal which taught me how to live.

Knowing how to live is part of what it means to be human. We are born with this knowledge, and if we listen to it, it will bring us closer to others. Lusseyran speaks of the terrible consequences of becoming anxious with others, or trying to take advantage of them, and feeling the "light" leave him. In the classic *Star Wars* movies, Darth Vader and his evil emperor say to Luke Skywalker, "Give in to hate, Luke. It's the only way you can win." They knew that giving in to hate would nullify the power of the Force and that this would destroy Luke and his fight for liberation from the Dark Side. It is hate, fear, anger, resentment, and all of the other negative, blaming emotions that darken our minds and lead us to do that which divides us from others and provokes them to respond in kind. When we look for the light and respond to the quiet but real whisperings from within, we can know what others need from us and know what we can do for them that would bring both of us joy. Responding to this light from within is critical for finding joy. Turning away from it, giving ourselves over to anger and resentment, causes the light to fade, and we become engulfed in emotions that confuse us and fill us with fear.

When our vision becomes clouded with the fog of self-betrayal, nothing is clear anymore. We see ourselves falsely as someone else's victims. We set traps for ourselves that we cannot fully see, yet they are real and have the power to dull our senses to the extent that we no longer know what it means to be truthful. Hence, failing to do what we know is right has myriad consequences to us personally and to those with whom we interact on a regular basis.

A Review

Let's take another look at some points about the dance of doom.

1. As human beings, we are under the influence of a moral law, expressed in our consciences, that we feel compelled to follow and expect others to follow as well. This moral law is common to all and thus connects us to others in important ways. In effect, we agree on the "rules of life"—on what represents fair play or decent behavior. Thus we are all imbued with a standard of right and wrong.

2. Because our consciences are so deeply tied into our deepest values and self-images, when we feel compelled to do one thing or not do another, it is as if we are giving ourselves direction. This direction comes to us in many ways, such as promptings, impressions, or flashes of thought or insight that we recognize as a summons that calls us to do what we feel is right.

3. We can follow or reject the law of human nature. To live truthfully and honestly with ourselves and others, we must follow our sense of right and wrong. When we do not, our internal vision is clouded and dulled, preventing us from seeing things completely and truthfully. This soul struggle produces tremendous internal stress. When we go against what we feel is right, we bring upon ourselves a host of troubles and sever the natural ties between ourselves and others. This produces great havoc in our hearts and in the hearts of those we fail to serve.

4. Most, if not all, personal stress and interpersonal conflict has its roots in turning away from what we know is right and doing what we know is wrong. The way we do wrong and still think we are doing right is through rationalizing away our behavior. We often blame someone else for preventing us from doing the right thing.

5. The most optimistic truth in all of this is the peace, harmony, and love that come when we simply follow our consciences and do for others what they need from us. If we listen, our consciences will whisper to us of others' needs and help us know how we can build trust and peace with others and avoid the pain brought by self-betrayal.

Over the past 20 years I have had the opportunity to work with hundreds of thousands of people who have had interpersonal relationship challenges. As a marriage counselor and family therapist, I saw it every day in my work: people embroiled in problems that they could not fully understand or resolve. Large corporations trapped in frustrating interdepartmental rivalries and warfare had similarities to couples' problems. We worry so much about who starts a fight that we fail to spend time looking for ways to stop it. And in all of these diverse settings there is one great truth that shines through the darkness in our eyes. It's our ability to see others honestly and to live truthfully in the light we receive from our consciences.

When I talk with people who have wrestled with a problem boss or a frustrating employee or a difficult teenager, I always ask them a simple question: "What do you feel is the right thing to do in this situation?" It may not be the easy thing or the convenient thing or the quickest thing, but it is the right thing. Rarely have I had people say, "I don't know." When they do, it is because they have lived for so many years with the pain and the blame and the resentment and the justifications that they are literally past feeling. Years of negative history drown out the calm voice of reason that conscience usually brings. Signals are being sent but are not being received. The truth stands before us, but our lenses have become so clouded and obscured that we can no longer see things as they really are. We do know what is right if we will only consult our consciences and then follow their advice.

I close this chapter with the words of C. S. Lewis.

> *The moral law or law of human nature is not simply a*
> *fact about human behavior . . . [and] it is not a mere*

fancy, for we cannot get rid of the idea. And most of the things we say and think about men would be reduced to nonsense if we did. And it is not simply a statement about how we should like men to behave for our own convenience. For the behavior we call bad or unfair is not exactly the same as the behavior we find inconvenient, and may even be the opposite. Consequently, this rule of right and wrong or law of human nature or whatever you call it must somehow or another be a real thing, a thing that is really there, not made up by ourselves.

Lens Five
Dancing the
Dance—Getting Stuck

What is right is often forgotten by what is convenient.
—Bodie Thoene, author of *The Twilight of Courage*

I still recall turning 12 years old and entering seventh grade, which was the year they introduced boy/girl afternoon dances at my school. I was petrified. I walked into the gymnasium with my buddies and saw a strange sight that soon became a familiar one.

All the girls were lined up on one side of the room against the wall or in little clusters, whispering to one another, and all the boys were lined up on the opposite wall. It looked more like two armies getting ready for battle than a bunch of kids at a dance. Thinking back, the term *battle* probably describes it pretty well. The real battle took place inside each of us as we wrestled with our powerful but conflicting emotions: "I think I want to dance, but I'm terrified of girls," I would reason with myself. "I could never go ask one to dance; that would be too hard. What if she says no? But, on the other hand, I think I like girls. I *think* . . ."

I don't know if the girls had a similar struggle inside themselves, but my buddies and I just stood there staring at one another, trying to make fun of the whole experience but knowing that we were all going through the same horrible pain.

During the first dance, with all the emotional battles raging inside me, I was stunned when a girl I didn't even know walked across the floor, stood directly in front of me, and asked, "Do you wanna dance?" I don't even remember who she was or what she looked like or anything else about her. I do remember the sheer panic that washed over me at that moment. I didn't know what to say, but before I knew what was happening, she grabbed my hand and led me to the center of the floor, and we started to dance. I had never danced before and didn't know how, but while Davey Jones and the Monkees blared in the background, I began to dance with this girl whom I had never met before in my life.

I realized while we were dancing to "Last Train to Clarksville" that the worst part of this gathering was not the dancing itself but the terrible moment when the song ended. In those days, before CDs and other fancy technology, it took the deejay a while to take the record off the record player, decide what the next song would be, and put that record on the machine. So while the student officers stood on the stage arguing about which song to play next, this girl and I and everyone else stood around waiting, with no clue as to what to say.

That was a torturous moment for me, as the song ended and she stared and waited for me to say something. I didn't even know her, so I just stood there, looking around and wondering how to get out of the situation. If she had just walked away, I could have dashed back over to where my buddies were standing near the wall, but she didn't. Before I realized what was happening, the next record was playing, and we were dancing again. That's how things went for the next hour. Between songs, we stood there, speechless, awkward, and embarrassed—dance after miserable dance.

On the bus ride home from school, all my friends peppered me with questions. "Who was that girl? Why did you dance with her?" And the most painful: "Why did you *keep* dancing with her?" My mind was swimming, searching for answers to what seemed like reasonable questions, especially since I had never danced before. "I didn't know the girl," was the answer to the first question. "She asked me," was the answer to the second. To answer the third, I remember saying something like "I don't know why I kept dancing with her. I hate dancing, and when we went to the dance, I had no idea I would dance with anyone. I hated it and wanted to run after every dance, but I felt stuck. I was trapped."

Dancing with this stranger was not in my plans. I was simply standing there talking with my two buddies, Wolf and Fish, about the previous night's baseball game; then she appeared, and the rest is history. For the first time in my young life, I felt trapped in a dance and resented the girl who had trapped me. I made sure that it never happened again by avoiding dances for the next few years. I always developed a headache, a sore throat, or some other serious ailment on the days when dances were scheduled. Luckily, my mom believed me and kept me home.

When I talk with people about relationship challenges that they are facing, they say several things that sound as if they are feeling about the same way I felt in seventh grade. They don't know how things started, they just know that the situation doesn't feel good. Some are angry and filled with blame and resentment. Others are more confused than anything else, wishing things could be different but not knowing how to bring about the changes they need. In nearly every case, the feeling of being trapped is one that people in the dance of doom can relate to. They want the dance to end, but they have no idea how to make it stop. They go on and on, sometimes for years, stuck on the "dance floor."

One day I was at home working when a friend called and wanted to come over to talk. I knew his job wasn't going well, but I didn't know the details. As Jeff sat in my office and started to describe his work situation, I saw a man who was clearly stuck, or at least felt that he was.

He told me a pathetic story of misery and frustration that went back nearly 12 years. He had been asked by an old college buddy whom he thought he knew well to work at a new company. After a few weeks on the job, he felt unappreciated by the people in charge. In particular, his college friend Roger seemed disinterested in his knowledge and ideas. Over the years, their relationship eroded from one of honest friendship to one of seething anger and resentment. Roger was vice-president of the company and decided much of what went on in the business. The more the company grew, the farther behind my friend felt. He felt that the business was leaving him in the dust.

"I remember a meeting where we were talking about future products for our customers," Jeff recalled. "I made a few suggestions, and Roger told me that the company was going in a different direction. He more or less told me that he didn't like my ideas and that the company would be fine without them."

"Did you go and talk to Roger about what had happened?" I asked.

"Well, sort of," he replied. "I tried to let him know why I thought some of the things they were doing were problematic, but he would never listen."

Jeff spun out story after story, illustrating how stupid and selfish Roger had become and how horrible it was for him to remain in a company where he felt so unappreciated. He pleaded for answers to what he felt was a terrible dilemma.

"What do you feel is the right thing to do at this point—the thing that would likely improve the situation?" I asked him flatly. "After all, you have done many things that have not helped. The situation is worsening every day. What do you think would help turn things around?"

Jeff laughed the hollow laugh of an angry, hopeless victim and said, "I know what you're getting at. I need to take responsibility for fixing this problem." Then he paused, as if collecting his thoughts, and struggled to say what he had been feeling for years. "But I'm just not ready to go to him. I don't want to give him the satisfaction."

For years he had labored under the growing frustration of going to work each day feeling that no one wanted to hear his ideas. What made it worse was that the very man who had hired him, an old friend, was leading the naysayers. He felt betrayed and resented Roger for his mistreatment. Curiously, everything he tried seemed only to make matters worse and did nothing to resolve the ongoing feud that had evolved between them. Their relationship had grown so stiff and cold that they hardly spoke to one another.

These were two grown men, both bright, capable, and very good at their technical specialties. Yet even with all of this intellectual knowledge, they had created a pattern of relating to one another that was very destructive to both. Everyone saw what was happening, even their wives, who wondered what it would take for Roger and Jeff to set aside their differences and rebuild their relationship. Each man felt innocent of any wrongdoing, and they had slipped into silent resentment and accusation of each other, inviting and provoking the very behavior that each disliked, thus keeping the painful dance alive. Whatever Roger did was viewed as a put-down by Jeff, and whatever he did in return was seen by Roger as a negative accusation. Round and round they had danced for over 10 years. Both hated what was happening and wanted it to end, but neither could see the situation clearly enough to make a correct move. They were stuck in the dance of doom.

Regardless of whom we are dancing with, the precise moment at which it started, or why it began, it is normal to eventually feel stuck in the middle of something we don't like but cannot seem to stop. It may be a difficult teenage child, a spouse, a close friend, someone at work, or someone in another relationship with whom we begin a pattern of interaction that is not working. In these cases, everyone on the dance floor is, in one way or another, miserable. When we are in such relationships, we generally experience some or all of the following emotions and perceptions.

- We feel trapped, and we see someone else as the cause of that feeling.
- We feel innocent of any wrongdoing. We say, in effect, "I was just standing there, leaning against the wall, listening to the music and talking with my friends, when all of a sudden I was out on the dance floor dancing, and I hated it."
- When we feel as if we have been forced into dancing against our will, we have all of the natural emotions of a victim. The negative emotions we experience are usually so strong that we cannot accept that we are choosing those emotions.
- We feel the need to search out those who are making us feel the way we do. We blame them because, from where we view the situation, they are the cause of our problems and pain.

• The other person feels our resentment toward them and becomes defensive. In fact, their feelings become the mirror image of ours as we bounce off each other.

We finally reach a point where we are so completely convinced of our innocence that we see no way out. So we wait it out and cope as best we can with a terrible, frustrating situation.

We don't dance exactly the same dance with the same person forever. With every new step, both partners change, however subtly. Time passes, emotions harden, opinions become more entrenched, and the feeling that nothing can ever change grows more and more believable. As we dance back and forth, stepping on one another's toes, we continue to give each other reasons for the dance to continue.

In its simplest form, the dance of doom is one-dimensional. A husband feels his wife is always nagging him to help more around the house, and it seems that the more she nags, the less he is willing to do. But to view such relationships as challenges in this way is to miss the dynamics of human interaction that lead, in part, to people staying in such patterns for years. Over time, her nagging changes and feels different as it continues day after day. After years of such behavior, she looks different to her husband than she did the first time she asked him to do something and he held back. Similarly, the first time he held back and failed to do what she needed, she may have been mildly frustrated, but after what seems like a thousand times, she sees him differently, too.

The situation that is created is something quite different from the simple tit-for-tat interchange that took place early in their marriage. It has now grown into a deeply rooted way of responding to each other, and it is deeper than either fully understands. All they know is that if they do not continue doing what they are doing, the situation will become worse. This belief and the years of history they have now created keep them dancing, even though both claim that they hate the dance and would do anything to get out of it. Anyone who has ever felt stuck in a difficult relationship can relate to what happens over time. Everyone changes as the interaction continues to wear them down, further convincing them that there is no way out.

Watching two people embroiled in a dance of doom is painful, for

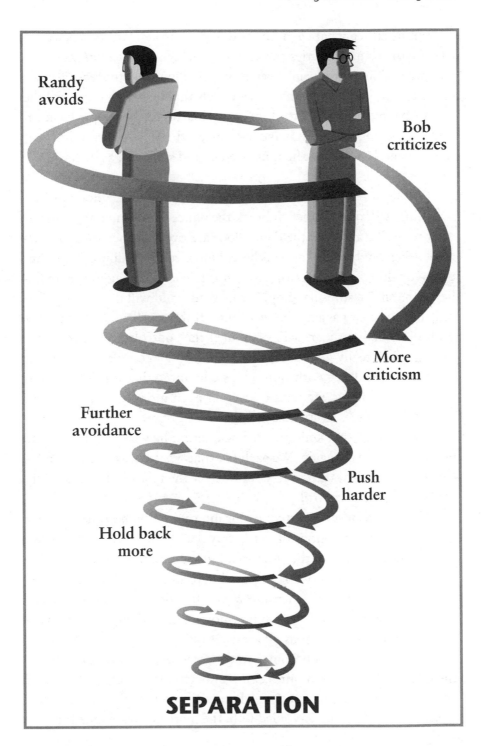

we can often see what each one is doing to make matters worse. We can see the teenager's cries for attention being met by a parent's controlling response, producing even more rebellion from the teenager. We can see how, when the manager who feels that he needs to control the "lazy" people who work for him exerts his authority, people back off and stop trying to be proactive in their work. This in turn reinforces the manager's belief that he must step in and supervise as he has done in the past.

On the sidelines, as we watch people on the dance floor of life, wrestling with one another to break the dance of doom, it all seems so clear to us. But those on the dance floor are overwhelmed by one powerful belief: "Whatever happens here, I must continue doing what I am doing or things will deteriorate even further." The nagging wife believes that if she stops nagging, her lazy husband will do nothing. It is only her constant nagging that gets him off the couch at all. The parent with the rebellious teen believes that if the controls are relaxed, the teenager will really go crazy and things will fall completely apart. In my frustrating dance with Bob, I was convinced that if I didn't avoid him as I was doing, we would interact even more, thus giving him more opportunities to criticize me. From his perspective, it was his regular "coaching" that kept me on track, and if he were to back off, he would never see me again. We each felt that what we were doing, frustrating though it was, had to continue, or the relationship would fly completely out of control.

This reveals just how myopic our internal vision becomes when it is clouded by the emotions of self-betrayal and the dance of doom. We can see only our side of the situation, but we cannot see it clearly. The other person's perspective is impossible to understand. Since we see our dance partner as our victimizer, we often don't care how he feels. We see him not as a real person but more as something that stands in our way and brings upon us all kinds of misery.

Our internal vision becomes so distorted that we cannot fully see the relationship between our feelings and actions and the feelings and actions of the other person. I was blinded from the wider perspective of seeing that the more I avoided Bob, the more he pressed me for con-

I betray myself or
follow a negative script.

I justify and rationalize
my wrongdoing.

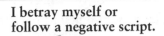

May I have
this dance?

Produces anger,
frustration,
resentment,
and blame of
others for my
negative emotions.

When others
are defensive,
I feel accused
and justified.

Distorts how I see
myself and others.
"I am a victim of
your mistreatment."

**DISTORTED
THINKING**

- Judge others'
  intentions

- Remove
  responsibility
  from myself

- Focus on people,
  not interaction

- See others as
  things

- Take a defensive
  position

tact. I felt that avoiding him was my only real choice, other than rushing into his office and pouncing on him in a fit of rage and frustration. That option seemed completely unacceptable and dangerous considering that he was my boss, so I opted for the only alternative I could come up with, which was to cope as best I could with an overbearing, nasty man who had no right to treat me as he did. The problem, I came to see later, was my inability to see the entire dynamic of our interaction. As it turns out, this is always the root problem in this kind of ever-worsening situation. Both parties are blind to any solution that will bring them anything other than greater pain and frustration.

This leads to a second question: What would a person have to do to keep a bad relationship in check and make certain that it doesn't improve? When I ask people this strange question, answers fly out of their mouths. It is easy to list numerous things that we can do to keep a bad relationship from improving: continuing to torment others, refusing to forgive, ceasing to communicate, blaming them for what they are doing, and so on.

When we step back and look at the relationships we currently have that are less than we would desire, it's hard not to see that we are to some degree engaging in exactly these kinds of actions. Think of it this way: If someone came to you and asked you what they could do to maintain a negative, frustrating relationship, what would you say? We intuitively know the answer from our own life experience and from observing those who get stuck in relationships that are painful. In essence, the key to maintaining a poor relationship is to keep doing that which got us into trouble in the first place. I resented Bob for his mistreatment, and as time passed, my resentment grew and I directed my anger and resentment toward him. As I did, I provoked him to deepen his defensive position toward me, which only served to justify my mistreatment of him. This kind of patterned interaction feeds on itself in many ways and ensures that nothing will improve.

If it were as straightforward as it sounds, we would still be left with a crucial question: Why, in the face of all this logic, do we persist at something that brings us pain? We can see it is not working and so can the other person, and yet we persist at a losing strategy. Why would we continue to do that which does not work when we know it is fraught with all kinds of peril? The answer to this question lies in the overwhelming role that our emotions play in these kinds of negative relationships. It is our emotions that make it all so real and so difficult and which blind us to the real solutions to the dance of doom.

The Power of Emotion

When we go against our own sense of right and wrong and reject the inclination to do right by others, certain things happen. First we must find a way to justify our actions. If I feel that I should go into Bob's office and visit with him about our troubles, for example, and then I do not, I have to come up with an argument against this feeling. Because we feel strongly compelled to live by the law of human nature inside us, we cannot violate it or reject it without a solid list of reasons. That is what justification offers. It is our way of doing what we know is wrong and feeling as if we had no other choice. "I would go talk with Bob, but the last time I did he got upset and made matters worse," I might think. The excuse "releases" me from doing right. When we know what is right and what would help produce a positive relationship but turn away from this feeling, we turn our back on others.

Resentment is almost always woven through the emotions of anyone who goes against what they feel is right. Resentment comes as if we say "Your mistreatment of me made me do the wrong thing, and I resent you for it!" We feel victimized by the other person, trapped, cornered, and helpless. In the self-justifying story that we create when we go against what we know is right, it is always someone else who is to blame, not ourselves.

The justification and rationalization that follow wrongdoing are not merely intellectual exercises. The negative emotions like anger, frustration, irritation, fear, and resentment help convince us that we are right even when we do wrong. Hence, we don't tell a self-justifying story with words alone. We are fully and completely caught up in the experience *emotionally*, and these emotions help convince us that we are justified in not doing what we feel is right.

One day, when I was talking with a woman who had strong negative feelings about her manager, I asked her a question: "If you did not feel the way you do toward your manager, how would you go about solving the problems between you?"

"What do you mean?" she asked, a bit confused.

"Well, if you didn't dislike her as you do and feel manipulated by her as you say you do and resent her for what she has done to you, how would you solve your problems?" I asked.

Then a light came on and she answered simply, "Well, I would walk down the hall and ask to meet with her so that we could talk things out and come up with some kind of resolution."

"I think that's right," I replied. "So what is it that keeps you from doing that this afternoon?"

She had to stop for a minute and think about that one. Before she had thought carefully she blurted out, "Well, that's just it, Randy, can't you see? If she weren't so hard to work with and so difficult, I would just work it out and be done with all of this."

I listened as she explained that if it were not for this person's weaknesses and her own feelings toward her, things would be easily resolved. "That's exactly what I am saying," I pointed out. "If you had no such emotions toward this woman, in spite of her weaknesses, you would walk down to her office and talk. It is your strong negative emotions and the judgments that you are making that prevent you from doing the right thing, the only thing that will ultimately turn this relationship around."

This prompted the woman to think differently than she had before. When she began to remove her negative, blaming emotions, the situation became much easier to work through. It is the fog of the emotions that obscures the right path and prevents us from stepping forward. Emotions come back on us again and again as the fundamental reason that we fail to do the right thing. After a few more minutes of talking it through, this woman resolved to make an appointment that afternoon. She and her manager met and talked openly about how they would like things to be different, and the relationship began to turn around.

Carol, a friend of mine, told me the following story, which clearly illustrates just how emotions play their role in the dance of doom.

> *I had been traveling a great deal for my new job, and I felt guilty about leaving my family so much. One night while in a hotel, I called home and talked with my five-year-old daughter. We talked about what she was doing, and she asked me if I would come home and play with her. I told her that I would and promised that as soon as I got home, we would play house. Two nights later, I drove into my driveway and was greeted by Jessica at the front door. I had hardly set my bags down before she was begging me to play with her. I was completely exhausted after a grueling week on the road. I tried to put her off until after I had had time to relax, but she persisted. Before I realized it, I was getting upset with her pesky pleading for me to play with her. "But you promised, Mommy," she said, whining. I tried to explain that I was tired and that I would play the next day, but she insisted that we play that night.*
>
> *The more demanding she became, the more I felt that she didn't deserve any of my time. She started to cry when I told her we would play the next day, and that really made me angry. I remember thinking, "Can't she show a little consideration here?" Finally, after a few minutes of trying to explain to her what was happening, I told her that if she was unwilling to be realistic, she would have to go to her room. She ran upstairs, crying, "You lied, Mommy. You lied." That really made me angry.*

This story is not about whether the little girl was demanding or not or whether her mother should or should not have made a long-distance promise to her. It is simply about a woman who felt pressured to play with her child and made a promise to do so but failed to follow through. It was that act of going back on her word that lit the fire of discord between her and her daughter. Carol's anger and irritation were not caused by her daughter. They were her own doing, but even so, they were real to her. She wasn't just pretending to be angry; she actually was upset with Jessica and was convinced that her daughter caused her anger.

It is this real emotion that helps build the self-justifying stories we create. Our emotions, which we believe are caused by another person, convince us that we are innocent and that the other person is guilty.

Was Carol living truthfully with her little girl? Did Jessica cause her mother's irritation and frustration? Did punishing Jessica by sending her to her room help build the relationship? Did it draw mother and daughter closer together or push them farther apart?

Play this scenario out differently and see where it likely would have gone. Suppose, for example, that Carol had, in spite of her fatigue, sat down and read her daughter a story or found some other way they could play together that wasn't too demanding. Jessica and her mother would have enjoyed each other's company, which they both missed while being separated for 10 days, and the rest of the story would never have happened. The anger, the irritation and blame, Jessica's tears and her feeling that her mother had broken a promise would have been avoided. Jessica would not have gone to her room sad and angry at her mother, and Carol would not have sat in the living room for an hour afterward, steaming over Jessica's childish behavior.

If Carol had followed her impression and lived in harmony with the truth in this situation, everything would have been different. It was the act of self-betrayal and the resulting rationalization and blaming that made the rest of the story come to life, and it was all a lie. When we follow our sense of right and wrong, on the other hand, we will always be directed to do for others what they need from us at that moment.

The greatest evidence that the law of human nature is real and living inside each of us is what happens when we follow it. We feel the peace that comes from doing what we feel is right, regardless of the consequences. Furthermore, we find that when we do the right thing, it builds the bonds of love and respect between us and those we interact with.

When we violate or reject this basic human law, we allow others to mistreat us and believe that it is their mistreatment that leads us to resent and blame them. The truth is that we are resentful because of our mistreatment of them. This is one of the greatest truths that I have learned in the area of human relationships and how to strengthen them. When we mistreat others in any way, it serves as a vivid reminder that we have gone against what we know is right. We can see ourselves clearly as we really are—and we usually don't like what we see.

How blurred and distorted our vision can become when we fail to do what is right! This is the simple but significant truth that the 20/20 Insight point of view provides. We can realize how deceived we often are by strong negative emotions. We bring these emotions upon ourselves when we fail to do that which we know is right and decent for others. These emotions can serve as a red flag signaling us that we have, in all likelihood, failed to follow a course that we know is right.

Tunnel Vision

There are two primary ways that people lose their physical eyesight. Some lose their central vision, as I did, and can use only their peripheral vision. Others lose their peripheral vision and are left with a small, tunnel-like visual area; this is called tunnel vision. Its implications are just what you would expect: Anything that falls outside of that visual tunnel is not apparent, and so people with tunnel vision fail to recognize much of what takes place around them.

Tunnel vision can also afflict the clarity and accuracy of our internal vision. It is the natural fallout of the dance, and it plays out in this way: When we view our relationship challenges, we are able to clearly see only a small part of the problem. With such a small view of what is really taking place, we can never arrive at an accurate understanding of the problems we face with others. Our internal vision is so myopic and narrow that we are blind to the dynamics of the relationship that we are part of, and as such, we focus exclusively on the behavior of the other person. Our actions are invisible to us, for they fall outside of what we can see clearly with our mind's eye. So we develop a simplistic and skewed understanding of the problem, which in turn leads us to try simplistic and ineffective solutions.

The point of view that we take on any situation dictates not only how we see or understand the situation but also the solutions we invent. If I view my relationship problems through a peephole, unable to see the full spectrum of the interactions between myself and others, I will understand only a small portion of what is taking place, and when I try to resolve the problem, I will be unsuccessful. My resolution to the dance of doom is no better than the clarity and completeness of my understanding. This principle holds true in any situation but particularly as we attempt to understand why we get stuck in difficult relationships and are unable to extricate ourselves. We can't see clearly enough to arrive where we really want to be. It is a vision problem, not a relationship problem.

I truly believed that my problem with Bob was caused by Bob. Parents struggling with a difficult relationship with their teenage son grow to believe that their teenager is the cause of the problem. Managers believe that if they could only fire all their "lazy" people and hire some real workers, everything would be fine. The distortion of our internal vision prevents us from seeing the fundamental interaction *between* people that defines the kind of relationships they create.

Jeff, the friend who came over to tell me about his 12-year feud with his company and its managers, said, "They have never trusted me from the beginning. I presented ideas that they rejected, and they made me feel unappreciated." Even so, he had stayed on board for all those years, with his resentment of them for what they had failed to do for him deepening daily. He told me about all of the vice-president's weaknesses and broken promises and how he had offended several people who had already left the company. As he poured his heart out to me, he talked about the sacrifices he had made for this company and the hours he had spent working late just to help them in times of crisis. To add insult to injury, he wasn't being paid what he was worth, and he and his former friend no longer even greeted one another as they passed in the hallway each morning.

Jeff's tunnel-vision viewpoint was evident. His company was at fault; he had done everything conceivable to make things work, and they still treated him poorly. He was consumed with deep-seated anger and resentment. Furthermore, he had all the telltale signs of following a course of action that he knew was wrong. He justified all of it in the name of "look what they have done."

A few days later, after I had gathered my thoughts, I told him the things that I'll outline here.

I believe that there are two very different ways of viewing a situation like Jeff's. These principles apply to any individuals or groups embedded in a negative relationship that seems to be getting worse, not better. The two viewpoints are the "I hate him" perspective and the "May I have this dance?" viewpoint. Let me talk a little about each. Depending on which viewpoint you adopt, your options and feelings will differ greatly.

If you adopt the "I hate him" perspective, there are few options available to you. From this viewpoint, you see yourself as an innocent victim and him as the nasty man who makes you feel the way you do. You feel attacked and mistreated by him, and all you can do is hope that somehow he will change. Your role is to hang in there and cope with his mistreatment until you can't take it any longer—or you can try to change him.

While you are merely coping with him or trying to change him, place yourself in his position. Have you ever been "coped with" by another person? How does it feel? Or have you ever had somebody try to change you to get you to do something that you feel no need to do? What is the message they send? Does it make you want to open your arms to them and say, "Thank you for pointing out my flaws and weaknesses. I'll change by morning"?

From this frustrating place, it's likely that you feel you have been doing everything you can think of to keep things from getting worse, and yet things have steadily eroded. This is likely to make you feel helpless because you feel that you are part of a bad situation that you cannot seem to turn around.

If you adopt the "May I have this dance?" perspective, you see your relationship with the other person as a pattern that the two of you have helped create and sustain day by day. From the dance perspective, you don't focus on each partner individually; rather, you see the pattern that both of you have created. He can't play his part without your cooperation, and you can't play yours without his. Moreover, you need each other in order to keep dancing. If either of you leaves, the dance officially ends. The other thing that ends a dance is a change in either partner's behavior, since the behavior of one supports the actions of the other. For example, if you have both agreed to the fox trot and all of a sudden you begin to waltz, you change the dance. What your partner was doing before no longer works with you doing different steps. To keep the dance alive, you both need to continue doing what you have been doing so the pattern can proceed uninterrupted.

There are several things that you need to know about viewing your own relationships of this type.

1. Our attitudes and behaviors help maintain the behaviors that we hate. If we said to the other person, "Can we talk? I've felt terrible about how things have been going on around here between us. I'd like to find a way to improve the way we work together," the response would be different. The dance of doom would end.

2. Another person's mistreatment of us is almost always a mirror image of our mistreatment of them. Imagine how relationships would change if we began to view others' behavior toward us as a reflection of our treatment of them. I'm not referring to casual interactions but rather to important and ongoing relationships at work and in the family, where we have regular contact. Is it possible that our child's irritability and misbehavior is a reflection of our harsh mistreatment of her? Is it also possible that when people have a hard time trusting us, it is because of the way we have acted toward them? This is not an attempt to say that we should blame

ourselves for all the human interaction problems we will ever have but rather a statement that to a large degree, people treat us depending on how they feel we are treating them.

As simple as that may sound, it is a point we often miss as we dance around with someone, feeling angry at what they are doing and blind to how they experience our behavior. Do we really believe that we can dislike or resent another person for their actions and not have them know it? And when they do, and they are defensive toward us, isn't that a clear indication that we have said or done something to invite their defenses, to cause them to feel the need to defend themselves?

3. When we see all interactions as a dance, it becomes clear that the situation is not about blame or who's right and who's wrong. It's about the interaction, the pattern that the two people have co-created. Once our vision clears to see the patterns we are part of, we start to see the absurdity of it all instead of being angry.

When you see interactions from this point of view, you begin to see solutions that the "I hate him" mentality will never yield. Knowing that you are dancing and have been dancing for years offers great hope for an end to the insanity that you have helped produce. Let me say a few things about the anger, blame, and resentment that are a big part of this whole pattern.

What you need to do is shift the anger off the individual and onto the interaction pattern that you are producing. One way to do this is to walk around to the other person's side of the dance and look at yourself through his eyes. What do you see? What might it feel like to be "hated" by one of your old friends? As you get inside the other person's skin, try to imagine what it is like to be on the receiving end of your current anger.

Here's another suggestion: Pretend that you aren't angry with the other person. Suppose that you were neutral toward him right now. Without the emotion and the historical baggage that you lug around each day, what would you do? My guess is that you would go to him and talk it out, find out what's wrong, and discuss ways to improve your interaction. It is your anger that prevents you from doing that.

Let me try to describe what I think is one of the most important insights I have ever received. When we are angry with someone else, when we are filled with blame and accusation, it absolves us from doing anything and convinces us that there is nothing we can do. So we do nothing and feel completely helpless to change things.

Anger is our justification for continuing to do what we are now doing. If my anger suddenly went away and I continued to act the same way, I would be a jerk. The minute that anger goes away, I see my treatment of the other person for what it is, and it isn't pretty.

That is why if Roger did something good—really, genuinely good—for Jeff tomorrow, Jeff would interpret it as insincere or manipulative. Viewing it any other way would require Jeff to check his anger and blame of Allen and to stare his own negative behavior in the face. None of us wants to do that, so we find ways to keep our anger alive and burning hot, thus keeping our justifying story alive.

"Getting stuck" in the dance of doom happens when we fail to see clearly the nature of the interaction of which we are a part. When we remove ourselves from the formula, we prevent ourselves from being an active part of the solution. In other words, like Jeff, if we don't feel that we have done anything to create this negative relationship, we cannot see how we can be part of fixing it. Failing to see our part in the negative relationships we face is being blind to half the truth. We are like children riding a see-saw. One looks over at the other going up and down and says, "Hey, how do you do that?" He fails to see that he is helping to make it go.

The stories in this chapter plainly illustrate that with a narrow, false view of a relationship, we become trapped into doing the very things that ensure that the dance will continue. When I am offended by another person, I become angry at that person. My anger causes me to either attack or defend myself. This attacking/defending behavior serves only to elicit similar behavior from the other person, which confirms my original judgment about him.

Can you see the trap? My boss calls me on the carpet in front of others and humiliates me. I think that only an insensitive lout would do such a thing. In my anger and resentment, I refuse to acknowledge him when we pass in the hall. Why should I after how he treated me? My anger and resentment are visible and palpable even when I am trying to not let them show. He feels my anger and senses my accusation. Not surprisingly, he feels defensive and responds in kind. But what else could I expect from someone like him?

Following the Script

Scripts are nothing more than conventions or rules that unconsciously tell us what to do in certain situations. There is a script for how we think, feel, and respond when we feel that a person has wronged us. This script is followed by virtually everyone when they feel offended, and the person on each side of the interaction plays his role perfectly. Try the following exercise to see how powerful and taken-for-granted these scripts are.

Think of a recent negative interaction that you had with another person. Then sit down with a third party who was not involved and share with her only the first few remarks exchanged between you and the other individual. In other words, tell the third party what was initially said or done, how you responded, and so forth, then ask her to predict where the interaction went and how it ended. Amazingly, you will discover that she can predict with incredible accuracy what took place and perhaps even quote exactly what was said. How can she do this? Because such negative interactions are carefully scripted and take a very similar path every time.

When we come to understand the scripted nature of interactions, our insight sharpens and we come to see our own involvement in the dance with others more clearly. Then we come to see with 20/20 Insight that it is what happens between us that creates the interactions we experience. How we behave *in relation* to others dictates how we dance and how long we remain stuck in the dance of doom.

Taking the Defensive Position

Soon after the dance of doom begins, one of the most predictable events is the taking of a defensive position. Usually we feel that the other person is doing things "to us," and we need to defend ourselves from their "attacks." When Bob was communicating with me in what seemed to be critical and punishing ways, I felt his sharp comments as dangerous "arrows" from which I needed to continually protect myself. In the dance, both parties feel defensive and thus assume a position to protect themselves from what they feel the other person is doing.

It is natural when we feel threatened in some way to take a defensive, protective position, because we are afraid of somehow being hurt by the other person. But while we are protecting ourselves from some real or perceived threat, we are not building anything productive. All of our effort, energy, and attention go into keeping ourselves safe, so the very best that we can hope for in the defensive position is that nothing worse will happen. Our resolve to keep defending ourselves is strengthened when we are successful in keeping something more terrible from occurring.

The principle here is important to emphasize: *We cannot simultaneously take a defensive stance with another person and still build the relationship*. Nothing positive can occur from a defensive position. From this position, our focus is on the other person and what we feel he is doing to us.

The root of the problem goes back once again to how we see the other person and how we see ourselves in relation to him. When I change, I give the other person a different person to respond to.

The Solution Becomes the Problem

One of the serious effects of the tunnel vision brought on by the defensive dance is our inability to arrive at productive solutions to our problems. With such a narrow view of what's going on, any solution we invent will ultimately fail; in many cases, it will make the situation worse. It all begins with how we define the problem while embroiled in a dance.

What was my problem in my relationship with Bob? It was Bob's mistreatment of me, his constant badgering and criticism. From this perspective, I could see only two solutions: either to attack Bob or to avoid him. I chose to avoid him, and in so doing, I presented him with his own perspective of the situation.

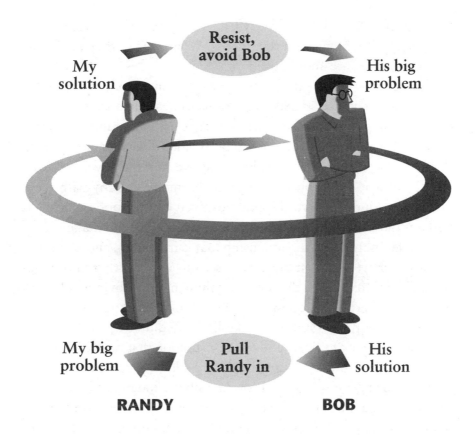

What was the problem Bob had to resolve? It was my avoidance and unwillingness to communicate with him, as my boss, and involve him in important matters. What was his solution to this problem? It was to initiate more contact by calling me in and talking with me. Amazingly, as shown in the illustration above, my definition of the problem and the solution I invented became the problem that Bob had to resolve. And his solution to that problem became the problem I had to resolve.

When we fail to do what our consciences tell us to do, we immediately step into a world where other people appear as things, objects to be moved about or manipulated for our own purposes. From this mode, we cannot see each other clearly. The needs of others become unimportant to us. We become preoccupied with getting what we want, protecting ourselves from others, and defending ourselves from their attacks. When we turn away from our own consciences, we also turn away from others and their needs. When we do, they justifiably feel our indifference and accusation.

Our decision to live life in the person-to-thing mode is of immeasurable consequence. It sets in motion predictable and destructive events that make us and everyone we engage with miserable. The great irony is that all this destruction can be avoided if we open our eyes to things as they really are and really can be. We have the power to create a different world, one filled with peace, harmony, and joy with those around us. Our choice to respond positively to the good inside us is perhaps the most basic and far-reaching decision we can make.

While embroiled in a relationship that is frustrating and painful to us, however, we often simply cannot see our way clearly to do things that help improve it. We think of everything but the obvious solutions to our most perplexing questions. I have looked back many times on my relationship with Bob and asked, "Why didn't I just go to him early on, share my feelings, and create a solution that both of us could live with?" Such an easy course of action could have prevented months of pain and anger on my part. I was literally far too busy blaming Bob to ever think about productive solutions to the problem. And all the blame I heaped on Bob never accomplished anything except to prolong the pain and blind me to the choices I was making and the choices I could have made to change.

Lens Six
Dancing a New Dance—Getting Free

> *To dance is to discover and to recreate, above all when the dance is the dance of love. It is the best mode of knowledge.*
>
> —Léopold Sédar Senghor, Senegalese poet

Several years ago, something mysterious happened in Canada. The rabbit population diminished dramatically. Intrigued by this, scientists searched for an explanation. Although they thought the drop in the number of rabbits must have been caused by a disease, they could not identify one. A few years later, scientists again noticed something unusual. The rabbit population increased, but again they were not able to discover an explanation for the variation. Additionally, at approximately the same time, fluctuations in the population of foxes were noticed. As before, scientists investigated diseases that might have accounted for these fluctuations, but again, none were discovered.

By coincidence, reports of the cycles in the rabbit and fox populations were read by another scientist, who noticed a correlation between the changes in the two populations. He figured that as the rabbit population multiplied, they provided an ample food source for the foxes, which resulted in a large number of foxes. When the increased number of foxes ate the rabbits, the food supply vanished, eventually resulting in the foxes dying off. When the fox population declined, the rabbit population again increased, creating a new food supply for the foxes. This cycle was self-perpetuating.

Canadian scientists who observed the fox and rabbit saga found it mysterious at first and were intrigued by the events surrounding these two apparently unrelated issues. That was their mistake. They were studying rabbits separately from foxes and failed to see the relationship between the two events. Then they studied foxes apart from rabbits and once again were baffled by what they found. It was the relationship between the two that helped a different scientist, who looked at both rabbits and foxes, discover the truth that led to an understanding of the curious cycle.

For many, the dance of doom as discussed thus far is equally mysterious. Most people I have met who are in the dance of doom are just as perplexed as the scientists in that story. They have studied and analyzed the situation in their own way and have been brought to tears by the pain and frustration of it all.

What is going on here? Why is it that otherwise bright, capable, and caring people can become enslaved by a pattern of interaction that they do not understand and cannot change? In the last chapter we discussed the reasons that we keep dancing and how we get stuck in the pattern. In this chapter we will find out how to get out of the dance.

Everyone wants their own dance to end so that they will be able to move on to better things, but a feeling of hopelessness engulfs most as they see things grinding further and further down to dust. So many people are dancing, and so few are able to see how to bring it to a halt. I once heard a senior manager say, in reference to the dance, "I would do anything if we could figure out how to stop this fighting and get back to work." Is that true? Are we willing to do anything to bring the peace we desire to our relationships with others? Are we willing to admit that, like the scientists in the fox-and-rabbit story, we don't have the whole story and have been blinded to the real truth all this time? Are we also willing to set aside preconceived notions about difficult people and troubled relationships and acquire a new view and a completely different perspective?

That is what we will do in the pages that follow. It is obvious that conventional wisdom is wholly inadequate for stopping the dance of doom as it plays out everywhere. In fact, much of what we do only makes matters worse, proving that our wisdom and insight are often blurred, distorted, and filled with blind spots and confusion. We need a new lens through which to view old problems.

Two Ways of Seeing and Being

Think about some of the things in your life—your car, your house, your furniture, your clothing, and so on. Our relationships with any material things are strictly conditional, based on how well they help us get what we want from them. If a car runs well and is reliable, we like it because it allows us to meet our needs. If, on the other hand, it breaks down continually and becomes unreliable, we hate it, resent it, and are deeply frustrated by it.

There is little real regard for things outside of their utility and no reason to invest in any kind of relationship with them. Hence, the ultimate value of a thing is based on its utility. Even an item that we keep around for sentimental reasons, such as my old baseball glove, has value because of its ability to produce nostalgic memories. When I'm dead, my child might keep the glove because it reminds him of me. But when it ceases to *work* in this way, it just becomes junk. When a thing meets our needs, we enjoy it; when it doesn't, we either try to fix it or we decide to simply get rid of it. Even though we get angry with things when they fail to work properly or get in our way, we would never think of having a relationship with something like a car or a couch.

When we look at people around us, they tend to appear as two types, those who help us get what we want and those who do not. As with material things, when they do, we like them and use them for our own purposes. But when they fail to perform as we want, we easily become frustrated with them and feel angry because they are no longer meeting our needs. Feelings of anxiety, resentment, and frustration with others are usually reliable indicators that we are seeing others as things and that those things are not doing what we want them to do.

When we relate to others in this way, we treat them with only superficial concern and friendliness. Underneath, we are on guard in case they behave in a way that frustrates our objectives. We feel that they are against what we want, and we spend most of our time worrying that something else will happen that will disappoint us. At worst, these feelings turn into bitter rivalries. Real people—former loved ones or work associates—are transformed into cold-hearted "things" that are attempting to undermine everything we want. I have met many people who have fallen victim to the person-to-thing point of view and who talk about others as if they were demonic robots, not real people with feelings, hopes, and fears.

The lenses through which we view others contain gross flaws that distort our views of them, turning them into ghastly beings with whom we must cope or against whom we must defend ourselves. We can no longer see them in any way as real people; as a result, we treat them just as we would normally treat a thing that is not performing as we would like. We resent them, blame them, accuse them, and feel frustrated by them. Building a relationship seems out of the question since they no longer appear to be people but things, and you just don't build a relationship with a thing.

The Person-to-Person Mode

The person-to-person way of being is strikingly different from the person-to-thing viewpoint. In the person-to-person mode, we experience harmony with others; we feel open, honest, straightforward, and secure. To the extent that we live this way, the needs, hopes, and desires of others are very real to us. We care about them for who they are, not simply for what they can do for us. People are not merely pawns to be moved around in order to meet our needs. Unsurprisingly, when we see others for who they really are, we experience peace and harmony in our relationships with them. We feel personally secure, with no need to resent, blame, or accuse for any reason. So, if we view others as people much like us, we find it hard to experience negative emotions toward them, because they are *like unto us*.

In the best relationships, there is real regard, a desire to understand, and a willingness to do what we can. The focus is on pleasing the other person, not on wrestling with him for position. We have no desire to change them, but rather we try to accept them and understand them. When we sense the real humanness in others, we are inclined to support, help, and understand them, not "fix" them, change them, or resent them. This is not to say that fulfilling relationships happen instantly once we adopt the person-to-person view, but this attitude is clearly effective in getting a new relationship started in the right direction.

Very few people remain in either one of these radically different perspectives all of the time. Most of us have been in both or shifted from one mode to the other. We have all had a relationship, perhaps with a child or a close friend about whom we cared deeply, that was deeply satisfying to us and brought us a great deal of peace. We experienced the unequaled internal resonance that comes from caring genuinely about another person as much as we care about ourselves.

Likewise, we have all had relationships in which we experienced pain, resentment, frustration, and blame. These relationships are draining and can, if left unattended, worsen and eat us alive emotionally. We are exhausted by such relationships and experience few positives. Those who have experienced a relationship characterized by a person-to-thing way of being hope never to have such a relationship again.

Let me share an example to illustrate the two very different ways of being in the world and being with ourselves and others. As you read this moving story, notice the dramatic differences between the two sets of parents. They are all very good people with wonderful potential and decent intentions. But the ways in which they see the world and live in it are vastly different; hence, the kind of life they live is very different.

Dan and Susan had recently graduated from college and were moving out of state with their baby daughter so Dan could take an exciting new job. Dan's parents were not enthusiastic about the move, but Susan's were. Since they lived close to both sets of parents, Dan and Susan stopped to see both as they headed their U-Haul to their destination three states away.

Dan's parents greeted them coldly. "We just don't see why you have to do this," they complained. "It seems to us that if you tried hard, you could find work here. And we don't like you taking away our grandchild, either!" His parents had never been overly supportive, which made everything that much more difficult. Dan and Susan felt lucky that he had even found a job, let alone such a good one with great promise. To receive only criticism and gloom from Dan's parents was almost more than they could take.

The next morning, Dan and Susan loaded up, said goodbye, and drove to Susan's parents' home. As they pulled into the driveway, her mom ran out to greet them and hugged them all enthusiastically. "We're so proud of you and what you're doing!" Susan's parents said. "It's hard to see you leave, but we'll be up there as soon as you get unpacked and have you give us a tour of the new house and town!" Susan felt fortunate to have her parents' support and understanding.

That evening they all sat up late and talked about this new phase of life, preplanning what needed to be done once Dan and Susan arrived.

"Before you leave in the morning, please wake us up so we can say goodbye," said Susan's mom.

"We will, Mom," Susan responded tearfully as they hugged before going to bed.

Very early the next morning, Dan and Susan got up, dressed the baby, and made final preparations to leave. It was still dark.

"Should we wake your parents?" Dan whispered to Susan.

She thought for a second and said, "Why don't we let them sleep? We kept them up pretty late last night." So they closed the front door and a chapter of their lives behind them and drove off into the darkness.

Later that day, they stopped at a hotel and called the respective parents. Dan's were still a bit annoyed that they were moving away, perhaps never to return. But when they called Susan's family, they were given yet another indication of their support and love.

"We wanted to wake you up this morning and say goodbye, but it was early and we just didn't want to disturb your sleep," Susan said, with tears in her eyes. "We love you so much, Mom and Dad, and we appreciate your love and support." Then her mom said something that neither Dan nor Susan would ever forget.

"We were awake long before you left, Honey, but we thought it might be easier for you if we didn't get up."

When Dan heard this, his jaw slackened and his eyes filled with tears. He pictured these two loving parents lying in bed, aching to get up and rush to their daughter, throw their arms around her, and tell her once more about their love, hopes, and support. He thought how much they must have yearned to kiss their granddaughter once more. But instead they stayed in their room because they thought it would be easier for Dan and Susan.

As Dan recalled this experience years later, he still marveled at the unselfish love demonstrated by his in-laws. He has never forgotten that day and what he learned from them about love and caring.

These two very different responses are more than just a one-time reaction to a difficult situation. They represent two very different ways of being in the world and responding to life. Even though the specific circumstances may vary, we still respond in two basic ways. And our response significantly affects our own emotions and the quality of our interactions with others.

From moment to moment, each of us chooses one of these two orientations, either person-to-person or person-to-thing. That choice affects not only how we respond to others around us but also the feelings we generate in our own hearts. Most people have had relationships of both kinds, moments or situations where they felt they were living in a person-to-person paradigm and others where the relationship was characterized by a person-to-thing paradigm. The first is a resonant, uplifting, straightforward, sincere, and deeply fulfilling experience. The second involves seeing others as threats, viewing them with suspicion and resentment, and feeling alienated from them.

The truth is that we probably operate from a mixture of these two paradigms, depending on our circumstances. This is the very problem that we will discuss in the remainder of this chapter.

What a stark contrast! One brings us peace and harmony with

others and the other brings us only misery. Why is this? Some say that this is just the human condition. Part of being human, they claim, involves pleasure and pain with other people. You get along with some people and don't get along with others. "That's just the way it is," they say.

I have a much different perspective. I am convinced that we begin life naturally and easily in the person-to-person mode. It is natural, normal, and effortless for little children to be with others in open, honest ways. Isn't this why we love them so much? They have a fresh, sparkling honesty that stirs something deep in almost all of us.

The person-to-person way of being is what we have at our core. It is the way we were designed to live in the world, and when we relate to others in this mode, we feel most comfortable and at ease. All of us want smooth relationships with others, relationships that are free of conflict, resentment, and friction. We want to like others and be around them; we want to feel that they like and support us. We want to "be ourselves." If we are given the choice between feeling harmony and peace with others and feeling fear, anxiety, and anger, the choice is easy.

This brings us to a critical question. Why would we ever choose to be fearful, anxious, and resentful and endure all of the internal stress that this feeling produces when we could just as easily choose happiness, harmony, and peace? At one level, the answer to the question "How do we stop dancing?" is simple. We simply stop. We stop doing the things that keep the dance alive and start doing the things that we should have been doing all along. In other words, we step out of the person-to-thing mode and its attendant blurring and distortions and start living in the person-to-person mode. In the pages that follow we will discuss various examples of people who have done this and how their changes came about.

The Person-to-Thing Mode

The person-to-thing way of being and seeing creates for us a lens that distorts everything and everyone around us. We begin to see ourselves as helpless victims and others as the causes of our frustration and pain. Our minds become clouded with confusion and our hearts turn away from others. The moral law of human nature discussed in Lens Four compels us to do for others what they need. It whispers to us of others' reality and of their "otherness." It calls us out of our own selfish and self-centered worlds into the world of another. It connects us to others in real and important ways, bringing us the peace that comes from the natural connection of all people.

When we turn away from what we know is right, consciously or otherwise, we bring upon ourselves the blindness of the person-to-thing way of seeing and the emotions that always accompany it. Turning away causes us to become obsessed with our own fears, frustrations, and pain. In this distorted mode, we are also unable to make sense of the relationship challenges we face.

In the person-to-thing mode, we think in narrow ways. We view the dance of doom from our own limited perspectives and fail to understand why the other person is doing what she is doing. We do not see our own involvement in the dance except as the victim of unfortunate circumstances. We essentially pull ourselves out of the formula and try to make sense of a mystery without all the facts. To study others apart from ourselves is to end up perplexed. Yet in the person-to-thing mode, the fog created by our strong negative emotions clouds our vision and prevents us from looking at all the facts; thus, our understanding is predictably distorted.

When we enter the person-to-thing mode, it is much like entering a room with four high walls that prevent us from seeing out. We are fully aware of our own pain and discomfort in the room and what others outside the room are doing to us, but we are unable to see ourselves clearly as we relate to others. Because we are unaware of what is happening outside the room, we invent solutions that simply do not work, solutions that assume, incorrectly, that those outside are not real.

Imagine that you are in this room and that someone or something is slipping notes under the door. When you read the messages, they make you angry, so you write your own nasty replies on the backs of the notes and send them back out. Back and forth you go, sending messages to one another. Separated by the walls of the room, you can't see each other. The other person no longer seems real to you, with a name, a face, and real feelings. He is just something "out there" that is making you upset, and you aren't going to stand for it. You do notice that the nastier your messages get, the nastier his get as well, until finally you are threatening that if you ever get out of this room, you are really going to give him a piece of your mind. For each of you, the other person's humanness is lost in the ensuing exchange of words and emotions, until you reach a point where you don't even realize that you are being nasty and hurtful to another *person*, not just a *thing*.

When we view ourselves as separate from the interaction between us and others, we end up with two possible ways to end the dance. We can either change ourselves or do what we can to change the other person. I remember once in a workshop talking about this idea of

TIT FOR TAT

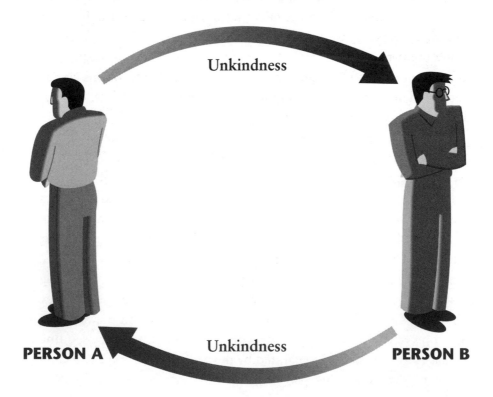

Unkindness

Unkindness

PERSON A   **PERSON B**

changing ourselves first in order to influence another person to change. At the time, I didn't fully appreciate the danger in this approach. One woman raised her hand and revealed her real motives when she said, "You mean that if I change how I respond to my husband, he might change?" As she talked, it was clear where she was headed: "I want my husband to be a certain way, and I can't seem to get him to change. But if it is true that I can get him to change by giving him a different me, then I'll do it." Her intentions were twisted. She was still operating from a person-to-thing mode, looking for ways to get what she wanted without having to make real changes.

When we make superficial attempts to change merely to get other people to treat us differently, they feel our duplicity and sense our true intentions.

Have you ever had a manager who learned in a workshop that if he went around and talked with people casually throughout the workday, he could build rapport and strengthen trust? He goes around trying to do MBWA (managing by wandering around), and it backfires because after years of working with him, you know his nature and his real motives. He does it in hopes of getting something out of it, something that he wants—more work, higher productivity, more loyalty from employees, and so forth—but what started out as a seemingly innocent gesture backfires when people feel undermined and manipulated. The manager's efforts to increase morale and strengthen loyalty actually make things worse.

An approach that fails to take into account the connection between us is built on a sandy foundation and will surely fail. Workshops abound on how to deal with difficult people, detailing strategies for coping with such people and ways to confront them in a way that will let them know that you will not accept their mistreatment.

Unfortunately, in many cases, these strategies only feed the problem and make matters worse. What if you are helping to create difficult people in your life? What if you have created a pattern together that both of you are helping to sustain? What will happen when you try to apply a strategy for dealing with the other person? If it pulls you out of the interchange, implying that you have nothing to do with what is going on, then the other person will feel unjustly accused of causing the whole problem. This will provoke her to respond in ways that cause greater problems for both of you.

It is obvious that conventional wisdom is really inadequate for getting out of the dance of doom. Strategies for negotiating agreements, managing your boss, or getting other people to do what you want are often grounded on a flawed assumption and a shallow understanding of the connectedness between us. That's why they don't work. That's why so many people give up and leave after years of dancing: They feel that they have tried everything and nothing has worked. In fact, much of what they have tried has worsened the situation. Why? Because their hearts have remained unchanged, even though cosmetic changes have taken place. Their hearts are still full of anger, resentment, anxiety, blame, and accusation, and they feel justified because they believe that others are making them feel this way. These strategies are a great, unjustified sham, for they purport to have real answers that they never deliver.

Such strategies always represent superficial changes in behavior while our hearts remain hard and unchanged. When we try to change others by directly attacking their mistreatment, we invite their resistance.

When Things Are Transformed into People

According to the insanity principle, it is insane to continue doing the same old things and hope for different results.

I once read an interesting little book about traveling around the country on a touring motorcycle. The story was about a man and his 11-year-old son, who were traveling with a married couple who knew the man well but had not spent much time with his son. Two days into the trip, the boy was getting on the couple's nerves. He refused to do what was needed in camp at night, he was often moody, and he irritated everyone. One night as they all sat around the fire while cooking supper, the boy announced that he wasn't hungry. "This is all there is, Chris," his father said. "If you don't eat now, you won't eat until morning." The boy stomped off into the darkness in disgust, and his father let him go.

He glanced over at his traveling companions, who were visibly bothered by his son's childish antics. "I've never told you why I brought Chris on this trip, have I?" he asked.

"No," they replied.

"Well, he's been struggling lately in school and at home," the father explained. "We're having him tested, and from the initial reports, it looks as if he has some mild mental retardation. We're still trying to find out exactly how this is affecting him, but what you see is part of what the disease causes."

After receiving this information, the couple looked at one another, and all their anger, resentment, and frustration with Chris melted. In that instant he was transformed from a "thing," an irritation to be dealt with, to a boy, a real 11-year-old boy with problems and burdens that they now understood. All of their negative emotions evaporated and were replaced with compassion and a desire to help Chris in any way they could.

It is this transformation that we need to understand in order to ever escape the dance of doom. It is the change of heart that these people experienced that we must all pass through in order for us to leave the person-to-thing room and enter the person-to-person world. When we understand what others are dealing with and the extra burdens that we may be making for them, our hearts melt, and we have no desire to do what we have been doing anymore. Their humanness comes out and the scales fall from our eyes, revealing who they really are.

I heard another story that describes this powerful change-of-heart experience. A mother, Janelle, described her nine-year-old daughter, Erin, like this.

> *Erin doesn't care if her schoolwork is done correctly and even cheats sometimes to get it done. Like any concerned mother, I make certain that she does her homework, even if it takes her all night. She whines and complains about*

it, and I try as cheerfully as I can to encourage her—as cheerfully as you can when a child acts like that. Usually she continues to doodle until I grow sterner and begin yelling at her.

The situation with Erin is especially frustrating because for years I have given her my best effort. Our first daughter, Carrie, was the most beautiful, talented, and delightful person I have ever known. She lit up a room when she entered it. But she was tragically killed on the way to kindergarten nearly 10 years ago.

Erin isn't as naturally gifted as Carrie was. Fearing that I would compare Erin to Carrie, I vowed to give Erin physical attention every day of her life, meaning warm hugs and lots of attention. Unfortunately, it must not have worked.

When her schoolwork continued to decline, her teacher finally recommended that Erin repeat second grade. I was assigned to help Erin with her flash cards. Sometimes she guesses the answer or counts on her fingers, and, I swear, at times she just gives the wrong answer even when she knows the right one. Working with her is as frustrating as anything I have ever done. I wonder if she's doing it on purpose, but why would she? I'm doing everything I can to help her, so why would she act this way? For some reason she just refuses to cooperate with me.

I haven't just provided a home for Erin. I've done everything I can do to help her out. I've loved her, cared for her, and tried my best to support and help her in everything she has ever wanted to do. I honestly don't know what more I can do.

Janelle's description of Erin tells us much more about Janelle than about her daughter. Janelle feels she is doing everything right but is still getting kicked in the teeth. She spends hours "helping" her little girl, yet all her efforts seem fruitless. She is deeply frustrated with and puzzled by this painful situation. It seems that everything she tries only makes the situation worse. Erin appears to be purposely driving her mother crazy.

Perhaps you can relate to Janelle's predicament. Maybe you have been in a relationship in your family or with a friend or colleague that just doesn't work. You honestly feel that you are doing everything you can to change the situation and improve it. But nothing you do seems to help.

Several months after writing the description above, Janelle wrote down her feelings after experiencing a mighty change of heart toward Erin and this irritating situation.

> *Over the past few weeks, I have been trying to look at my relationship with Erin differently. What I have learned about myself will remain with me for the rest of my life. My eyes were opened to something I had never before noticed, and it melted me, changed me in significant and transforming ways.*
>
> *As I began to think about my relationship with Erin, I realized that I had always been harder on her than on any of my other children. When we worked on the flash cards, I was encouraging her outwardly, but inwardly I was angry at her and didn't trust her, and she surely felt this coming from me. I cried when I realized the price she had paid for my inability to love her without reservation.*
>
> *Remarkably, once I came to this realization of how I had been treating Erin, I became a different person. I felt differently toward Erin and felt empathy for her and what she had been going through. One afternoon we sat down to work on her flash cards. I believe she sensed something different in me, because on this day she missed only 3 out of 30 problems. Usually she only gets about 3 or 4 correct. To top it off, she left the table with a smile on her face instead of the usual tears.*

Things went fine for a couple of days, and then a real test came. On Sunday Erin seemed to be trying everything she could to frustrate me and make me angry. We try to make Sunday a family day, and she said emphatically, "I hate being with my family all the time. I want to be with my friends." My normal response would have been to get angry and say, "Now listen, young lady, you shouldn't talk like that. Sunday is our family day; you will be with the family, and you will have fun."

Instead, I sat down, pulled her onto my lap, and looked into her eyes. I felt this overwhelming sense of love for her. I held her close and told her how much I loved her. I realized that this moment was the first time in nearly eight years that I had expressed true love for her. I had hugged her many times before, but inwardly I had felt anger or frustration, not love. But this time the love and affection for my daughter were natural and right and true. It was as if I were holding a new baby for the very first time. I felt so much love for her.

Tears filled my eyes and ran down my cheeks as I looked in her sweet face. "Mommy," she said, "are you crying because you love me?" I nodded. Then she said with a smile, "I want to stay with you forever, Mommy."

Like all of us, when Janelle was embroiled and engulfed in her emotionally frustrating situation, she could not see her way out. Everything she tried failed. She worked on her behavior, tried to be a nice mother, held her daughter, and spoke the words of love, but they were hollow words and actions, and her daughter knew it. Everything Janelle did, even though her intentions seemed pure, made matters worse. Ironically, Janelle thought that Erin caused the problem, so she did everything she could to change Erin. That is why nothing she did produced the results she longed for. Her actions were not a result of love and empathy for her daughter but of a selfish need to change Erin to alleviate her own frustration.

For years, Janelle's disappointment and anger prevented her from seeing the truth in this relationship—that nothing could change until she experienced a change of heart toward Erin. Janelle's resentment and anger at Erin even prevented her from realizing that a change of her own heart was possible.

Janelle came to see that only with a change of heart can anything else change. Anything less cannot help a transformation happen.

This is the great paradox in relationships: It is when we ourselves most need to change that we least believe that we can and must do it. It is when we alone are responsible for our emotional troubles that we are most likely to blame them on others. This is a paradox that few people ever see.

Blue Elk, the famous holy man of the Oglala Sioux, expressed this paradox eloquently when he said, "It is in the darkness of their eyes that men get lost."

When we find ourselves in painful, frustrating relationships and our way becomes dark and gloomy, we think that the darkness is coming from "out there" somewhere—from the other person's behavior or from the frustrating situation that we are caught in. But alas, the darkness that surrounds us does not come from outside. It comes from the darkness in our own eyes that prevents us from seeing things as they really are.

Janelle's predicament and others like it teach us this great principle: As human beings, we hold the keys to healing the relationships that produce such emotional turmoil for us. The darkness in our eyes prevents us from seeing the truth that it is ourselves in great measure, not others, who are responsible for our troubled feelings, and it is we alone who can drive them away. The people we blame for our troubled emotions cannot relieve our pain.

It's like being in a place you really don't like and feeling that you can't get out. You beat on the door and scream at those outside whom you feel have put you there. But in your pocket you have the key to the exit—you just don't know it. You're so busy blaming those outside the room that you don't even stop to notice the key. We hold the key to the door of peace, happiness, and resonance with other people. Ironically, however, we think that someone else must change for us to feel these positive emotions.

Janelle tried to do everything conceivable to influence Erin to do what she wanted her to do. But the more she persisted, the less cooperation she received. It seemed that the more Janelle pushed, the more Erin pushed back.

Then, in an instant, all of this changed. What finally brought about this long-awaited change? It happened when Janelle stopped trying to change her daughter and instead allowed herself to be influenced from within. When she was open and honest with herself, there was an immediate softening; she saw her daughter in a new light. Janelle realized that despite what she thought, she had not been helping her daughter at all.

> *I was resenting Erin; I was irritated and angry at her for not doing what I wanted her to do. I'm horrified now to imagine how all of my resentment must have looked to my precious daughter. By sending her the message that she was an inconsiderate and irritating person, I made her believe that I was an obstacle in her path. Her defensiveness was nothing more than a reflection of my mistreatment of her.*

Take a Heart Test

What about you? You might be thinking that a change of heart is too rare, beyond the scope of your abilities or perhaps too fantastic for you to relate to. Before moving on, I'd like to give you a chance to think about yourself in some everyday situations that most of us have experienced. As you read these brief scenarios, think about your feelings and how they change. In many ways, the process that Janelle went through and what you may experience as you read the stories below are very much the same in that they all involve a change of heart.

You recently bought a new car—not just any car, but the dream car that you have wanted for years. You love the color and the brilliant shine of the new paint. It looks great sitting in your driveway, and all your neighbors have been over to admire it. This is your dream come true.

One day as you are driving down a narrow country road, you notice a young boy by the side of the road. As you pass him, you hear the sickening thud of something large and heavy crashing into your car. You pull over and see a large, ugly dent in the door on the passenger side. In an instant, you realize that the boy hit your new car with a rock.

Immediately you begin to boil. "Of all the rotten, irresponsible things to do!" you think. "I'm going to go back there and give this kid a piece of my mind! I wonder if his parents know what he's doing out here."

As you walk quickly back to where the boy is standing, you grow angrier and angrier. You want to rip the little brat's head off. As you get closer, you notice that the boy has tears rolling down his face. "Well, at least he's crying," you think, "because if he weren't, he would be by the time I got through with him."

As you reach the boy, ready to explode from all your pent-up anger, he says tearfully, "I'm sorry for hitting your car. I have been trying to stop a car for a long time." Then he points to another child half-covered by the tall grass. "My little brother is hurt bad and I needed someone to help. Can you help me, please?"

How have your feelings changed? As you glance over at the little boy curled up in the long grass, what runs through your mind? Don't you want to reach out to this terrified child? Don't you want to do whatever you can to get his injured brother some help?

Let's consider another situation.

Your sister is married to a successful attorney, but lately things have been getting very strange. Your mother complains that your sister's husband has been acting very possessive. "He won't let her out of his sight," your other sister comments. "It's as if he's afraid that she'll leave him or something." The whole family is upset about how possessive he has become; they decide that he is just insecure and needs to feel important by keeping her under his thumb. They select you to talk to him. You're supposed to let him know that his actions are un-acceptable and that he'd better shape up.

One morning, as you are thinking about having lunch with him to give him a talking to, your phone rings. It's your brother-in-law. "I don't know if you realize it, but I'm under a great deal of pressure right now," he confides. "Your sister has been diagnosed as having an eating disorder and has been caught stealing from a local department store. It seems she has a whole host of uncontrollable addictions."

You're shocked. "My sister?" you ask in disbelief.

"Yes," he says. "I wanted to hide her problem from the family and not cause her any embarrassment, but I feel that I can't handle it alone anymore. I don't dare let her out of my sight for fear of what she'll do. I've even stayed up all night sometimes just to make certain that she won't do anything to hurt herself."

What just happened to your feelings toward your brother-in-law? Do you still resent him and want to give him a piece of your mind? Do you still think that he is insecure and overbearing? You may have feel-ings exactly opposite from those you had before his phone call. Do you feel compassion and empathy for your sister and her difficulties? Do you wonder how you would behave in the same circumstances, if your wife developed the same problems? Does your heart go out to this man whom you were going to blast out of the water minutes before?

Let's look at one last situation.

You are on a plane headed for a distant city on a business trip. As you sit down, you politely say hello to the woman in the seat beside you. She grunts and turns her head away.

"I'm just trying to be friendly," you mutter to yourself. Then the flight attendant comes by with drinks, and the woman acts rude to her as well. "What's wrong with you?" you want to ask her. Once again you try to strike up a conversation, but she seems totally disin-terested. You offer to lend her a book to read, and she seems bothered by your gesture. After about an hour, you want to get up and sit somewhere else. You've never met such a cold, unfriendly person in all your life.

Then she pulls something out of her purse—a newspaper clipping. As you glance over, she looks up and sees you looking at her. Tears are running down her face as she folds the clipping. With her eyes still filled with tears, she says, "I'm sorry I'm not very good company. My only brother was killed two days ago in a tragic accident, and I'm going to the funeral today. He left a wife and three little children. I don't know what they're going to do."

Now what do you think of this "unfriendly" woman? Are you still annoyed by her huffy attitude? Is it still a huffy attitude, or do you now see something else? Do you still want to get up and move to another seat and glare at her on your way out? Or do you want to reach over, touch her hand, and express your heartfelt sympathy? Do you wish there was something you could do to ease her pain at this moment? Don't you want to say something, to do anything you can to support her at this tragic time? Has she changed, or have you?

What happened to you as you read each one of these scenarios? How did your feelings change as you imagined yourself in the situations described? It's likely that you experienced dramatic changes in your feelings and attitude. You learned something that changed your perspective on the situation and the people involved. Your eyes were opened and you understood clearly what was really happening; your understanding caused your heart to soften. This change was automatic, requiring no forethought on your part. Even so, the facts in each situation remained the same. Nothing changed except your level of knowledge, your attitude, and your perspective on the situation.

These kinds of changes can and do happen. They are the keys to helping us transform the relationships in our lives into harmonious, resonant, loving situations, free from blame, accusation, and pain—if we can only open our hearts and minds to see them!

This kind of change happens without any mechanical, artificial effort on our parts. We don't have to sit down and create action plans or "to do" lists of things to say or not to say to improve a relationship. Those kinds of deliberate efforts to change are often manipulative, designed to get other people to change. The strategy is to subtly make them think that we are changing or to cleverly convince them of their need to change so that our problem will go away. But the only true mechanism for lasting change is our own change of heart.

Conditions for Change: Emotional Honesty

Part of what prevents us from creating free-flowing and harmonious relationships with others is our unwillingness to be emotionally honest. Emotional honesty involves recognizing what is really happening in a relationship and admitting it. It includes a realization of what our behavior has done to another person, how it has made him feel, and how it may have hurt him. When we become emotionally honest, we not only see the other person differently as he becomes very real to us, we also perceive ourselves differently. This is the key to breaking out of self-betrayal, justification, and blame.

A change of heart starts when we begin to respond to others compassionately, by perceiving them truthfully and not taking offense at anything they are doing. When we try through sheer willpower to change ourselves, we change only superficial behavior, not our hearts. It is virtually impossible for us to change emotion or attitude directly. Only through seeing others differently do our emotions, which flow from how we see, also change.

A friend, Brad, shared with me this powerful story of emotional honesty.

> *My wife and I decided to join a new health club. While I was at work, Lisa called for information about the facility and fees. They offered us a free one-week trial membership, at the end of which we needed to join or walk away. We worked out for a week, and then we sat down to talk with the manager about whether to join.*
>
> *She explained a little more about the membership fees, but I wasn't listening. I felt that this was Lisa's decision and that she had already thought it through. When the manager finished, Lisa turned to me and asked, "Well, what do you want to do?"*

I was caught off-guard and felt stupid. "What do you mean 'what do I want to do'?" I asked angrily.

"Well, do you want to join or not?" Lisa asked.

I felt so dumb sitting there with the manager looking at me, waiting for me to say yes. Finally I said, "Let's go home and talk about it first," and we left.

When we got into the car, I laid into Lisa. "Why did you embarrass me like that?" I asked her loudly. "I felt stupid in there. Are you trying to make me look like a fool?"

"No," she said a bit defensively. "I just know that we need to make this decision together."

"Well, you didn't even know what the place was going to cost us. I thought you had talked with this lady and had it all worked out," I continued. I was still very upset.

All the way home we argued back and forth—me telling her why I didn't like what she had done and her telling me why she had asked me. By the time we got home, neither of us was talking.

Brad was making a sweeping accusation of his wife. He felt that she was setting him up, trying to make him look stupid in front of the manager. His response to her insensitive treatment of him was to blame her for what she had done to him. And then something changed.

When we got home, Lisa went upstairs, and I went into my office. I was still angry at what she had done to me. As I sat there, I started to rethink the situation. It hit me that perhaps she wasn't trying to embarrass me at all. In fact, I realized that I was putting on airs, wanting to act cool in front of the club manager. I didn't want to look foolish, and because I felt foolish when Lisa asked me what I wanted to do, I blamed her for trying to embarrass me. I realized that I had failed to see her question for what it really was—a simple way to involve me. I knew that if she had just joined without my input, I would have been angry at her for not asking me what I wanted to do. But when she did, I was angry at her because I was caught off-guard.

Then I started to think about how she must have felt when I acted so stupid at the club. I must have embarrassed her by my angry response to her simple question. And then I had followed it up with all the angry arguing on the way home, blaming her and accusing her, but of doing what? Asking me my opinion? The more I reflected on the experience, the sorrier I felt for Lisa and how she must be feeling at that moment.

The longer I sat there, the worse I felt; I knew I needed to go to her and tell her honestly how I felt, so I did. She wrapped her arms around me and immediately forgave me, and the topic was closed.

Brad faced the truth by admitting that his wife had not been trying to humiliate him in any way and that he was taking offense where none was intended. Admitting the truth destroys our resentful emotions. Brad's initial assessment of the situation with his wife was blatantly wrong. His actions and the emotions generated from his assessment were all part of a colossal lie that he was living. Thus, when he recognized his folly, all the emotions that he held within the lie disappeared. His recognition of the truth made his lie absurd.

The lie that Brad was living was essentially, "What you did upset and embarrassed me." The truth actually was, "I am choosing to be upset and to blame you." This lie, like so many others we have discussed, became the detonator in the breakdown of Brad's relationship with his wife.

This simple interchange could have turned out much differently. My friend could have mulled over this incident for days, continuing to blame his wife and hold it over her. By so doing, he could have chilled the relationship and created permanent defensiveness on Lisa's part as she tried to defend herself from his judgments of her. He could have held a grudge and never let her live it down, bringing it up again and again every time they went to the health club. This, and so much more, could have happened and would have obviously created a much different ending than the one you just read.

Holding grudges is an interesting path to self-betrayal. We drag along behind us some event that we still have feelings about. We hold it over someone else as if to say, "You were wrong then and you're still wrong and I'm never going to forget it." Then there's the other part. "If I forget it, then you might forget it, and I don't want that to happen because I want you to always remember how wrong you were and the pain you caused me."

I know two sisters, now in their eighties. When they were in their fifties, their father passed away. One sister felt that she was slighted in the will because she didn't receive something that she felt she deserved. But instead of blaming her dead father, she blamed her sister because she accepted the item. For more than 20 years, they have refused to have anything to do with one another. In that time they have been in the same room twice, at funerals of relatives. But even though they stood only a few feet apart, neither acknowledged the other's presence.

For more than 20 years, these sisters have held grudges. As with so many similarly terrible tragedies, it would be impossible and irrelevant to determine who started the mess. Each would have her own perspective and be prepared to argue, almost literally to the death, that she was right and the other was wrong. Today they live in the same city, only 30 minutes apart, and both are alone and lonely. But neither is willing to forgive and move on.

For every extreme case like this, there are thousands upon thousands of smaller examples of grudges held against others whom we feel have wronged us. The grudges course through our hearts like poison, hardening our emotions, feeding our resentment, and making us miserable. For many, resentment, blame, and holding grudges have become a natural way of life. If holding a grudge led to effective solutions, I would strongly encourage it. If holding a grudge made us truly feel better about ourselves and others, I would recommend it. If holding a grudge worked, I'd highly support it as a form of problem-solving. But it doesn't. It serves no purpose other than to poison our hearts and harden our minds. It is self-destruction in slow motion.

Opening Ourselves Up to Others

There is great irony in the fact that the primary way in which we undergo significant changes is to open ourselves to be touched by others. On the one hand, because we see others as threatening, we are afraid to open up. It seems like the worst possible thing to do. But on the other hand, this is the one response to others that will end our fears. Moreover, opening ourselves to others involves admitting honestly to ourselves any wrongdoing we have done.

When we approach the truth, we tend to draw back, sensing that it will be too painful to admit, yet only by this honest admission can we rid ourselves of the lie that we fear facing and the troubled feelings that surround that lie.

When we no longer need the other person to validate the lie we are living, she becomes a real person to us. And the same factors that earlier we would describe with irritation can now be described with compassion. When we perceive others and ourselves truthfully, we see neither ourselves nor others accusingly, but rather compassionately. The truth and love always go together, two aspects of the resonant way of being with others in life.

Opening up to others and becoming emotionally honest requires us to admit to ourselves any wrong that we have done to them. Admitting that we have done wrong is often very difficult because of its implications. First, it transfers responsibility for change back to us and away from those whom we have blamed for causing all the problems. Second, admitting our part in a problem destroys the elaborate scheme of justification that we have labored under for so long. As we blame others and then mistreat them further, we justify it by accusing them of starting the problem. Thus, when we finally admit that we have done wrong, this justifying story is done away with and we must face things as they truly are.

In relationships in which we experience resentful feelings, we must understand that we choose those feelings. No one forces us to feel the way we do. There are numerous other responses that we can choose. When we feel angry and resentful but still try to act lovingly, the inconsistency eventually breaks down and is revealed. The irony is that when our inconsistency is revealed and our negative feelings win over our positive superficial behavior, we blame the other person. Here's an example of what I mean.

Jack and Mike have been neighbors for five years, and over that time, they have developed a pretty good friendship. Jack is a handyman and has lots of tools, which Mike occasionally borrows. The problem is that sometimes Mike forgets to return them or returns them dirty. Once Mike borrowed an electric sander from Jack and returned it broken. Jack was livid.

"Mike, this is the last straw. I don't mind you borrowing my things, but when you break them, well, that's going too far." He made sure that Mike knew how irresponsible he was for mistreating his tools, and before Mike could respond, Jack slammed the door.

"Of all the nerve," Jack groaned to his wife, Carol. "This guy has the gall to borrow my sander and ruin it, and then just come over and hand it to me as if nothing was wrong."

"I heard what you said to him, Jack," said Carol. "You really lost your grip. Don't you think you should go over there and apologize? We don't want hard feelings between us and our next-door neighbors."

"Apologize?" Jack exclaimed angrily. "He's the one who ought to apologize. He borrows my stuff, then ruins it! He should be here right now writing me a check. I didn't do anything wrong. He did!"

But the next day at work, Jack couldn't stop thinking about the incident. Carol's words kept racing around his mind, crashing into his anger and resentment at Mike and what he had done. "You really ought to go over and apologize to him, Jack," Carol's words echoed. He couldn't concentrate on anything.

After work, Jack walked into the house to some unexpected news. "We've been invited to a neighborhood party at George and Merry's," announced Carol. "Some of our old friends who have moved away will be there, and we'll get a chance to meet the new people down the street."

Jack jumped to his feet. "I'm not going if that rotten Mike is going to be there!"

"Jack," his wife said, "you and Mike have been friends for a long time. You're not going to let this sander stand between you, are you? Come to the party with me, and when you see Mike, I want you to try to be nice. You don't have to act stupid in front of all our neighbors."

Jack finally gave in and went to the party. As they were walking in, Jack said, "I'll try to be nice to the guy, but after what he did, it'll be hard." Inside the house, Jack saw Mike and coolly waved to him, but then quickly turned away. Twice Mike walked right past Jack but said nothing. Jack was steaming inside.

"After all I have done, to come to this dumb party and try to be nice to him, and then he treats me like this. This is a side of Mike I have never seen. I'm glad I found it out now before it was too late," he thought.

"I tried to be nice to the guy," Jack said in frustration on the way home. "Mike acted as if I wasn't even there. He even walked right by me."

"Maybe he was afraid you would jump down his throat again like you did when he returned the broken sander," Carol suggested. "That's how I would feel if I were Mike."

This was not what Jack wanted to hear, but as Carol spoke, he knew she was right. He also knew that he needed to apologize to Mike for acting the way he had. He also knew that Carol was right about their friendship being more important than a $20 sander that was worn out anyway. All of this he knew—but he didn't want to hear it.

Over the next few days, Jack continued to mull over the situation with Mike. He knew that something needed to change, but he struggled to accept the feeling that it was he who should approach Mike. "After all," he reasoned, "it was Mike who started this by returning my sander the way he did." Even as this thought ran through his mind, he heard Carol's words: "Surely you're not going to let a sander stand between your friendship" and "Jack, you know what the right thing is, and you need to do it. Don't let this problem continue to eat away at you."

Conscience can seem so demanding when we resist it as Jack did. His conscience continued to call to him. In his heart he knew what was right, but his head was trying to talk him out of it by filling his mind with justifications. The only question left was which would win out.

A few days later, Jack saw Mike working in his garden. "I guess this is as good a time as any," he thought, taking a deep breath. "I have to do this." He walked over and said, "Mike, I've been a real jerk the last few days, and I want to apologize. That sander thing really caught me off-guard, and I'm sorry for what I said."

Mike looked up and smiled. "I've been wondering how to bring it up to you, too. I should have offered to have it fixed or something."

The two men stood and talked for an hour or so, trying to overcome the awkwardness of the moment. They shook hands, and Jack walked back home. "What a relief that is," he confessed to his wife. "I think Mike and I have finally put this behind us."

Certainly, not every story ends this way. For too many of us, pride and an unwillingness to follow our consciences stand in the way of the peace we claim we want with others. When we resist our sense of right and wrong, conscience can be a hard taskmaster. It simply will not leave us alone. Even though the loud, blaring sound of rationalizations has a tendency to drown out the soft whisper of conscience, we cannot turn away from ourselves and what we know we should do without hearing the echoes of those promptings.

Jack learned the painful irony that we all learn when we do the wrong thing, choose resentful feelings, and then try to act as if we don't have those feelings. Negative feelings always win out over superficial positive behavior. And we blame others when this takes place. The chain of events in such situations is interesting.

1. We choose anger and resentful feelings toward another person, an indication that we have engaged in some form of self-betrayal.

2. Then we try to act nice, even though we still have the negative emotions. This is a facade, a lie, an insincerity.
3. Others sense how we really feel despite our facade and defend themselves against our resentment.
4. We view their response to our real feelings negatively, as if they have broken our code and seen through our disguise to how we really feel.
5. We blame them again when our negative emotions win out over our disguise and they see it.

Jack didn't stop to think how Mike had experienced the tongue-lashing. And when Jack pretended not to be angry, putting on a happy face that he didn't feel inside, it took virtually no provocation on Mike's part for Jack's true feelings to show. No matter what Mike did, Jack would have seen something blameworthy in his behavior. What Jack was really angry about was his inability to fake Mike out, to hold resentful feelings while acting as if he didn't. Mike took the rap for that as well. What a twisted irony all the way around!

What makes emotional honesty difficult is that we must examine our feelings, our choices, and our attitudes and admit that they might be unfair. Jack found it difficult to be honest about what he was feeling and why those feelings had come upon him. He had done something that he knew was wrong by his own standards, but he refused to admit it. Admitting it would have then required something of him, an apology, a visit to Mike's house, something other than what he was now doing. Being emotionally honest involves admitting not only that we have negative emotions but that we have chosen those emotions.

It would have been easy, for example, for Jack to admit to Carol, "Yes, I'm angry at Mike for what he did and I resent his mistreatment of my things, I admit it." It would have been quite another for him to admit that he had chosen to respond angrily and was choosing to hang on to those feelings to justify himself. That kind of emotional honesty is far different from simply recognizing that we feel the way we do. We know when we're angry or resentful. We just don't know why and don't see that there are other ways of responding that are far less destructive to us and our relationships. But when we learn to see differently, it changes not only how we see now but also how we view the past.

Bob and Randy: Why Don't We Talk?

You may be wondering what happened between Bob and me and how we were able to break the dance we were dancing. Much of the reason that I am able to write about getting in a dance of doom, getting stuck, and getting out of it is that I have lived in all three places and have danced the dance of doom far too often with far too many people. Here's what happened.

Our dance went on for nearly six months. Inside, I was dying. Every morning when I went in to work, my heart pounded with anxiety about what might happen. I feared Bob, despised him in many ways, and resented him for what he was doing to me and my family. My wife had become such an intricate part of this dance that she was "stepping in" while I rested. She had almost as much frustration and ill will built up for Bob as I did, but with all of this emotion and the time I spent talking about it and complaining about it, things only got worse.

I reached a point nearly six months into this where it became clear that I could not dance this way for one more day. I knew that something had to happen. It seemed then that I had two choices: to leave and simply find another job or to talk with Bob directly, honestly, and thoroughly about what we were doing to one another and how it could be stopped. I decided to talk.

I must admit that the days that preceded my talk with Bob were anxious ones. I was afraid of this man and had become so wrapped up in my own pain that Bob had become a monster in my eyes. I had friends who agreed with me, and we had built a case that portrayed me as the innocent victim and Bob as the mean and nasty boss abusing his authority. Still, I knew that if we were going to sit down and talk, I could not do so angrily or accusingly. It was probably more out of fear than compassion that I came to this point. I knew that if I went to Bob and said anything that accused him or blamed him for what was happening, he would explode and the whole conversation would end abruptly, leaving the two of us dancing harder and faster than ever.

I worked on my feelings for several days, trying to sort through how I really felt and why I had allowed myself to get so deeply wrapped up in all of this. When I felt I was ready, I went to Bob and asked him if he could drop by because I had something I wanted to talk with him about. He agreed, and before I knew it he was sitting across from me, waiting to hear what it was that I wanted.

Pay close attention to what happened in this discussion, because it illustrates in some ways what must happen for all of us as we try to extricate ourselves from the pain of the dance of doom.

I first thanked him for meeting with me and then explained what it was about. "As you know, we have been struggling lately. Our relationship has become pretty negative and nonexistent. I'm sure it must be hard for you, too. It sure has been difficult for me, and I haven't really known what to do. I'm sorry if I have done anything to hurt you or offend you. I sincerely want things to be different between us."

He stood up and looked out the high-rise window, thinking about what I had said. "Yes, we do need to fix this, don't we?" he responded. Then he explained how he had been seeing me and that he understood my need for independence. "I know it's fun to do your own thing and to work without a lot of supervision. I'm a lot like that, too," he said. As he talked, I could see that he was honestly trying to understand why I had been behaving as I had and was giving me the benefit of the doubt. The trouble was that he thought that while I was avoiding him and doing my own thing independent of him, I was having the time of my life.

"If I'm having so much fun out there doing my own thing, Bob, then why do you think the last six months have been the most miserable six months of my professional career?" I asked him.

He glanced over at me in surprise. "What do you mean?"

I explained how miserable I had been and how difficult it had been to work day after day with our relationship so tenuous. He was completely surprised by my comments. He had assumed that I was having a great time doing my own thing, when all along it was killing me. He now had information that he did not have before, and so did I. We had a place to start reconciliation.

Over the next two hours we talked about what had been going on and why. I shared my concerns about his treatment of me, and he shared his need for further communication. Then he said something that I found really interesting. "I need your help. Sometimes when I am critical, I really don't know that I'm talking to people in that way. If you ever hear me do it or feel that I'm talking in ways that cause you to feel defensive, tell me about it and I'll try to change." He was asking for my help in his efforts to change, which led me to ask for his.

Bob and I bared our souls that day, and in so doing, we laid the groundwork for honest problem-solving. I saw his side of the situation for the first time, and he saw mine. I stepped out of my myopic box and saw him for the first time as a man just like me, with fears, anxieties, and hopes just like mine. I also saw what a burden I represented for him and how hard he had struggled under it, trying to figure out how to work with me. Through our discussion we saw each other in completely honest ways, and our hearts underwent a change that was much more than skin deep. It changed how we saw one another and how we felt about what had been happening. It changed both of us.

When Bob walked out of my office that day, I felt as if a 1,000-pound weight had been lifted off my heart. "Why didn't I do this five months ago when this first started to spin out of control?" I asked myself on the way home that night. I had anticipated this experience being painful and ugly, but it was not. In the days that followed this conversation, my feelings for Bob changed as well. I could no longer see him as I had before because he was no longer being that kind of man. I had seen him before as a critical, distant, judgmental boss who didn't care for me and what I was going through. After our talk, he changed in my eyes, and I no longer saw him as a thing to be dealt with but as a man who did care and honestly wanted to make things better.

The very act of asking Bob to visit with me about our relationship served to break the dance that we were caught in. I was giving Bob a different Randy to respond to, and he gave me a different Bob. Together, over the weeks that followed, we created a positive pattern, a different dance in which he treated me with respect and I responded in kind. He admitted honestly that he had weaknesses in the area of relationships, and I admitted that I, too, had some rough spots, revealed over the past few months. From that point on, we began to create a different style of interacting and were committed to never again dance that dance.

What If . . .

Often when people hear me tell how Bob and I stopped dancing, someone will ask, "I can see how this worked for you and Bob, but what if the other person really is a jerk? I used to have a partner whom everyone hated and who caused problems everywhere he went. He was a bona fide jerk and everyone knew it. There was nothing you could do. What do you do in a situation like that?"

The very nature of this question shows how deeply scripted we are to think of relationships in the wrong way. To separate an individual and examine his behavior independent from the treatment he receives from others is to miss the point of this chapter. The only way we can really understand any person's behavior is to view it in relation to and in the context of his treatment by other people. I said to this man, "Did your old partner have anyone who liked him?"

"Sure he did. He was married and had four children who all seemed to get along with him pretty well. He played golf with a bunch of guys every week who seemed to be friends," the man replied.

"So he wasn't seen by everyone as a jerk, is that what you're telling me?" I asked.

"Yes, I guess so," he admitted.

"Then here's the question," I continued. "How do you think your partner would have behaved if he had not been mistreated by everyone in your office? In other words, if people had accepted him, communicated with him openly and honestly, tried to work out their problems in an up-front way, with no games or back-biting behind the scenes, how do you think he would have been different?"

"I don't know," he said honestly.

"One thing we do know is that he would no longer be under the burden of people's anger and resentment," I pointed out. "If you and others had given him different people to respond to, would you not predict that he would have been a different man?"

"Yes, I guess he would have," he said.

The only way that we can know what people might be like is to see how they respond when they are not being mistreated—when they are not being judged, accused, or blamed in some way. How would Bob have responded if after our first negative exchange, I had gone back to him and said, "Bob, that discussion we had this morning was a difficult one for me, and maybe it was for you as well. I want to have a good, open and honest relationship and do whatever I can to support you in your demanding work. I'm sorry for what I have done and want to make sure that no matter what, we can always be open with each other about what's on our minds and look for ways to make this work. Could we talk about how to do that?"

It is impossible to know exactly what would have happened, but in all likelihood we could have prevented six months of hell by addressing our concerns openly and honestly immediately after our first difficult conversation. Instead, for six months I gave him a negative, resistant, avoiding Randy who blamed him in a hundred ways for bringing all of this on, and I provoked him to mistreat me in a similar way. It doesn't matter who started it and what the specific event was that lit the fire. All that mattered to me after six months was that we find a way to stop. I believe now that had I gone to him sooner, it would have ended sooner. To stop dancing we need to simply stop dancing! Stop doing what you are doing, which you know is not working, and start doing what you know you should. Many times, the way out of the dance is really that simple.

Secrets of Getting Free

Getting out of the dance may not always follow a pattern like mine and Bob's. Sometimes it may take much longer. Maybe the other person will not respond as Bob did. Other times we may find that it takes several conversations and experiences with another person before we can start to notice that our feelings are changing. There are three important elements illustrated in my story and in every story of breaking the dance of doom once you know you're dancing.

Drop your agenda. We create all kinds of problems with others when we try to fix a broken relationship the same way we would fix a thing that is not working as we would like. When our cars break down, we take them to be fixed. We have agendas, things that we want to get out of the deal. When we approach people as things and try to fix them, we go in wrong. We stand and face them as things that are bothering us, irritating us, and inconveniencing us. But when we try to fix people, we invite their defensiveness. People can sense our intentions long before we say a word.

Set aside pride. What is it really that prevents us from going to others in open and honest ways? As one man put it, "I am not ready to talk with him. I don't want to give him the satisfaction." Is it the satisfaction that he thinks the other person will gain by his going to him for reconciliation? The irony in all of this is significant. On the one hand, the primary way in which we break the dance is to open ourselves to be touched by the otherness of other individuals. But because we see others as "the problem" and as threats to us, we are fearful of opening up to them; in fact, they are often the last people we want to open up to. Being open and honest with someone we are dancing with seems like a ridiculous and even stupid thing to do. But as we saw in my story, being open and viewing our "partners" as real people is the quickest way to end our fears and end the painful dance.

There is a host of reasons why we are fearful of opening up to others. For starters, it requires us to be honest about our own complicity in what has taken place between us. Our own "sins" must be acknowledged personally and with another person. We must say, "I am not all at fault here and neither are you, but I am not blameless, either." For so long we have woven a complex array of arguments about our innocence and their guilt that to now admit that we had a part in the painful interaction is very hard and requires us to set aside the pride that screams at us not to proceed any further. Yet it is only by our honest admission of complicity that we can rid ourselves of the lie that we have been living and the troubled emotions that surround it.

See the burdens of others. Finally, a critical aspect of emotional honesty with others in breaking the dance is the realization of what we have done to others. What burdens have we created for them that they have carried because of our mistreatment? When we begin to see the burdens that we have created, we see others differently, not as things deliberately trying to make us crazy but as people who, like us, have burdens, some of which are brought upon by our mistreatment.

We are at our best when we are with others in real and honest ways, when they are real people to us and we are real people to them.

Everything Changes

I still remember meeting a woman named Rachel years ago. She was consumed with rage against her mother's poor parenting. She was 35 and still fuming over her mistreatment as a child. "When I talk with my friends about their mothers, they tell me how their mothers took them shopping, how their mothers were their best friends," she exclaimed. "My mother did nothing."

Rachel had several serious personal problems, including food addiction, alcohol problems, and substance abuse. Her life since leaving home at 18 had been one pathetic experience after another. Nothing had worked out for her. At some point, someone told her that her problems were likely the result of a poor relationship with her mother, and Rachel had grabbed that idea with a vengeance.

For years she held a grudge against her mother and was certain that her mother disliked her and treated her unfairly. No matter what her mother did, Rachel had decided long ago to see it negatively. In the darkness of her eyes, her mother could do nothing right. Unsurprisingly, their relationship was stressful for both of them. Her mother had more or less quit trying, since everything she did seemed to make Rachel angry. And when she did that, Rachel used the silence and distance as further evidence that her mother didn't care. In all those years, they had never learned to talk their feelings out. Their relationship had become a cold war. Then one day something changed.

Rachel went to a family reunion, where she met, for the first time, a cousin who had grown up with her mother in the same small country town. "You know," Rachel told this relative, "I know virtually nothing about my mother's early life. She never talked about her upbringing or her parents or anything. Tell me, what was my mother like?"

For nearly three hours, this cousin told Rachel about her mother's difficult life, her early upbringing in poverty, and the stresses the family had experienced. Rachel learned for the first time that her mother, the youngest of seven, had been raised mostly by her older sisters. "Your mother," the cousin told her, "really never had a mother very much. She more or less had to figure it out on her own. That was very difficult."

Story after story sank deep into Rachel's hardened heart. She started to look at her mother from a different perspective. With this new understanding, her mother's parenting pattern seemed to make much more sense. Learning of her mother's turbulent past helped her better understand not only her mother but also many experiences that they had had as Rachel was growing up. "Your mother is a wonderful, loving soul," the cousin said as they hugged goodbye. "I love her. You should feel lucky to have a mother like her."

These words hit Rachel like a freight train. She had never felt lucky to have her mother. She had mostly been ashamed of her, resented her, and blamed her for most of her own problems. That night she couldn't sleep. She got out old pictures of herself and her mother when she was a child. She remembered things they had done, and with her added perspective, she saw her entire upbringing in a different light. Her eyes were opened. The darkness was replaced with marvelous light and illuminating understanding. Rachel was changed and so were her feelings about all that had happened so many years ago.

The more she pondered her life and her relationship with her mother, the worse she felt. She knew that she had been a source of great concern and pain to her mother. She realized that she had been acting resentfully toward her mother for years because she felt that her mother had ruined her life. Now she knew that all of that was a lie—a huge untruth that began to break her own heart.

She wondered what pain she had caused her mother and even started to picture her mother at home crying over her daughter's life and her inability to reach out and help. Rachel's feelings of resentment were replaced with empathy, love, and understanding. Her entire past now looked different to her, and her present emotions were transformed from resentment to a heartfelt love for her mother.

Several weeks later, Rachel went to her mother's house to talk. Her heart was so full that she could barely control her emotions. She felt terrible about the years of anger and resentment toward her mother that had brought pain to the entire family. They talked, they cried, and together they buried the past, with all of the negative emotions it contained for them, and began building a new story together.

Rachel's story illustrates one important aspect of emotional honesty—realizing what we have done to others. When we become emotionally honest at last, we perceive ourselves differently, along with the situations we find ourselves in. In addition, we see the other person with new eyes, and the emotions we hold against them melt away.

When we see how we have mistreated another and honestly come to a realization of the truth in a situation, we are transformed in our relationship with them. When our hearts change, deep down we become different; we move from being anxious and resentful to being loving, empathic, and resonant—with 20/20 Insight.

Seeing with Perfect Vision

The effects of going against our sense of right and wrong are blinding. Our vision of ourselves is distorted and we become preoccupied with our needs, our frustrations, and our anguish, seeing others as the cause of it all. Additionally, we view others in accusing ways, blaming them for what we feel and provoking them to do what they know is wrong. All of this is a prelude to the dance of doom and is one of the most predictable patterns I have ever seen. When one person (or a group or nation or community) justifies wrong action, he violates the law that has the power to bring us together. It is only when we reject this moral law that the dance begins and we become trapped by its seductive pattern.

We have talked about being emotionally honest and truthful with ourselves and others. This lies near the very heart of 20/20 Insight, for when we are in any way untruthful and living a lie, we are naturally blinded to the reality around us. Living truthfully is ultimately the only way we can live, for all other options are dead-end streets, leading nowhere.

In the stories in this chapter, we saw that anything less than a change of heart is really no change at all. When our hearts remain full of anger, resentment, and blame, any solution that flows from those negative emotions will lead us deeper into the dance and farther from what we really want. It is through giving up these negative emotions that we come to see clearly, so that the truth of what is really unfolding is revealed.

For some, all of this sounds far too simple. They look for a laundry list of things that they can do to get out of the dance and to "manage" their way to success. But as we said at the outset, conventional answers to interpersonal problems simply do not work. They provide us with lists of things to do and fail to recognize that unless and until our hearts change and we see others differently, those things will not work. They will enable us to modify the dance, but the dance will go on.

Nothing less than a change of heart will do. This is not the kind of change we can engineer or set a goal to achieve. It comes naturally as we give up our act, come clean with full emotional honesty about what is really taking place, and stand up to others as they really are—people who have needs, hopes, and fears just like ours and who feel the same law of human nature flowing through them as we do. Our rejection will invite them to ignore this voice, but our compassion will invite them to live true to it.

Our influence on others and their influence on us are natural and interconnected. It is what happens between us that tells the story of any relationship; it is not about who started it or who is most at fault. The fault-finding approach, in which we keep score of who did what to whom, only reinforces our blaming spirit and strengthens the others' defensiveness, and before long we both assume a defensive position from which nothing positive can ever take place.

So stopping the dance and breaking free from its painful effects are simple but challenging actions. To do so requires us to do as love requires, to step away from ourselves and toward others and to recognize that the only way we can achieve the peace we long for in life is to respond to ourselves and others in truthful ways. It is here in the sunshine of truth that we find the warmth and comfort we look for in our relationships with others. Stop blaming, resenting, harboring grudges, accusing, and self-excusing, for it is these things that invite others to do the same. Unsurprisingly, it is our kindness, compassion, and openness with others that invite them to be kind, compassionate, and open with us. And yet there is no guarantee.

Final Critical Questions

In trying to get to the bottom line, I have found that a few simple but important questions take us there quickly. We all want to create harmony and to feel at ease with ourselves and others. We have talked in this book thus far about several ways to bring that about. Now here are some guiding questions that may be helpful in staying on track when you feel a relationship starting to slip into the dance of doom.

What is the problem? What is my part in it? I list these two questions together because they are so intertwined. When we have a relationship problem with another person, the question "What is the problem?" is a useful one to ask, but it usually leads us to the wrong place. In my relationship with Bob, the answer to this question was clear: "Bob's shabby treatment of me is the problem." Or in other words, "Bob is my biggest problem, and if I could just get him to stop, everything would be fine." Notice that in answering the question I removed myself from the formula as if I had nothing to do with the sad state of our relationship. This is exactly what blurred tunnel vision yields. It prevents us from seeing the entire picture and from including all the parties. It causes us to focus microscopically on ourselves until the time comes to solve the problem; then we leave ourselves out of it.

The second question was also easy for me to answer when Bob and I were dancing. I felt, at least in the beginning, that I had no part in the problem. I felt that Bob's mistreatment was uncalled for and arbitrary and that he had not been provoked into communicating with me in this nasty way. I felt innocent of any wrongdoing, and that made it all the more painful. It follows that when we feel that we have no part in the problem, we cannot see ourselves as part of the solution.

I suggest that the question be modified in a way that will produce a more truthful answer: "What is the problem in this relationship?" This question is like asking the first and second question simultaneously. It focuses our attention where it must be placed—on the interaction between us. It also brings the two separate but interlocking stories created by two people who are dancing together into one story. I could not tell my story without Bob, and he could not tell his story without me. Hence, when either of us changed our response, we changed the story we were creating and the story others were spinning as well.

Do I approve of my actions? A friend of mine got married a couple of years ago, and during the first year of marriage, he and his wife had numerous relationship problems. Soon they found themselves dancing, and the pain index shot up for both of them. After several weeks of marriage counseling, the counselor asked one question that turned everything around for this couple. He looked at my friend and asked, "Do you approve of your feelings and actions toward your wife?"

At first my friend was caught off-guard by this question and didn't know what to say. Perhaps his silence was an answer. As he reflected on what he had said about his wife during the previous hour, his criticism of her, his anger with her, his frustration and accusations, he posed the question to himself and received the truthful answer. He knew that he did not approve, and it was answering this question honestly that opened his eyes to the truth between him and his sweet wife.

Many times in the midst of the dance, we have no idea how it all started. Sometimes it seems that one day something just started, and it has been going ever since. I have found that no matter where a dance began or what stage it may be at now, asking this question is incredibly helpful. Think of one of your most troubled and frustrating relationships. Think about how you feel toward this person and how you are treating them and ask yourself, "Do I approve of my emotions and actions toward this person?" If we are willing to set aside our pride and defensiveness, we will likely discover that we in fact do not approve of what we are feeling and doing.

Am I in the defensive position? Earlier I said that when we are in the defensive position with regard to others, we cannot simultaneously build the relationship. This may sound self-evident, but I've met people who are confused about why a bad relationship does not improve even though they admit that they feel the other person is mistreating them and they feel the need to protect themselves.

When we feel the need to defend ourselves, we can be assured that we have gone against ourselves in some way and have violated the primary laws of human nature. We feel that if we do right, we will in some way be hurt or lose ground or lose power. In this state of mind and heart, we cannot find our way out of the dance's eternal grip. We must break free from defensiveness by asking the question, "Do I approve of what I am now doing?" We must answer it honestly and then do what love requires.

What's my agenda? When we are in the dance of doom, our agendas are generally clear: We want to change the other person. To break the dance, we need to give up our agendas or shift them from getting the other person to change to creating an open and honest exchange that will stop the present pattern from continuing. I have found that whenever we have hidden agendas, people can sense our real motives. Our agendas must be transformed into simply doing what we feel is right and what others need from us. When we do this with sincerity and honesty, we will find that not only have our hearts changed but we have invited the other person to change with us. In most cases, he does.

Questions such as the ones I've mentioned can help focus our minds and hearts on the issues that lead to getting out of the dance of doom. I've discovered that we can dance with someone in many different ways and for a variety of reasons. Some people can relate to my dance with Bob. Others find that they do fine at work but dance on occasion with a spouse or child. Leaders find that leading people requires far more empathy than brilliance. Other people's behavior can only be understood in relation to our actions. We are bound to others with an invisible cord, and when we turn away from others and their needs, the cord jerks and others jerk back.

Some people may say, "This all sounds too simple, doing the right thing and all. There must be more to it than that." But surely what we have been talking about is not simple, or more people would do it. It requires a level of honesty that most have never experienced. It forces us to admit responsibility for things that we could just as easily blame on someone else. It disallows foolish pride and egoism, for these are the enemies of emotional honesty. If you really think through the subject carefully from beginning to end, there are depths of understanding and insight aplenty. What begins as a simple declaration to "do the right thing by others" takes on dimensions scarcely before imagined. It is not hard to understand, but it is difficult to do. I wish you well on the journey.

Epilogue
Rediscovering Who We Are

Into the hands of every individual is given a marvelous power for good and evil—the silent, unconscious, unseen influence of his/her life. This is simply the constant radiation of what man really is, not what he pretends to be.

—William George Jordan,
author of *The Vision of High Ideals*

So here we stand on the precipice, at a new level of understanding about things that affect us directly and personally. Insight has opened our eyes to see in ways that we did not know existed. Understanding has been raised to a new level, and our minds and hearts have undergone a mighty shift.

I once talked with the mother of a teenage boy who was driving her crazy. "He's so rude to his younger brothers, so abrasive and harsh, calling them names and doing whatever he can to torment them," she complained. "We have tried everything we can to help him understand how he hurts other people's feelings, but still he continues. I don't know what we can do." Many parents have seen things in their children that go completely counter to what they have been taught in the home. In their hearts they wonder if anything is sinking in and what kind of people their children are becoming.

Later the mother came over to visit and told me a different story about this same young man.

> *We were down at my office getting something and my son noticed a Down's syndrome boy in the car next to ours. The young boy called my son over and hugged him and my son hugged him back. Then the most amazing thing happened. For nearly 20 minutes I watched my seemingly cold, uncaring son treat this boy with kindness and sweet respect. They talked about all kinds of things, and my son seemed sincerely interested in what the boy was telling him. Then they embraced again and the young boy said to my boy, "Call me sometime," and my son said, "I'll call you tomorrow."*
>
> *I don't think I have ever seen this side of my boy, at home so much the aggressor and the cause of so many hurtful feelings and now here with this boy, so thoughtful, kind, and considerate. I kind of wondered if this was really my son, because he surely didn't act like him.*

After sharing this story with me, she paused briefly and then said something very profound. "It was so good for me to see him in such a positive light because now I know that he has the capacity to love and care for people in very sweet and tender ways. That helps me realize that he's not all bad, and believe me, I was beginning to wonder." And then her final insight. "I believe the kind, caring person I saw recently is who my son really is, and his gruff, hurtful side is a facade he puts on. It's not who he is when he's really himself."

This mother had the opportunity to witness something that felt like a mini-miracle as she observed her son transformed before her eyes. She was struck with wonderment as she compared what seemed to be two very different people: the son she saw at home who was the source of so much conflict, and this kind and generous son.

Witness to a Miracle

In many ways, the stories throughout this book are stories of small but real miracles in the lives of the people involved. The dictionary defines *miracle* as "something to wonder at." Perhaps you have wondered at many things as you have moved through this book, examining yourself in new ways. "I wonder if this could really be true? I wonder if I can make the kind of changes the author is suggesting? I wonder if I have the courage to step into the darkness and experiment with a new way of seeing myself and others?" A sense of wonderment and curiosity is critical to any effort to change, for it serves as the fuel that propels us forward into new areas and opportunities.

There is another part of the definition of miracles that is equally intriguing. A miracle is "a divinely natural occurrence that must be learned humanly." Often things around us that seem too fantastic to be true must be understood humanly. To our Creator, miracles are natural occurrences that we "wonder at" because we cannot explain or understand them. They lie beyond our natural ability to comprehend, and that is what makes them seem miraculous to us.

In part two, we looked through the three lenses of personal vision in order to see ourselves more accurately and clearly. Our focus was at a level where we do not often look—on our beliefs and assumptions, our automatic thoughts and opinions that create in large measure the kind of world we experience day by day. We discussed how we process or *re-present* life in ways that lead to outcomes, sometimes positive but other times negative and in the opposite direction from where we want to go. We then discussed how we hold within us the power to choose and looked at several ways to expose distorted thoughts and beliefs and change them for greater effectiveness and peace.

In part three, our focus shifted slightly to relationship challenges with others, called the dance of doom. Our focus was on how we get into, get stuck in, and most important, get out of such frustrating and tiring interactions. Throughout, we have been talking about returning to basic truths and living truthfully and honestly with ourselves and others. Living truthfully is really the overarching answer to all of the many things we have discussed, for when we learn to live truthfully, we learn to see things as they really are and really can be. This is when miracles begin to happen. When we come to see things in clear and precise ways, our hearts change and we become different.

Normally, when we think of change, we think of things moving from one state to another, like a convertible car changing from having a top to not having one. Here we have talked a great deal about a change of heart, but this is not as precise as we need to be. It is not that our heart and feelings change or progress but rather that we return to being who we were before we began seeing falsely. In other words, we have the capacity to see ourselves and others with perfect clarity. That is part of who we really are.

When we start to see the world falsely, "through a glass darkly," we begin to see ourselves and others in false ways. When our hearts change, we return to the truths that were always there but became lost in the darkness. It is much like when we are physically ill and we say, "I'm not well and I don't feel like my old self today. Give me a few days and I'll be back to normal." We don't feel the way we want to feel, the way we normally feel. Getting better is obviously not about becoming a new person but about getting rid of that which ails us and prevents us from feeling like ourselves. So what do we tell people when they ask us how we're doing once we've recovered? "Great; I'm feeling like my old self again."

Emotional illness, even seemingly common forms such as depression, deep discouragement, frustration that lingers, blame of another, resentment of what others are doing or not doing, and all the attendant emotions brought about when we go against what we know is right, does not describe who we are but merely who we become when we are not being ourselves. It is when we turn away from others and fail to do as love requires that we bring upon ourselves all kinds of "illness."

It follows that the nasty, negative personality traits that we often see in ourselves and others are not permanent "attachments" to our real nature at all but merely manifestations of the "virus" that always shows up when we dance with others and betray ourselves. They show up when we go against ourselves, and then they vanish as soon as the dance ends. We get better and return to our old selves. Even though our language isn't used in this way, when we are dancing with another person we could just as easily say, "I don't feel so hot. I feel terrible and wish I could feel open, honest, and up-front with people again, the way I am with my close friends and family."

No one who has ever gone against what they know is right, either knowingly or unwittingly, has felt good about what comes afterward. We may blame, resent, or feel trapped and victimized by another, but this all feels wrong to us and makes us sick inside. It serves as the breeding ground for stress, ulcers, and all manner of physical manifestations that arise when we fight an internal battle between our consciences—what we know is right—and our wrongdoing, which we need to justify. But all the justification in the world doesn't make our wrongdoing right; it just convinces us that it might be so. The way we feel should be our first clue that something is wrong and needs to be corrected before it gets worse.

Understanding this truth should help us exercise far more patience with others and with ourselves when we find ourselves doing wrong and suffering the painful consequences. We would never criticize hospital patients in intensive care for looking pale and preoccupied. Why then would we criticize those who are under anesthesia as they undergo surgery on their soul? There's no need for us to stare and impatiently wonder how long their recovery will take. The stitches will come out at some point, and they will be themselves once again.

As we view the behavior of those around us, it also helps to keep in mind a simple truth that I learned years ago: *All human behavior is either an expression of love or a cry for love.* As I danced around painfully with Bob those many months, this truth eluded me. Had I looked upon him with greater compassion and learned to see his irritable behavior as a cry for love and acceptance, I would have responded differently. Instead I became so caught up in my own pain that I forgot to think about him and his side of the wrenching relationship. If you test this principle by beginning to look at others through this lens, you will come to see them differently and your heart will respond more compassionately and far less judgmentally.

Sometimes when we are looking for answers to specific challenges, we long for tactical solutions that we can implement immediately. We have become accustomed to a fast-food, quick-fix, cookbook approach to life that leaves most of us exhausted and still having problems that need mending. Returning to ourselves is not a process marked by goal-setting, action plans, and strategic initiatives.

The Ebenezer Scrooge Phenomenon

The story of Ebenezer Scrooge and his mighty change of heart may provide us with the finest illustration of returning to our old selves that has ever been written. We all know the story. A mean, tight-fisted old man who treated everyone as an irritation and a bother, Scrooge seemed to have no feeling whatsoever for anyone, including his tired assistant Bob Cratchit. Here's how Charles Dickens describes Scrooge.

> *Scrooge! A wheezing, wrenching, grasping, scraping, clutching covetous old sinner, hard and sharp as flint from which no steel had ever struck out generous fire; secretive and self-contained, solitary as an oyster. The cold within him froze his old features; nipped his pointed nose, shriveled his cheek, stiffened his gait, made his eyes red, his thin lips blue, and spoke out shrewdly in his grating voice. He carried his own low temperature always about with him; he iced his office in the dog-days, and didn't thaw it one degree at Christmas.*
>
> *External heat and cold had little influence on Scrooge. No warmth could warm, nor wintry weather chill him. No wind that blew was bitterer than he. No falling snow was more intent upon its purposes, No pelting rain less open to entreaty. Foul weather didn't know where to have him.*

No one stopped to visit Scrooge or talk with him in the street. Neighbors didn't come over for a pot of tea, children were afraid of him, and dogs ran from him. Everyone found him mean and nasty and filled with bitterness to the center of his soul. But Scrooge didn't care. This was the way he liked it. As he edged his way along the crowded paths of life, warning all human sympathy to keep its distance, Scrooge could find few reasons to be happy. On special holidays like Christmas, when everyone else was happy and filled with cheer, he seemed even more irritated than ever. He resented other people's attempts to cheer him up. He was miserable and unhappy and he intended to stay that way. Scrooge was also selfish. He kept the coal box in his office and doled out the coal so sparingly that his employees were always cold.

As Scrooge retires on Christmas Eve, he has no idea what the night holds in store for him. First his long-time but now dead partner Jacob Marley appears to him in a vision to tell him that on this night, he will be visited by three ghosts—the ghosts of Christmases past, present, and future. This means little to the crusty old man until the first ghost appears. Throughout the night, Scrooge is taken back to see events earlier in his own life that had shaped him. He sees himself playing with old friends he has long since lost touch with. He views his present life and those around him who are affected by his cruel, cold treatment. Finally he looks into the future to see what will be if things do not change. He even looks in on the family of his loyal employee Bob Cratchit, whom he has mistreated for years. He sees things he had never seen before and recognizes Bob not just as an employee but as a decent and good father and husband.

Scrooge sees himself and those around him in the visions of the night until finally he is led by the last spirit to a cold, mysterious, haunting place filled with gravestones. He is instructed to look at one stone, but he shrinks back, afraid.

"Before I draw near to the stone to which you point," says Scrooge, "answer me one question. Are these the shadows of things that will be or are they shadows of things that may be only?"

The ghost answers nothing and continues to point to the stone. Then Scrooge conjectures aloud, "Man's courses will foreshadow certain ends to which, if persevered in, they must lead. But if the courses be departed from, the ends will change. Say it is thus with what you show me!" he pleads with the spirit.

The spirit says nothing but continues to point to the headstone. Finally, Scrooge looks at the stone and sees two simple but chilling words: EBENEZER SCROOGE. He has been up all night seeing his life in ways he had never before imagined. Now, as he stands looking at his own gravestone, he realizes that his life is deplorable. He sees what he has done to himself and to others and where it will all lead if nothing changes. This heartbreaking realization is more than he can bear.

"Spirit!" he cries, falling to his knees, "Hear me, I am not the man I was. I will not be the man I just have been. Why show me this if I am past all hope?"

"Assure me," Scrooge begs, clutching the spirit's robe, "that I may yet change these shadows you have shown me, by an altered life!"

The lessons of this night are bitter and cruel for Ebenezer Scrooge. He sees his life and where it is all heading, and he shrinks in agony as he watches it unfold before him. But he is never to be the same again. He experiences a mighty change of heart, not just a simplistic, cosmetic change in his attitude or his behavior. He undergoes a miraculous transformation that shakes him to his very soul.

Waking from his night vision, Scrooge's face is wet with the tears he shed while pleading with the spirit. Suddenly he realizes that it is all over and he is at home, in his own bed, alive and well. He leaps up in ecstasy for what he saw and for the chance to make amends.

Before this stirring vision, Scrooge had looked at life through a dark and dismal peephole. He hated life and almost everyone he met. He resented people who were happy and was irritated by nearly everything and everyone. But this crusty, miserable old man underwent a change—a mighty change of heart. "I am as light as a feather," he shouts. "I am as happy as an angel, I am as merry as a school boy, I am as giddy as a drunken man!" He leaps and whoops with delight at his newfound insight and the chance he now has to create a different life.

The world now looks vastly different to him. Twenty hours before, the children's singing grated on him and angered him. But now it is the most pleasant sound he has ever heard. People who had come asking for contributions to a charity and were tossed out by Scrooge now find him shaking their hands and giving generously. He walks around town and finds that "everything yields him pleasure. He had never dreamed that anything could bring him such happiness." He meets people on the street and smiles genuine smiles of sublime happiness. He takes great satisfaction in doing everything possible to help his struggling assistant, Bob Cratchit. He becomes a second father to Bob's little boy Tiny Tim, and he becomes a good old man. "His own heart laughed and that was enough for him," says Dickens.

Scrooge had undergone a fundamental shift that led to a profound clarifying of his vision. The darkness in his eyes had been lifted and he became a different person living in a much different world.

Will the *real* Ebenezer Scrooge please stand up! Which one of these very different men was the real Scrooge? Was it the ornery, selfish, ungrateful man who seemed to enjoy belittling others and hoarding everything in the world, or was it the kind, generous, loving man who emerged from that terrifying night vision? Is it possible that for all those miserable years, while Scrooge was *acting* the way he was and alienating everyone around him, he was like a person suffering from an illness that prevents him from feeling like himself? And once his eyes were opened to see what he had always missed, he dropped the facade, gave up the act, and returned to himself? Is it possible that the kind, generous, giving man so full of joy was the real Scrooge, healed from his emotional illness? Could you predict what would have happened to this lonely man if he had not had his eyes opened by the visions of the night? It was clear where his life was headed, and he saw every bit of it in the terrible vision of the future. He saw where his life was going and didn't like it.

What Happened to Scrooge?

How do we explain what happened to Ebenezer Scrooge? Was it a miracle? Did he really see all those terrifying figures in the night, or was it all just a bad dream? Can it be explained simply by psychological means, as delusions? How or why it happened we can only speculate. Dickens doesn't elaborate. The reasons behind Scrooge's experiences are less important than the results. The important thing we do know is that he underwent a mighty change. During the long and wrenching night vision, he looked backward and forward at his life and saw it for what it really was. His views of the future terrified him as he saw where he was heading. They softened his hardened heart in fundamental ways. His desires changed; his emotions changed. His response to those around him spun 180 degrees from where they had been just 24 hours earlier.

When he awoke from this dreadful vision, he looked at the same world as before, but oh, how different it looked to him then! The children singing on the street who had so annoyed him just the day before now sang like angels to his transformed ears. His eyes saw things that had always been there but that he had been too blind to see.

Scrooge experienced what we are calling a change of heart, a return to who he really was before his heart became hardened. His basic emotions, feelings, and attitude underwent a significant change, an enormous transformation from one state of being to another. Scrooge didn't just make simplistic alterations in his behavior, such as trying to be kinder to the little children so they wouldn't be afraid of him or trying to not be so grouchy to poor Bob Cratchit. These were deep-down, head-to-toe changes that made him a new man. And as a new man, he saw and created a new world for himself that was filled with joy, opportunities to serve and give, and a desire to bless everyone he came in contact with.

Before his transforming experience, Scrooge lived in the person-to-thing mode. Others were irritations and sources of frustration to him. They were not real people with real feelings. Even Bob Cratchit, his long-time clerk with a sick little boy, had become mannequin-like to the hard heart of Ebenezer Scrooge. But all of that changed when his heart changed.

Conscience Is the Cord

In the pages of this book, I have talked a great deal about the power we all have to create our own future and about how our heads create our world. Our vision and how we see ourselves and others sets the boundaries for our lives and the kinds of success we experience. I have talked about conscience, the power we have within us to know what we should do in a given situation if only we learn to listen. Listening to our conscience is so important because of where it leads us, if we will only follow. Conscience is the cord that ties us to other people. As we follow it, it helps produce harmony and compassion for others, and when that happens, we are expressing our deepest emotions of love and caring. Ironically, the more we care for others, the more we come to correctly value ourselves, and we begin to live with integrity and do what we feel is right. The quiet but reliable impressions we receive also remind us what brings us the greatest joy and what will bring us peace and harmony.

Conscience is like a constant companion whispering to us, "This is not you. This is not what you know is best. This is how you should treat this person or respond in this situation. You know what is right. Do this. Don't do that." This internal voice, if we will only learn to follow it, is our sure link to who we are when we are not being somebody else. It calls us back to who we really are and pleads with us to think and feel and respond in ways that will pull us closer to others. For these many reasons, our consciences are sure scouts on the horizon, beckoning us home.

The power we have to break the dance of doom is within each of us if we will only open our eyes to see things as they really are and really can be. We do have the power to create peace inside our hearts and between ourselves and those we live and work with. In fact, this is our natural state, the way we are meant to be when we live and think and see clearly. When we come back home to ourselves, we let go of the emotional viruses that infect us and weaken our souls and break down our important relationships.

When we turn away from blame, resentment, and anger, we can then turn fully back to ourselves and feel healthy again. When we cling to these destructive viruses, they eat at us, and we don't feel like ourselves anymore. Blame, resentment, anger, and all the other symptoms we have discussed in this book are blaring warning signals to us that we are emotionally ill and not feeling like ourselves. Peace, harmony, and joy describe how we feel when we feel normal and right. The various lenses in this book can be used to clarify our vision of ourselves and others and lead us back home. We can't afford to lose our way. The journey is far too important. There's no place like home!

It is my prayer that the words, ideas, and stories in this book have helped you "come home to stay" and that you will never leave again. Creating peace, harmony, and success is within our grasp if only we come to see with perfectly clear vision, with 20/20 Insight. But the journey only begins here. It is from this point on that your greatest insights and discoveries will take place as you experiment with these words, try them on for size, and seek to live in harmony with your true self, with all of its attendant magic and joy. I pray that your trip home will find you rediscovering who you are and who you have the possibility of becoming. The journey is far too important to leave it in the hands of anyone else.

More Insights?

Share your stories of personal or interpersonal transformation with the rest of the world by sending them to the address below. Your story may be included in a forthcoming book dedicated to the principles of inner vision, highlighted by real-life examples of applying these powerful ideas. Understanding and awareness are essential. Solid application that plays out in everyday life still rules supreme, for it is the evidence of real learning. Send your stories and experiences to:

Gibbs Consulting Incorporated
20/20 Insight
P.O. Box 1898
Orem, Utah 84097
Fax: (801) 224-0202

Also, visit our Web site at http://2020gibbs.com, which provides e-mail information and so much more.

Seminars, Lectures, and In-Sight Tools

You can also contact us at the above address for further information on workshops, audiotapes, other books, learning aids like CD-ROMs, application exercises, videotapes, and more. Also, tell us how we can best assist you in applying the ideas in *20/20 Insight*. We welcome your suggestions.

Recommended Reading

This list of books represents some of my most cherished reading, as they have inspired and helped me to formulate my own beliefs. These are books that you can go back to again and again, and I hope that you will have a chance to read some of them.

And There Was Light, Jacques Lusseyran (Parabola Books, 1987)

Beliefs, Robert Dilts (Metamorphous Press, 1990)

Discovering the Future: The Business of Paradigms, Joel A. Barker (ILI Press, 1985)

Mere Christianity, C. S. Lewis (Simon & Schuster, 1997)

Miracles, C. S. Lewis (Macmillan, 1978)

Your Own Worst Enemy: Understanding the Paradox of Self-Defeating Behavior, Steven Berglas and Roy F. Baumeister (Basic Books, 1993)

Index

Italicized page references indicate illustrations.